business solutions

Pivot Table
Data Crunching

Bill "Mr. Excel" Jelen

Michael Alexander

800 E. 96th Street
Indianapolis, Indiana 46240

D0323275

Pivot Table Data Crunching

Copyright © 2006 by Que Publishing

International Standard Book Number: 0-7897-3435-4

Library of Congress Catalog Card Number: 2005924224

Printed in the United States of America

Tenth Printing: July 2010

10 11 12 13 14 15   14 13 12 11 10

Trademarks

Warning and Disclaimer

Bulk Sales

Que Publishing offers excellent discounts on this book when ordered in quantity for bulk purchases or special sales. For more information, please contact

U.S. Corporate and Government Sales
1-800-382-3419
corpsales@pearsontechgroup.com

For sales outside of the U.S., please contact

International Sales
international@pearsoned.com

Publisher
Paul Boger

Acquisitions Editor
Loretta Yates

Development Editor
Songlin Qiu

Managing Editor
Charlotte Clapp

Project Editor
Seth Kerney

Copy Editor
Bart Reed

Indexer
Ken Johnson

Proofreader
Tricia Liebig

Technical Editor
Juan Pablo Gonzalez

Publishing Coordinator
Cindy Teeters

Interior Designer
Anne Jones

Cover Designer
Anne Jones

Page Layout
Brad Chinn

Table of Contents

About the Authors

Bill Jelen is the principal behind the leading Excel website, MrExcel.com. As an Excel consultant, he has written Excel VBA solutions for hundreds of clients around the English-speaking world. His website hosts more than 12 million page views annually. Prior to founding MrExcel.com, Bill spent 12 years "in the trenches," working as a financial analyst for the finance, marketing, accounting, and operations departments of a $500 million public company. His duties included turning large amounts of mainframe data into meaningful reports. Working initially with Lotus 1-2-3 and then Excel, Bill honed techniques to take massive amounts of data and produce meaningful reports in record time. Bill is the author of seven books on Microsoft Excel.

Michael Alexander is a Microsoft Certified Application Developer (MCAD) with more than 13 years' experience consulting and developing office solutions. Michael started his career in consulting and development at the White House Communications Agency in Washington D.C., later parleying his experience with VBA and VB into a successful career in the private sector, developing middleware and reporting solutions for a wide variety of industries. He currently lives in Plano, Texas, where he heads an analytical services group for a $700 million company. In his spare time he runs a free tutorial site, www.datapigtechnologies.com, where he shares basic Access and Excel tips with intermediate users.

1. Select a single cell in your dataset. Choose PivotTable Report from the Data menu. Click Finish. You are given a blank pivot table, as shown in Figure I.7.

Figure I.7
After three mouse clicks, you have a blank pivot table report. Three more mouse clicks to go.

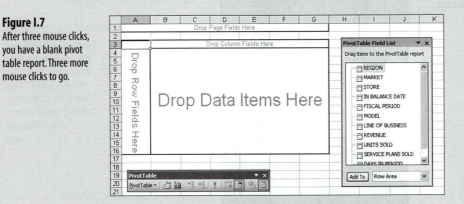

2. From the pivot table field list, drag Region and drop it where it reads "Drop Row Fields Here." Drag the Model field where it reads "Drop Column Fields Here." Drag the Revenue field where it reads "Drop Data Items Here." After a total of six mouse clicks, you have the required report, as shown in Figure I.8.

Figure I.8
Drag three headings to the report, and Excel calculates your report.

	A	B	C	D	E	F	G	H	I	J	K
1					Drop Page Fields Here						
2											
3	Sum of REVENUE	MODEL ▼									
4	REGION ▼	2500C	2500P	3002C	3002P	4055T	4500C	4500P	5001C	5001P	Grand Total
5	North	25893618	20621317	26590786	106393633	4157167	64532173	8707258	6443346	13653319	276992617
6	South	36711470	28153264	32652417	113242781	4778067	76674818	7562089	7015903	13029501	319820310
7	West	23976601	19594197	22529175	65359020	3841454	46967756	1249362	7619872	25444675	216582112
8	Grand Total	86581689	68368778	81772378	284995434	12776688	188174747	17518709	21079121	52127495	813395039

If you are racing, you can actually create the report shown in Figure I.8 in exactly 10 seconds. This is an amazing accomplishment. Realistically, it would take you about 50 seconds at normal speed to create the report. If you are a spreadsheet wizard and are instead following the steps in the previous case study, the non–pivot table solution would take you at least 12 times longer.

Further, when your manager comes back with the request to add Market to the analysis, it takes just seconds to drag the Market field from the field list and drop it on the report, as shown in Figure I.9.

Figure I.9
Creating a new report with the Market field is as simple as dragging the field to the report.

	A	B	C	D	E	F	G	H	I	J	K	L
1												
2												
3	Sum of REVENUE		MODEL ▾									
4	REGION ▾	MARKET ▾	2500C	2500P	3002C	3002P	4055T	4500C	4500P	5001C	5001P	Grand Total
5	North	Great Lakes	1929517	3269643	2864393	13963620	505943	9955238	516729	1327536	2660019	36992638
6		New England	6011684	3356078	3065267	13080189	466559	7744218	1136300	711092	1769837	37341224
7		New York North	3932881	4828599	3584264	14770735	1021718	10577200	377719	624445	1776112	41493673
8		New York South	1641970	1173574	2991008	12321868	312315	6587253	2706905	409673	1338327	29482893
9		Ohio	2381299	3960185	4130289	17035110	535677	10475995	2126208	710365	1348690	42703718
10		Shenandoah Valley	4244770	2329461	6761719	22991629	949272	12532535	1433878	1705928	3284389	56233681
11		South Carolina	5751497	1703777	3193846	12230482	365683	6659734	409519	954307	1476045	32744890
12	North Total		25893618	20621317	26590786	106393633	4157167	64532173	8707258	6443346	13653319	276992617
13	South	Florida	3783617	4823314	4761551	18810662	423298	8866059	1465039	1378033	3050898	47362461
14		Gulf Coast	5830888	2685703	4915966	17030692	585060	9997150	1071708	1086584	1955434	45159185
15		Illinois	2989788	3562893	4473116	16043130	551270	9530083	1681398	968999	2280764	42101421
16		Indiana	3616687	4958038	4031526	11570514	722557	13404905	508271	916869	1313087	41043454
17		Kentucky	5972430	3662458	3339436	11685568	1108919	9926609	388990	376749	1002473	37363632
18		North Carolina	3763158	2311733	4134523	13719904	543294	6083844	783871	1090512	1651515	34082354
19		Tennessee	6323837	3505028	2920257	10414153	355609	7802248	644914	621099	977236	33564381
20		Texas	4531085	2644097	4076042	13968158	488060	11063920	1006898	577058	768104	39143422
21	South Total		36711470	28153264	32652417	113242781	4778067	76674818	7562089	7015903	13029601	319820310
22	West	California	4020385	3570593	5195351	12494689	1345939	11582176	5346	3935376	19486877	61636732
23		Central US	3506717	3414010	3229599	10869224	358988	7076062	660777	464767	923698	30503842
24		Colorado	3113591	3124724	2743057	10523054	234431	5074260	4391	562917	836776	26217201
25		North West	3179141	2807395	4136112	9708920	322535	6292914	118550	1045684	1313892	28923143
26		Southwest	4532147	3465741	2822512	9621154	531280	6211995	131180	635042	1374236	29325287
27		Topeka	5624620	3211734	4402544	12141979	1048281	10730349	331118	976086	1609196	39975907
28	West Total		23976601	19594197	22529175	65359020	3841454	46967756	1249362	7619872	25444675	216582112
29	Grand Total		86581689	68368778	81772378	284995434	12776688	188174747	17518709	21079121	52127495	813395039

Conventions Used in This Book

This book contains the following special elements.

NOTE

Notes provide additional information outside the main thread of the chapter discussion that might still be useful for you to know.

TIP

Tips provide you with quick workarounds and timesaving techniques to help you do your work more efficiently.

CAUTION

Cautions warn you about potential pitfalls you might encounter. Pay attention to these, because they alert you to problems that otherwise could cause you hours of frustration.

Generally, a pivot table would serve you well in any of the following situations:

- You have a large amount of transactional data that has become increasingly difficult to analyze and summarize in a meaningful way.
- You need to find relationships and groupings within your data.
- You need to find a list of unique values for one field in your data.
- You need to find data trends using various time periods.
- You anticipate frequent requests for changes to your data analysis.
- You need to create subtotals that will frequently include new additions.
- You need to organize your data into a format that's easy to chart.

The Anatomy of a Pivot Table

Because the anatomy of a pivot table is what gives it its flexibility and, indeed, its ultimate functionality, it would be difficult to truly understand pivot tables without understanding their basic structure.

A pivot table is composed of four areas. The data you place in these areas define both the utility and the appearance of the pivot table. Keeping in mind that you will go through the process of creating a pivot table in the next chapter, let's prepare by taking a closer look at the four areas and the functionality around them.

Data Area

The data area is shown in Figure 1.5. It is a large rectangular area below and to the right of the headings. In this example, the data area contains a sum of the Revenue field.

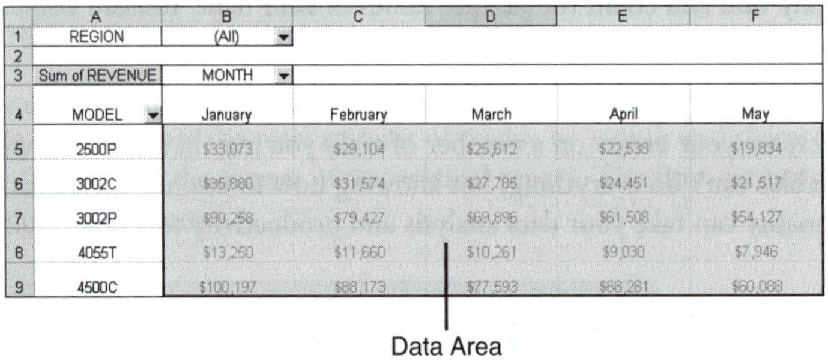

Figure 1.5
The heart of the pivot table is the data area. This area will typically include a total of one or more numeric fields.

	A	B	C	D	E	F
1	REGION	(All)				
2						
3	Sum of REVENUE	MONTH				
4	MODEL	January	February	March	April	May
5	2500P	$33,073	$29,104	$25,612	$22,538	$19,834
6	3002C	$35,880	$31,574	$27,785	$24,451	$21,517
7	3002P	$90,258	$79,427	$69,896	$61,508	$54,127
8	4055T	$13,250	$11,660	$10,261	$9,030	$7,946
9	4500C	$100,197	$88,173	$77,593	$68,281	$60,088

Data Area

The data area is the area that calculates. This area is required to have at least one field and one calculation on that field in it. The data fields that you would drop here would be things you would want to measure or calculate. The data area might include Sum of Revenue, Count of Units, or Average of Price.

It is possible to have many fields in the data area. You might include Sum of Quantity, Sum of Revenue, and Average of Price.

It is also possible to have the same field dropped in the data area twice, but with different calculations. A marketing manager might want to see Minimum of Price, Average Price, and Maximum of Price.

Row Area

The row area is shown in Figure 1.6. It is composed of the headings that go down the left side of the pivot table.

Figure 1.6
The headings down the left side make up the row area of the pivot table.

Row Area

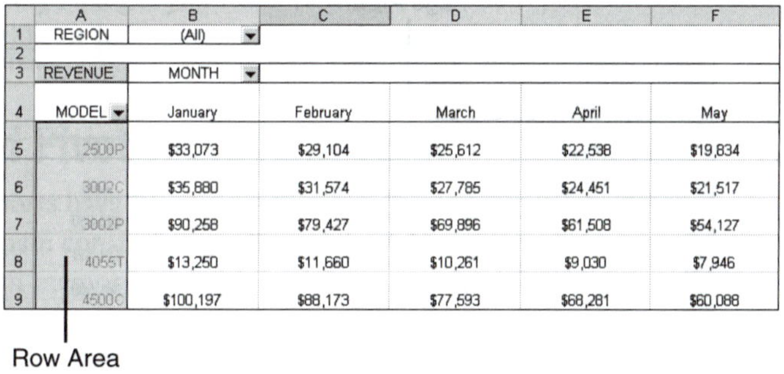

	A	B	C	D	E	F
1	REGION	(All)				
2						
3	REVENUE	MONTH				
4	MODEL	January	February	March	April	May
5	2500P	$33,073	$29,104	$25,612	$22,538	$19,834
6	3002C	$35,880	$31,574	$27,785	$24,451	$21,517
7	3002P	$90,258	$79,427	$69,896	$61,508	$54,127
8	4055T	$13,250	$11,660	$10,261	$9,030	$7,946
9	4500C	$100,197	$88,173	$77,593	$68,281	$60,088

Dropping a field into the row area will display the unique values from that field down the rows of the left side of the pivot table. The row area typically has at least one field, although it is possible to have no fields. The example earlier in the chapter where you needed to produce a one-line report of credits is an example where there are no row fields.

The types of data fields you would drop here are things you want to group and categorize—for example, Products, Names, and Locations.

Column Area

The column area is composed of headings that stretch across the top of columns in a pivot table. The pivot table in Figure 1.7 has the month field in the column area.

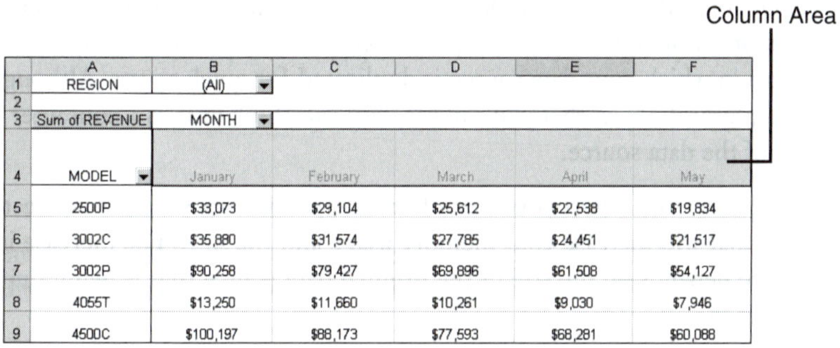

Column Area

Figure 1.7
The column area stretches across the top of the columns. In this example, it contains the unique list of months in your dataset.

	A	B	C	D	E	F
1	REGION	(All)				
2						
3	Sum of REVENUE	MONTH				
4	MODEL	January	February	March	April	May
5	2500P	$33,073	$29,104	$25,612	$22,538	$19,834
6	3002C	$35,880	$31,574	$27,785	$24,451	$21,517
7	3002P	$90,258	$79,427	$69,896	$61,508	$54,127
8	4055T	$13,250	$11,660	$10,261	$9,030	$7,946
9	4500C	$100,197	$88,173	$77,593	$68,281	$60,088

TIP

For a great book on learning VBA macro programming, read *VBA and Macros for Microsoft Excel* by Bill Jelen and Tracy Syrstad (ISBN: 0789731290, Que Publishing). It is another book in the *Business Solutions* series.

After you make the four changes described here, the data is ready for use as a pivot table data source. As you can see in Figure 2.5, there are headings for every column. There are no blank cells, rows, or columns in the data. The monthly data is now presented down column E instead of across several columns.

Figure 2.5
This data will take up six times as many rows, but it is perfectly formatted for pivot table analysis.

	A	B	C	D	E	F
1	REGION	MARKET	STORE	MODEL	MONTH	REVENUE
2	North	Great Lakes	65061011	4055T	April	$2,354
3	North	Great Lakes	65061011	4055T	February	$3,040
4	North	Great Lakes	65061011	4055T	January	$3,454
5	North	Great Lakes	65061011	4055T	March	$2,675
6	North	Great Lakes	65061011	4055T	May	$2,071
7	North	New England	2105015	2500P	April	$11,851
8	North	New England	2105015	2500P	February	$15,304
9	North	New England	2105015	2500P	January	$17,391
10	North	New England	2105015	2500P	March	$13,468
11	North	New England	2105015	2500P	May	$10,429
12	North	New England	22022012	3002C	April	$256
13	North	New England	22022012	3002C	February	$330
14	North	New England	22022012	3002C	January	$375
15	North	New England	22022012	3002C	March	$290
16	North	New England	22022012	3002C	May	$225
17	North	New England	12011011	3002P	April	$35,734
18	North	New England	12011011	3002P	February	$46,145

Creating a Basic Pivot Table

Now that you have a good understanding of the importance of a well-structured data source, let's look at the one you'll be using to build your first pivot table report. Figure 2.6 shows your data source.

Figure 2.6
The data source.

	A	B	C	D	E	F	G	H	I	J	K
1	REGION	MARKET	STORE	IN BALANCE DATE	FISCAL PERIOD	MODEL	LINE OF BUSINESS	REVENUE	UNITS SOLD	SERVICE PLANS SOLD	DAYS IN PERIOD
2	North	Great Lakes	65061011	01/03/03	200205	4055T	Parts	$3,454	0	0	19.0
3	North	Shenandoah Valley	62067017	01/03/03	200205	2500P	Printer Sale	$15,682	2	0	19.0
4	North	Shenandoah Valley	32139049	01/03/03	200205	2500C	Copier Sale	$12,968	6	0	19.0
5	North	New England	2004014	01/03/03	200205	4055T	Parts	$2,789	0	0	19.0
6	North	New England	72074014	01/03/03	200205	4500C	Service Plan	$32,605	0	23	19.0
7	North	New England	12011011	01/03/03	200205	3002P	Service Plan	$52,437	0	30	19.0
8	North	New England	2105015	01/03/03	200205	2500P	Printer Sale	$17,391	2	0	19.0
9	North	New England	22022012	01/03/03	200205	4055T	Parts	$2,468	0	0	19.0
10	North	New England	22022012	01/03/03	200205	3002C	Parts	$375	0	0	19.0
11	North	New York South	12118068	01/03/03	200205	4500C	Service Plan	$67,592	0	30	19.0
12	North	New York South	12118068	01/03/03	200205	3002C	Service Plan	$21,454	0	15	19.0
13	North	Ohio	44040030	01/03/03	200205	3002C	Parts	$979	0	0	19.0
14	North	Ohio	44040020	01/03/03	200205	4055T	Parts	$4,539	0	0	19.0
15	North	Ohio	44040020	01/03/03	200205	3002P	Parts	$3,209	0	0	19.0
16	North	Ohio	34037017	01/03/03	200205	3002P	Parts	$34,612	0	0	19.0
17	North	South Carolina	53154014	01/03/03	200205	3002C	Service Plan	$14,051	0	9	19.0
18	South	North Carolina	63064014	01/03/03	200205	5001P	Parts	$249	0	0	19.0
19	South	North Carolina	73179019	01/03/03	200205	5001P	Service Plan	$3,951	0	1	19.0
20	South	Florida	33130010	01/03/03	200205	3002P	Service Plan	$157,434	0	68	19.0
21	South	Florida	33130010	01/03/03	200205	3002P	Parts	$18,087	0	0	19.0

Introduction to the PivotTable Wizard

To get started, click on any single cell in your data source. This will ensure that the pivot table captures the range of your data source by default. Then go up to the application toolbar and select PivotTable and PivotChart Report from the Data menu.

This will activate the PivotTable Wizard, as shown in Figure 2.7.

Figure 2.7
Step 1 of the PivotTable Wizard allows you to choose from a variety of data sources.

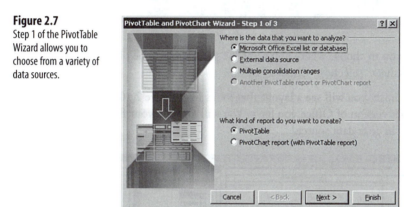

The first step of the PivotTable Wizard allows you to select the location of your data source. Other types of data sources will be discussed later in the book. For now, use the default "Microsoft Excel list or database." Choose Next.

Figure 2.8 shows step 2 of the wizard. If your data is properly structured without any blank rows or columns, Excel will properly sense the correct range for your data.

Figure 2.8
Provided you selected a single cell in your data source, the range se nsed in step 2 is usually correct.

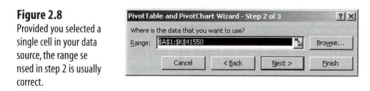

Step 2 of 3 allows you to specify the range of data. Note that the PivotTable Wizard is smart enough to read your data source and accurately auto-fills the range. However, you always want to take note of this to ensure you are capturing all your data. Choose Next.

5. Select the Revenue field from your field list and drag it into the data area, as shown in Figure 2.21. This is the first point where you have a completed pivot table.

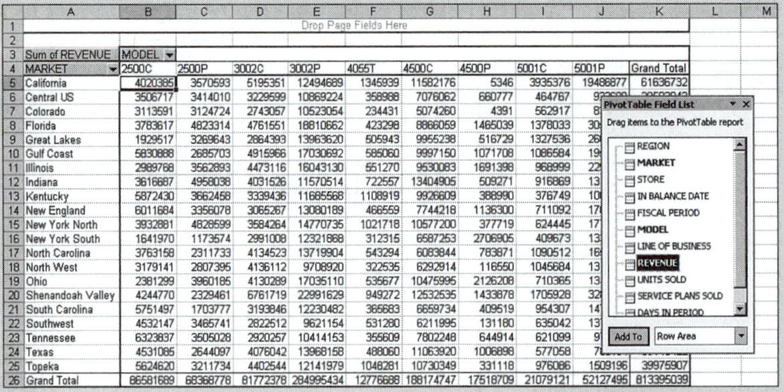

Figure 2.21
A pivot table needs at least one data field.

In five easy steps, you have calculated and designed a report that satisfies the requirements given to you. Select a cell outside of the pivot table in order to hide the pivot table field list, as shown in Figure 2.22.

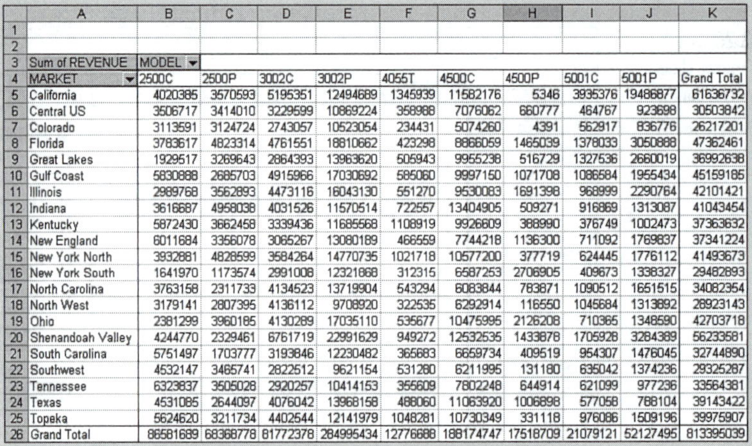

Figure 2.22
This summary can be created in less than a minute.

You can go the extra mile and add one more dimension to your pivot table report in order to allow for analysis by region.

Choose any cell in your pivot table report to redisplay the pivot table field list. Select the Region field from your field list, as shown in Figure 2.23.

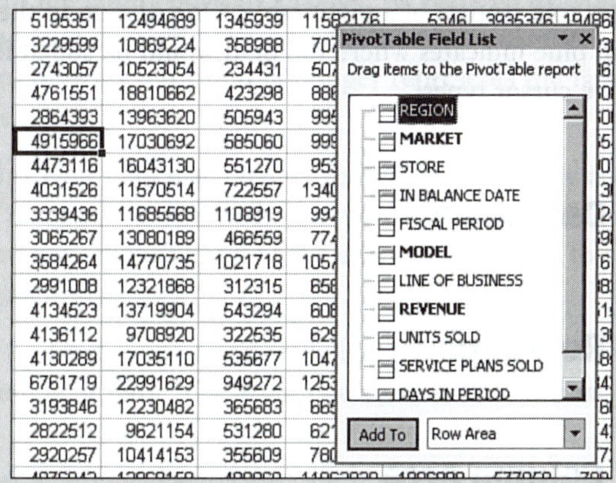

Figure 2.23
The field list will reappear whenever you select a cell in the pivot table.

With the field selected as shown in Figure 2.23, you could use the drop-down next to the Add To button to select Page Area. Or, you could simply drag the Region field into the page area, as shown in Figure 2.24. By default, Excel will show the data for all regions.

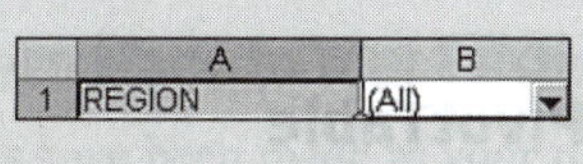

Figure 2.24
When a field is first dropped in the page field area, Excel chooses the option to display the total for all regions.

With the Region field placed into the page area, you can now create separate reports by region if needed. Select the drop-down in cell B2 to see a list of available regions, as shown in Figure 2.25.

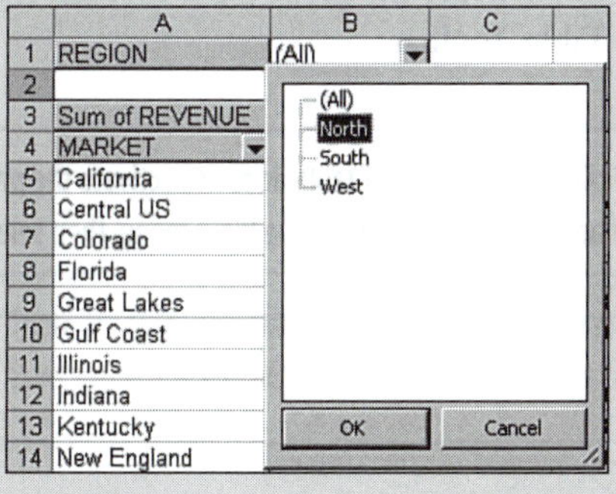

Figure 2.25
Select any region from the drop-down to filter the report to sales for just that region.

Your Data Source's Range Has Been Expanded with the Addition of Rows or Columns

When changes have been made to your data source that affect the range of your data source (that is, you've added rows or columns), you will have to update the range being captured by the pivot cache.

To do this, right-click on your pivot table report and select PivotTable Wizard. You will start in step 3 of the PivotTable Wizard, so choose the Back button to return to step 2 of the wizard.

In step 2, choose the Browse button, as shown in Figure 2.28, to respecify the new location of your data.

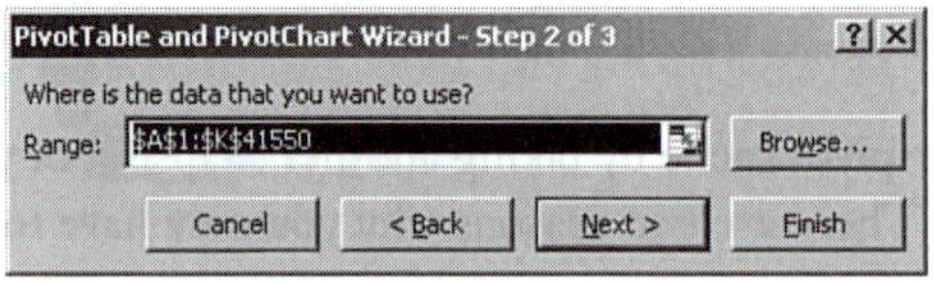

Figure 2.28
If you've added new rows, new columns, or have changed the field headings in your data, you need to respecify the data source using step 2 of the wizard.

Update your range to include new rows and columns and then choose Finish. Your pivot table report will now include your new data.

> **TIP**
>
> Selecting just the columns in your data source as the range (as in $A:$K) will capture all 65,536 rows of the current spreadsheet in your pivot cache. Although this does take up a bit more memory, you will be able to add new rows to your data source and refresh your pivot table report without readjusting your range.

Next Steps

In Chapter 3, "Customizing Fields in a Pivot Table," you will learn how to enhance your pivot table reports by customizing your fields, changing field names, changing summary calculations, applying formats to data fields, adding and removing subtotals, and using the Show As setting.

Customizing Fields in a Pivot Table

3

The Need to Customize

As you build your pivot table reports with the PivotTable Wizard, Excel is busily adding fields and performing calculations in the background.

The wizard is designed to always sum numeric data and to always count text data. The wizard allows you to produce a standard pivot table in a few seconds. However, sometimes the PivotTable Wizard doesn't quite hit the mark.

A common problem is that Excel chooses to count data that you wanted summed. This can happen when your numeric data inadvertently contains a single blank or text cell mixed in.

Sometimes, you want to create something other than the default pivot table. In addition to Sum and Count, Excel offers a total of 11 subtotal options that can be used separately or in combination. You can combine these with nine different running total options. That makes for 5,621 different ways to present each data field in the pivot table.

You can step in and take control of the calculations by customizing the pivot table. Customizations are controlled in the PivotTable Field dialog box.

Displaying the PivotTable Field Dialog Box

Each row field, column field, and data field has its own PivotTable Field dialog box. The easiest way to activate the dialog box is to double-click on the field name in the pivot table.

The new name will appear in the pivot table. Look at cell A3 in Figure 3.4. The name "Revenue " is less awkward than the default "Sum of Revenue."

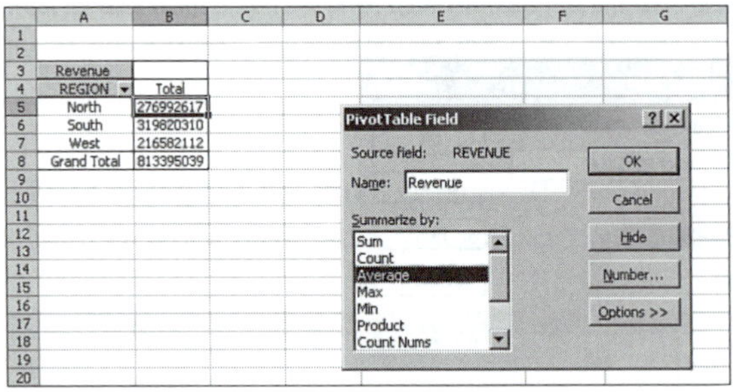

Figure 3.4
The name typed in the PivotTable Field dialog box appears in the pivot table. Although names should be unique, you can trick Excel into accepting a similar name by adding a space to the end of it.

Applying Numeric Formats to Data Fields

As on your standard spreadsheet in Excel, numbers in a pivot table can be formatted to fit your needs (for example, Currency, Percent, and Number). Rather than attempting to format the results of the pivot table using the formatting toolbar, you can easily control the numeric format of a field using the PivotTable Field dialog box. After you set the numeric format for a field, the numeric format will apply to all cells even after the report is pivoted into a new shape.

You'll notice that the PivotTable Field dialog box for data fields has a button on it labeled "Number." Click this button to access the Number tab of the Format Cells dialog box. Here, you can apply any standard or custom numeric format to your data items. Figure 3.5 shows the results of using a custom number format to display dollars in thousands.

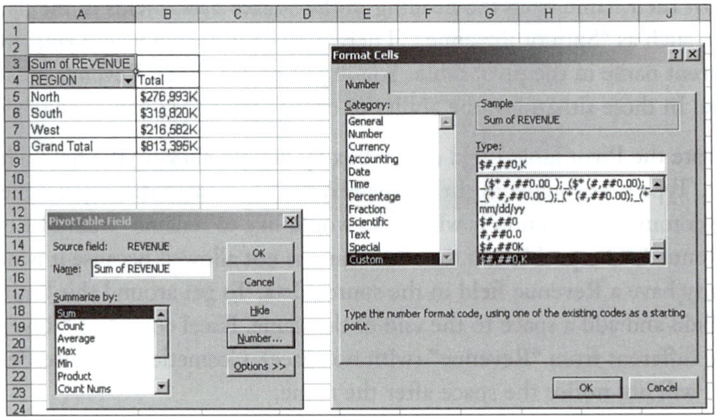

Figure 3.5
Use the Number button on the PivotTable Field dialog box to control numeric formatting for a data field.

Changing Summary Calculations

When creating your pivot table report, the PivotTable Wizard will, by default, summarize your data by either counting or summing the items. Instead of Sum or Count, you might want to choose functions such as Min, Max, and Count Numeric. In all, 11 options are available. However, the common reason to change a summary calculation is because Excel incorrectly chose to count instead of sum your data.

One Blank Cell Causes a Count

If all the cells in a column contain numeric data, Excel will choose to sum. If just one cell is either blank or contains text, Excel will choose to count. Be vigilant while dropping fields into the data section of the pivot table. If a calculation appears to be dramatically too low, check to see if the field name reads "Count of Revenue" instead of "Sum of Revenue." When you created the pivot table in Figure 3.6, you should have noticed that your company only had $41,549 in revenue instead of $800 million. This should be your first clue to notice that the heading in A3 reads "Count of Revenue" instead of "Sum of Revenue." In fact, 41,549 is the number of records in the dataset.

Figure 3.6
Your revenue numbers look anemic. Notice in cell A3 that Excel chose to count instead of sum the revenue. This often happens if you inadvertently have one blank cell in your Revenue column.

	A	B
1		
2		
3	Count of REVENUE	
4	REGION ▼	Total
5	North	13729
6	South	15361
7	West	12459
8	Grand Total	41549

You can easily override the incorrect Count calculation. Activate the PivotTable Field dialog box by double-clicking on Count of Revenue and then change the Summarize By setting from Count to Sum.

Using Functions Other Than Count or Sum

Excel offers a total of 11 functions in the Summarize By section of the PivotTable Field dialog box. The options available are as follows:

- **Sum**—Provides a total of all numeric data.
- **Count**—Counts all cells, including numeric, text, and error cells. This is equivalent to the Excel function =COUNTA().

You must remove subtotals from each of the outer row fields individually. After repeating these steps for Region, Market, and Line of Business, you'll find the report in Figure 3.11 to be much easier on the eyes.

Figure 3.11
After specifying None for three fields, you give the report a cleaner look.

	A	B	C	D	E
1					
2	Revenue				
3	REGION	MARKET	LINE OF BUSINESS	MODEL	Total
4	North	Great Lakes	Parts	3002C	357,898
5				3002P	2,180,810
6				4055T	505,943
7				5001C	600,978
8				5001P	174,507
9			Service Plan	3002C	2,506,495
10				3002P	11,782,810
11				4500C	9,955,238
12				4500P	516,729
13				5001C	726,558
14				5001P	2,485,512
15		New England	Parts	3002C	441,208
16				3002P	1,553,113
17				4055T	466,559
18				5001C	466,164
19				5001P	138,260
20			Service Plan	3002C	2,624,059
21				3002P	11,527,076
22				4500C	7,744,218
23				4500P	1,136,300
24				5001C	244,928
25				5001P	1,631,577

Adding Multiple Subtotals for One Field

You can go in the opposite direction and add customized subtotals by choosing Custom and selecting the types of subtotals you would like to see. The dialog box in Figure 3.12 shows five subtotals being selected for the Region field.

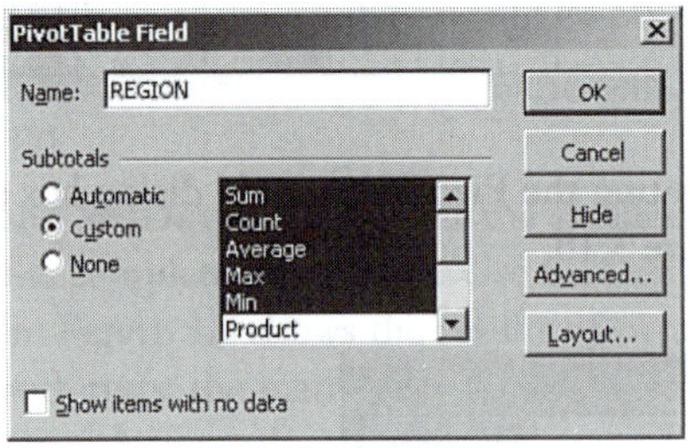

Figure 3.12
By selecting the Custom option in the Subtotals box, you can specify multiple subtotals for one field.

With this option, you can add a host of metrics as subtotals. The report in Figure 3.13 shows all five subtotals for the Region field.

Figure 3.13
Instead of just a sum or count, this report gives a variety of statistics in the Total line for the Region field.

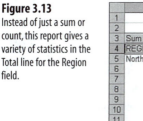

	A	B	C
1			
2			
3	Sum of REVENUE		
4	REGION ▼	MARKET ▼	Total
5	North	Great Lakes	36992638
6		New England	37341224
7		New York North	41493673
8		New York South	29482893
9		Ohio	42703718
10		Shenandoah Valley	56233581
11		South Carolina	32744890
12	North Sum		276992617
13	North Count		13729
14	North Average		20176
15	North Max		296091
16	North Min		1
17	Grand Total		276992617

Using Running Total Options

So far, every pivot table created has been using the Normal option. When you want to create running totals or compare an item to another item, you have eight choices other than Normal.

To access the list of choices, open the PivotTable Field and click the Options button. This opens a combo box called Show Data As.

The ability to create custom calculations is another example of the unique flexibility of pivot table reports. With the Show Data As setting, you can change the calculation for a particular data field to be based on other cells in the data area.

When you click the Options button, your dialog box is expanded to reveal the Show Data As settings. Figure 3.14 illustrates the eight custom calculations available on the Show Data As drop-down list.

Figure 3.14
Click the Options button to reveal additional choices for a data field.

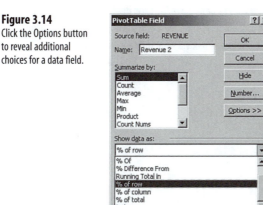

Display Change from Year to Year with Difference From

Companies always want to know how they are doing this month compared to last month. Or, if their business is seasonal, they want to know how they are doing this month versus the same month of last year.

To set up such a report, double-click the Revenue field and choose the Options button. In the Show Data As drop-down list, select Difference From. Because you want to compare one year to another, select Years from the Base Field option. In the Base Item field are several viable options. If you always want to compare one year to the prior year, select the (previous) option, as shown. If you have several years of data and want to always compare to a base year of 2003, you could select 2003.

Figure 3.15 shows both the dialog box settings and the report that results from the settings. The report shows that January of 2004 was $1,058,180 higher than the same month in 2003.

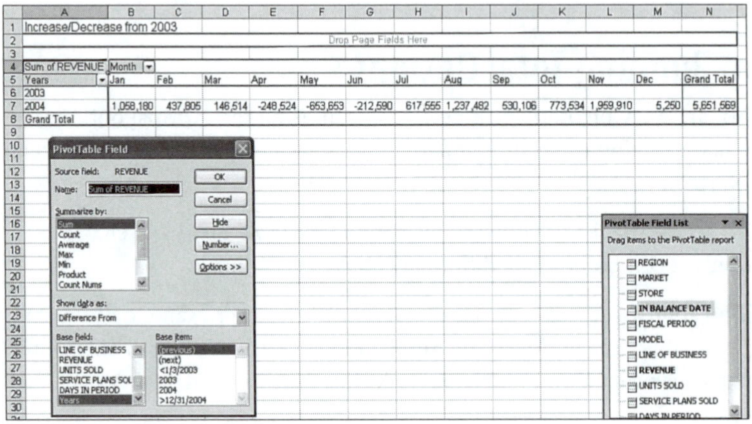

Figure 3.15
The Difference From option allows you to compare two different time periods.

CAUTION

When you use an option from the Show Data As drop-down list, Excel does not change the headings in any way to indicate that the data is in something other than normal view. It is helpful to manually add a title above the pivot table to inform the readers what they are looking at.

Compare One Year to a Prior Year with % Difference From

This option is similar to Difference From. The % Difference From option will display the change as a percentage of the base item. In Figure 3.16, you can see a report where 2004 is reported as a percentage change from 2003.

Figure 3.16
The % Difference From option shows that January 2004 is up 3.24% over January 2003.

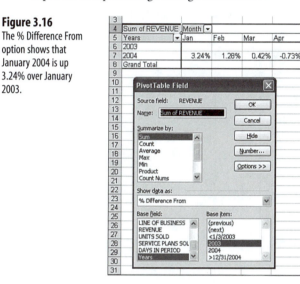

Track YTD Numbers with Running Total In

If you need to compare a year-to-date (YTD) total revenue by month, you can do so with the Running Total In option. In Figure 3.17, the Revenue field is set up to show a Running Total In by Month. With this report, you can see that the company did a total of $103 million through March.

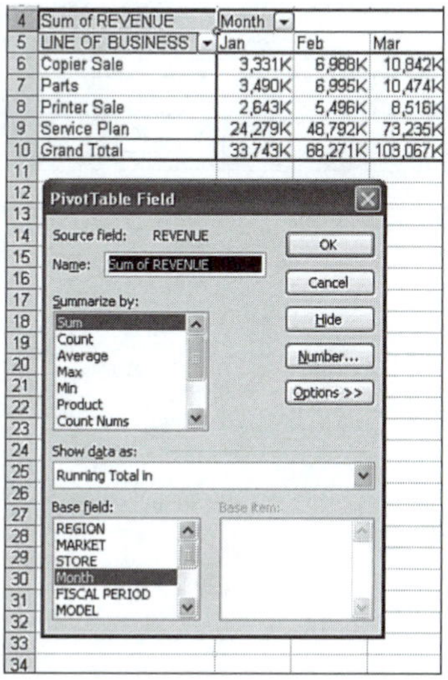

Figure 3.17
The Running Total In option is great for calculating YTD totals.

How Much Does Each Line of Business Contribute to the Total?

The head of the company will often be interested in what percentage of the revenue each division of the company is contributing. In Figure 3.18, you can use the % of Column option to show such a report. Each column will total to 100%. You can see that printers contributed 7.83% of the revenue in January, but only 6.5% in April.

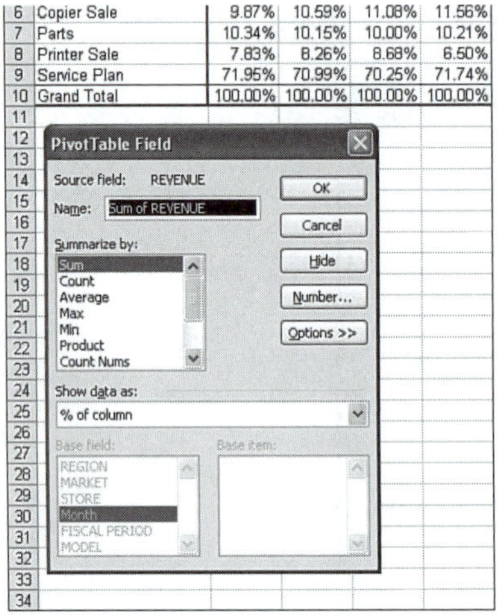

Figure 3.18
The % of Column option produces percentages that total to 100% in each column.

Seasonality Reports

This report is great for seeing the seasonality of your business. The % of Row option will produce percentages that total to 100% in each row. Figure 3.19 shows a report where Jan+Feb+Mar+...+Dec add to 100% for each year.

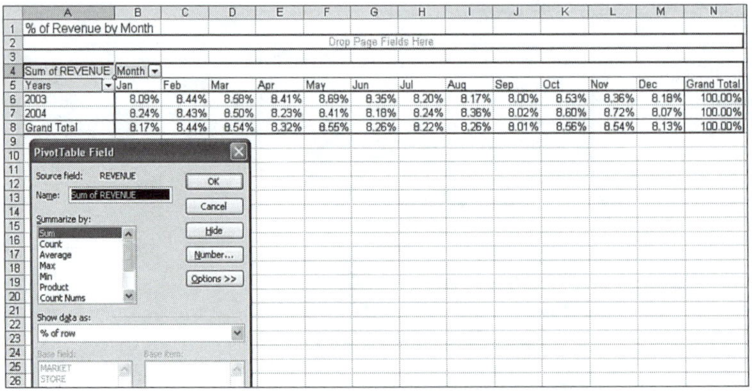

Figure 3.19
The % of Row option produces percentages that total to 100% in each row. This is great for measuring seasonality. Based on this report, copier sales are not very seasonal—people apparently make copies all year long.

Measure Percentage for Two Fields with % of Total

The option % of Total can be used for a myriad of reports. Figure 3.20 shows a report by Region and Line of Business. The values in each cell show the percentage of revenue contribution from that region and line. Cell E9 shows that sales from service plans account for 70% of the total revenue. The South region's sales of service plans account for 27% of total sales.

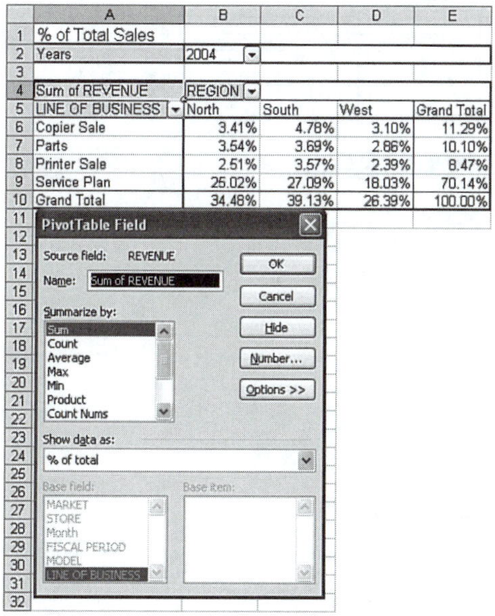

Figure 3.20
The % of Total option produces a report where every cell is a percentage of total sales. The manager of the South Region Service Plan department can use this report to explain why his department should get a raise this year.

Compare One Line to Another Line Using % Of

The % Of option allows you to compare one item to another item. This might be relevant if you believe that part sales and service revenue should be related. Set up a pivot table that compares each line of business to service plan revenue. The result is shown in Figure 3.21.

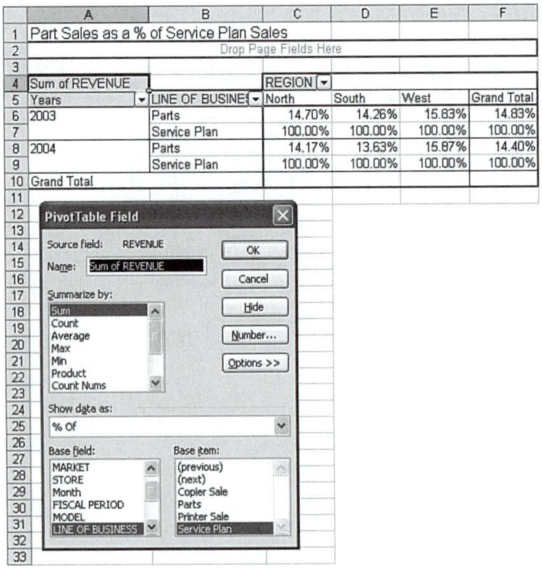

Figure 3.21
The West region is able to move more parts in relation to service plans than the other regions. This report is created using the % Of option with Service Plan as the base item.

Track Relative Importance with the Index Option

The final option is the Index option. This is a fairly obscure calculation. Microsoft claims that this calculation describes the relative importance of a cell within a column.

Look at the normal data in Figure 3.22.

Figure 3.22
Use these numbers when trying to follow the next example.

	A	B	C	D	E
1					
2	Sales	REGION			
3	Fruit	Calif	Tenn	Georgia	Grand Total
4	Banana	$200	$10	$10	$220
5	Kiwi	$200	$10	$10	$220
6	Peach	$100	$10	$180	$290
7	Apple	$100	$8	$10	$118
8	Grand Total	$600	$38	$210	$848

To calculate the index for Georgia Peaches, Excel first calculates Georgia Peaches × Grand Total Sales. This would be $180 × $848. Next, Excel calculates Georgia Sales × Peach Sales. This would be $210 × $290. It then divides the first result by the second result to come up with a relative importance index of 2.51.

The index report is shown in Figure 3.23. Microsoft explains that peaches are more important to Georgia (with an index of 2.51) than they are to California (with an index of 0.49).

Figure 3.23
Using the Index function, Microsoft shows that peach sales are more important in Georgia than in Tennessee.

12	Index	REGION			
13	Fruit	Calif	Tenn	Georgia	Grand Total
14	Banana	1.28	1.01	0.18	1.00
15	Kiwi	1.28	1.01	0.18	1.00
16	Peach	0.49	0.77	2.51	1.00
17	Apple	1.20	1.51	0.34	1.00
18	Grand Total	1.00	1.00	1.00	1.00

Even though Georgia sold more apples than Tennessee, apples are more important to Tennessee (index of 1.51) than to Georgia (index of 0.34). Relatively, an apple shortage will cause more problems in Tennessee than in Georgia.

CASE STUDY

3

Revenue by Line of Business Report

You have been asked to produce a report that will provide a comprehensive look at revenue by line of business. This analysis needs to include revenue dollars by line of business for each market, the percent of revenue that each line represents within the markets, and the percent total company dollars that each market represents within the lines of business. Here are the steps to follow:

1. Place your cursor inside your data source. Then go up to the application toolbar and select PivotTable and PivotChart Report from the Data menu.

2. When the PivotTable Wizard activates, simply choose Finish. A new worksheet will be created with the beginnings of a pivot table report and your field list, as shown in Figure 3.24.

Figure 3.24
After clicking Finish, you will get this blank pivot table report.

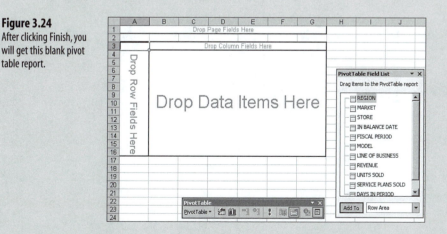

3. Drag the Market field into the row area. Then drag the Line of Business field into the column area, as shown in Figure 3.25.

Figure 3.25
Setting up the row and column fields.

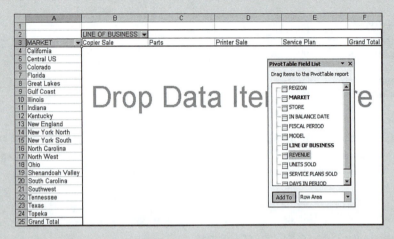

4. Drag the Revenue field into the data area three times to create three separate revenue data items, as shown in Figure 3.26.

Figure 3.26
Having three copies of Sum of Revenue doesn't look useful...yet.

	A	B	C	D	E	F	G
1							
2			LINE OF BUSINESS ▼				
3	MARKET ▼	Data ▼	Copier Sale	Parts	Printer Sale	Service Plan	Grand Total
4	California	Sum of REVENUE	4020385	8720027	3570593	45325727	61636732
5		Sum of REVENUE2	4020385		3570593	45325727	61636732
6		Sum of REVENUE3	4020385		3570593	45325727	61636732
7	Central US	Sum of REVENUE	3506717		3414010	21096068	30503842
8		Sum of REVENUE2	3506717		3414010	21096068	30503842
9		Sum of REVENUE3	3506717		3414010	21096068	30503842
10	Colorado	Sum of REVENUE	3113591		3124724	18118561	26217201
11		Sum of REVENUE2	3113591		3124724	18118561	26217201
12		Sum of REVENUE3	3113591		3124724	18118561	26217201
13	Florida	Sum of REVENUE	3783617		4823314	33718447	47362461
14		Sum of REVENUE2	3783617		4823314	33718447	47362461
15		Sum of REVENUE3	3783617		4823314	33718447	47362461
16	Great Lakes	Sum of REVENUE	1929517		3269643	27973342	36992638
17		Sum of REVENUE2	1929517		3269643	27973342	36992638
18		Sum of REVENUE3	1929517		3269643	27973342	36992638
19	Gulf Coast	Sum of REVENUE	5830888		2685703	31753026	45159185
20		Sum of REVENUE2	5830888		2685703	31753026	45159185
21		Sum of REVENUE3	5830888		2685703	31753026	45159185
22	Illinois	Sum of REVENUE	2989768		3562893	31718353	42101421
23		Sum of REVENUE2	2989768	3830407	3562893	31718353	42101421
24		Sum of REVENUE3	2989768	3830407	3562893	31718353	42101421
25	Indiana	Sum of REVENUE	3616687	4342101	4958038	28126628	41043454

5. Right-click on Sum of Revenue and select Field Settings, as shown in Figure 3.27.

Figure 3.27
Right-click to access Field Settings from a report with many data fields.

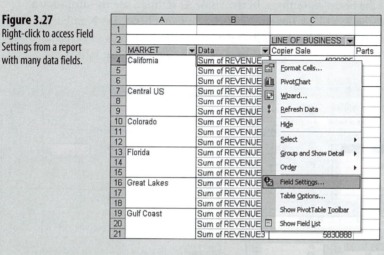

6. As shown in Figure 3.28, change the name of the data field to Total Revenue. Then click the Number button to open the Format Cells dialog box. Change the format of the data item to currency and then close out both dialog boxes by clicking OK.

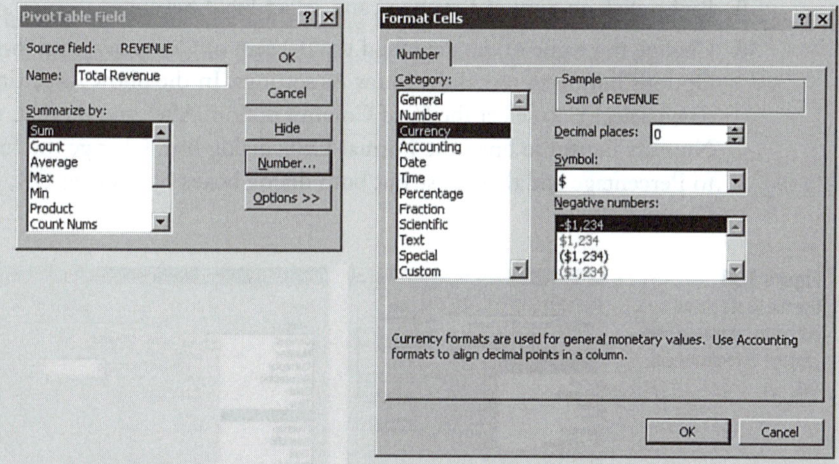

Figure 3.28
Set up the first Revenue item as normal.

7. Right-click on Sum of Revenue2 and select Field Settings.

The second icon on the pivot table toolbar is a lightning bolt over a table (see Figure 4.1). Use this button to open a special PivotTable version of the AutoFormat dialog box. Alternatively, you can choose any cell in your pivot table and then select AutoFormat from the Format menu.

Figure 4.1

The lightning bolt and table icon is the key to making this table look better.

You'll notice there are 22 different formats to choose from: 10 report formats, 10 table formats, the PivotTable Classic default format, and None.

This dialog box is as straightforward as can be. As shown in Figure 4.2, simply select the format you would like to see your pivot table report in and click OK.

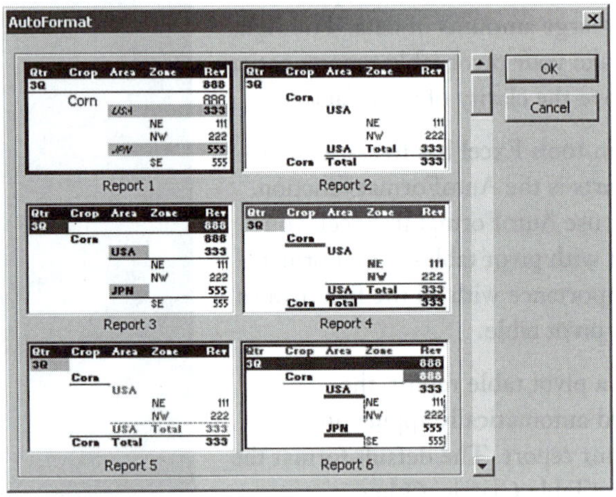

Figure 4.2

Select a predefined format and click OK. It is easy to select another format if the chosen one doesn't suit your tastes.

When you select one of the report formats (Report 1 through Report 10), your pivot table's structure will actually change. Compare the pivot table report in Figure 4.1 with the one in Figure 4.3. The only difference is that you selected Report 5 from the AutoFormat dialog box. Excel moved the Line of Business field from the Column Field area to the outermost field in the Row Field area. This allows for indenting and gives your pivot table report a layered look and feel.

Figure 4.3
Any of the 10 report-style AutoFormats will rearrange your data to eliminate column fields.

	LINE OF BUSINESS	REGION	MARKET	REVENUE
	Copier Sale			
		North		
			Great Lakes	1,929,517
			New England	6,011,684
			New York North	3,932,881
			New York South	1,641,970
			Ohio	2,381,299
			Shenandoah Valley	4,244,770
			South Carolina	5,751,497
		North Total		25,893,618
		South		
			Florida	3,783,617
			Gulf Coast	5,830,888
			Illinois	2,989,768
			Indiana	3,616,687
			Kentucky	5,872,430
			North Carolina	3,763,158
			Tennessee	6,323,837
			Texas	4,531,085
		South Total		36,711,470
		West		
			California	4,020,385
			Central US	3,506,717
			Colorado	3,113,591
			North West	3,179,141
			Southwest	4,532,147
			Topeka	5,624,620
		West Total		23,976,601
	Copier Sale Total			86,581,689

When you select one of the 10 table formats (Table 1 through Table 10), your pivot table report's structure is maintained while other attributes are changed. Figure 4.4 shows the original pivot table changes to use Table 7 from the AutoFormat dialog box.

Figure 4.4
Any of the 10 table-style AutoFormats will keep the table in the original format while applying styles to the various levels of subtotals.

REGION	MARKET	Copier Sale	Parts	Printer Sale	Service Plan	Grand Total
REVENUE		LINE OF BUSINESS				
North	Great Lakes	1929517	3820136	3269643	27973342	36992638
	New England	6011684	3065304	3356078	24908158	37341224
	New York North	3932881	4821041	4828599	27911152	41493673
	New York South	1641970	2530757	1173574	24136592	29482893
	Ohio	2381299	4692767	3960185	31669467	42703718
	Shenandoah Valley	4244770	6967670	2329461	42691680	56233581
	South Carolina	5751497	3165496	1703777	22124120	32744890
North Total		25893618	29063171	20621317	201414511	276992617
South	Florida	3783617	5037083	4823314	33718447	47362461
	Gulf Coast	5830888	4889568	2685703	31753026	45159185
	Illinois	2989768	3830407	3562893	31718353	42101421
	Indiana	3616687	4342101	4958038	28126628	41043454
	Kentucky	5872430	3687359	3662458	24141385	37363632
	North Carolina	3763158	3804215	2311733	24203248	34082354
	Tennessee	6323837	2830384	3505028	20905132	33564381
	Texas	4531085	2784152	2644097	29184088	39143422
South Total		36711470	31205269	28153264	223750307	319820310
West	California	4020385	8720027	3570593	45325727	61636732
	Central US	3506717	2487047	3414010	21096068	30503842
	Colorado	3113591	1862325	3124724	18116561	26217201
	North West	3179141	3660700	2807395	19275907	28923143
	Southwest	4532147	2355409	3465741	18971990	29325287
	Topeka	5624620	4584545	3211734	26555008	39975907
West Total		23976601	23670053	19594197	149341261	216582112

Selecting the PivotTable Classic option returns your report to its default formatting, as shown in Figure 4.5.

Figure 4.5
The PivotTable Classic format.

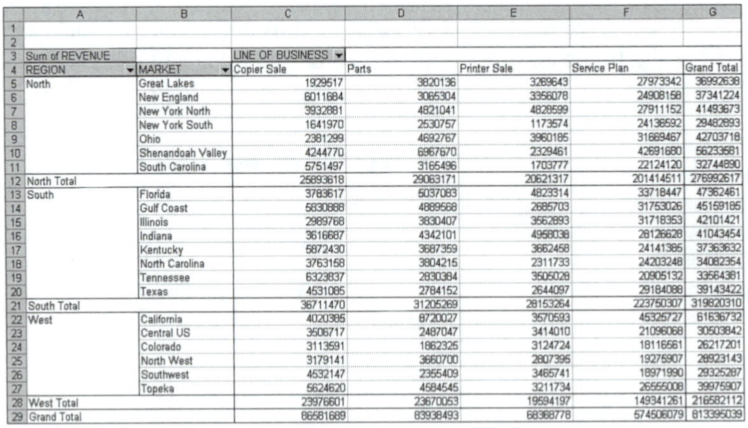

Sum of REVENUE		LINE OF BUSINESS ▼				
REGION ▼	MARKET ▼	Copier Sale ▼	Parts	Printer Sale	Service Plan	Grand Total
North	Great Lakes	1929517	3820136	3269643	27973342	36992636
	New England	6011684	3065304	3356078	24908158	37341224
	New York North	3932881	4821041	4826599	27911152	41493673
	New York South	1641970	2530757	1173574	24136592	29482893
	Ohio	2381299	4692767	3960185	31669467	42703718
	Shenandoah Valley	4244770	6967670	2329461	42691680	56233581
	South Carolina	5751497	3165496	1703777	22124120	32744890
North Total		25893618	29063171	20621317	201414511	276992617
South	Florida	3783617	5037083	4823314	33718447	47362461
	Gulf Coast	5830888	4889568	2685703	31753026	45159185
	Illinois	2989768	3830407	3562893	31718353	42101421
	Indiana	3616687	4342101	4968038	28126628	41043454
	Kentucky	5872430	3687359	3662458	24141385	37363632
	North Carolina	3763158	3804215	2311733	24203248	34082354
	Tennessee	6323837	2830384	3505028	20905132	33564381
	Texas	4531085	2784152	2644097	29184088	39143422
South Total		36711470	31205269	28153264	223750307	319820310
West	California	4020395	8720027	3570593	45325727	61636732
	Central US	3506717	2487047	3414010	21096068	30503842
	Colorado	3113591	1862325	3124724	18116561	26217201
	North West	3179141	3660700	2807396	19275907	28923143
	Southwest	4632147	2355409	3465741	18971990	29325287
	Topeka	5624620	4684545	3211734	26555008	39975907
West Total		23976601	23670053	19594197	149341261	216582112
Grand Total		86581689	83938493	68368778	574506079	813395039

Selecting the None option removes all color and border formatting.

Applying Your Own Style

Although the AutoFormat feature is a convenient way to apply formatting to your pivot table reports, you may run into situations where the available options don't give you the effect you're looking for. In these cases, you can manually apply formatting that will suit your needs.

When applying your own style, you can pinpoint an individual cell in your pivot table report or an entire section with your report.

For example, let's say that each market in the pivot table report in Figure 4.6 needs to be formatted to have a background color of black with white lettering. If you move your cursor over the Market field, your cursor image will change into a cross.

Figure 4.6
Notice the cross-style mouse pointer in cell B4. This will select only a single cell.

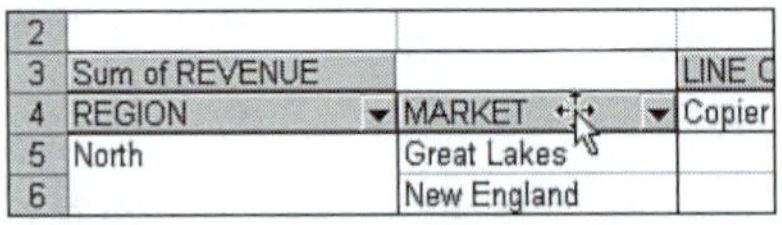

Sum of REVENUE		LINE C
REGION ▼	MARKET ⊹ ▼	Copier
North	Great Lakes	
	New England	

Moving your cursor a little higher will change the cursor image to a black arrow (see Figure 4.7), pointing toward the data items in the Market field. This indicates that any action taken at this point will affect all data items in the Market field. If you click your mouse here, all the data items in the Market field will be selected.

Figure 4.7
Move the mouse pointer up a bit and it will change into the black arrow. This will select all Market cells.

	A	B	
1			
2			
3	Sum of REVENUE		LINE (
4	REGION ▼	MARKET ▼	Copier
5	North	Great Lakes	
6		New England	

Now, when you apply your formatting using the standard toolbar, it will be applied to all data items under the Market field. Figure 4.8 shows the pivot table after selecting a white font and black background.

Figure 4.8
After you've selected the Market range, formatting changes apply to all the cells that contain a market.

	A	B	C
1			
2			
3	Sum of REVENUE		LINE OF BUSINESS ▼
4	REGION ▼	MARKET ▼	Copier Sale
5	North	Great Lakes	1929517
6		New England	6011684
7		New York North	3932881
8		New York South	1641970
9		Ohio	2381299
10		Shenandoah Valley	4244770
11		South Carolina	5751497
12	North Total		25893618
13	South	Florida	3783617
14		Gulf Coast	5830888
15		Illinois	2989768
16		Indiana	3616687
17		Kentucky	5872430
18		North Carolina	3763158
19		Tennessee	6323837
20		Texas	4531085
21	South Total		36711470
22	West	California	4020385
23		Central US	3506717
24		Colorado	3113591
25		North West	3179141
26		Southwest	4532147
27		Topeka	5624620
28	West Total		23976601
29	Grand Total		86581689

4

Using this method, you can format all data items in a given field, all instances of a single data item, subtotals, and grand totals.

Let's take the same pivot table and format all the "Region" field subtotals. Simply move your mouse to the left edge of one of the subtotals, as shown in Figure 4.9, until your cursor image turns into a black arrow. Then click your mouse to select all the Region subtotals.

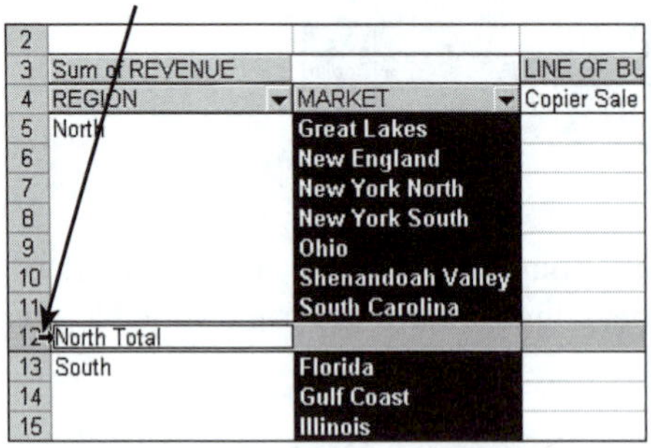

Figure 4.9

Move your mouse to the left of any subtotal and click, and all of that level of subtotals will be selected.

Choose a gray background and a bold font to change the subtotals as shown in Figure 4.10.

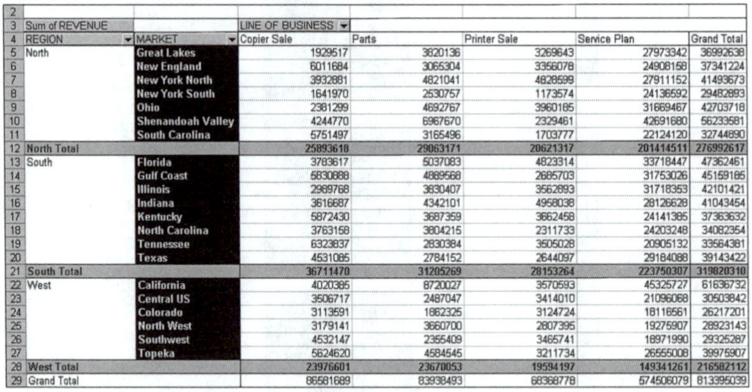

Figure 4.10

After using the preceding technique to select just the totals, it is a snap to format all the subtotals at once.

> **TIP**
> You can apply formatting to multiple sections of your pivot table report at one time by holding down the Ctrl key on your keyboard while selecting each section.

You can similarly choose all the data in the North region. Move the mouse pointer to the left of any of the cells in A5:A11 to select that region.

If you use pivot tables a lot, you might want to consider dragging three new buttons to the pivot table toolbar. Right-click any toolbar and choose Customize. The Customize dialog box shown in Figure 4.11 will activate. In the Categories list box, choose Data. In the Commands list box, scroll down to the three pivot table selection icons. These icons let you select all labels, all data, or both. Drag these to any visible toolbar.

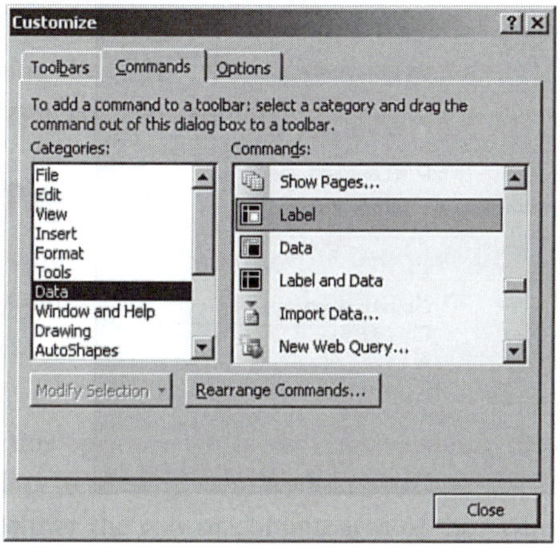

Figure 4.11
If you frequently apply your own formatting to pivot tables, consider adding these three icons to the pivot table tool-bar.

Setting Table Options

Beyond the formatting of colors and fonts within your pivot table report, you can tweak 13 format options to modify the way your pivot data is presented and printed. These options are found in the PivotTable Options dialog box. If you regularly set these options, you can access step 3 of the PivotTable Wizard by choosing the Options button in the lower left of the dialog box.

After creating a pivot table, you can activate the PivotTable Options dialog box by right-clicking inside your pivot table and selecting Table Options. Alternatively, the pivot table drop-down on the left side of the pivot table toolbar includes a Table Options selection near the bottom.

Repeat Item Labels on Each Printed Page

This option is checked by default. When you have two row fields, Excel uses an outline view for the outer row field. In Figure 4.15, row 51 will be at the top of a new page. When you are looking at page 2, you won't really know that rows 51 through 53 apply to the South region.

Figure 4.15
Due to the annoying outline view of pivot tables, you wouldn't expect to see a label of South at the top of page 2.

	A	B	C	D	E
28		200404		11,500,535	11,500,535
29	North Total		135,798,929	141,193,688	276,992,617
30	South	200205	12,727,533		12,727,533
31		200206	13,679,193		13,679,193
32		200207	13,469,631		13,469,631
33		200208	13,368,172		13,368,172
34		200209	13,830,922		13,830,922
35		200210	13,530,350		13,530,350
36		200211	13,094,448		13,094,448
37		200212	13,124,048		13,124,048
38		200301	12,937,835		12,937,835
39		200302	13,354,434		13,354,434
40		200303	13,319,244		13,319,244
41		200304	13,127,058		13,127,058
42		200305		13,372,402	13,372,402
43		200306		13,521,005	13,521,005
44		200307		13,704,411	13,704,411
45		200308		13,180,773	13,180,773
46		200309		13,500,566	13,500,566
47		200310		13,115,848	13,115,848
48		200311		13,182,356	13,182,356
49		200312		13,468,008	13,468,008
50		200401		12,792,406	12,792,406
51		200402		13,609,530	13,609,530
52		200403		14,011,254	14,011,254
53		200404		12,798,883	12,798,883
54	South Total		159,562,868	160,257,442	319,820,310
55	West	200205	8,720,476		8,720,476

This option is one of the more amazing options in Excel. When it is checked, even though the word "South" does not appear in cell A51, Excel will ensure that the word "South" does print as if it were in cell A51. Figure 4.16 shows the page preview for page 2.

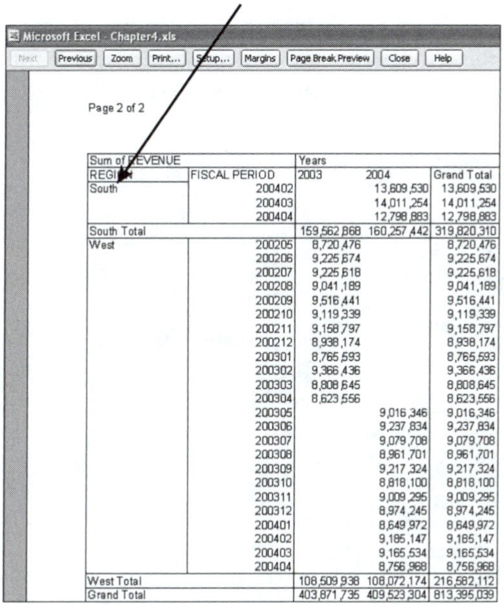

Sum of REVENUE		Years		
REGION	FISCAL PERIOD	2003	2004	Grand Total
South	200402		13,609,530	13,609,530
	200403		14,011,254	14,011,254
	200404		12,798,883	12,798,883
South Total		159,562,868	160,257,442	319,820,310
West	200205	8,720,476		8,720,476
	200206	9,225,674		9,225,674
	200207	9,225,618		9,225,618
	200208	9,041,189		9,041,189
	200209	9,516,441		9,516,441
	200210	9,119,339		9,119,339
	200211	9,158,797		9,158,797
	200212	8,938,174		8,938,174
	200301	8,765,593		8,765,593
	200302	9,366,436		9,366,436
	200303	8,808,645		8,808,645
	200304	8,623,556		8,623,556
	200305		9,016,346	9,016,346
	200306		9,237,834	9,237,834
	200307		9,079,708	9,079,708
	200308		8,961,701	8,961,701
	200309		9,217,324	9,217,324
	200310		8,818,100	8,818,100
	200311		9,009,295	9,009,295
	200312		8,974,245	8,974,245
	200401		8,649,972	8,649,972
	200402		9,185,147	9,185,147
	200403		9,165,534	9,165,534
	200404		8,756,968	8,756,968
West Total		108,509,938	108,072,174	216,582,112
Grand Total		403,871,735	409,523,304	813,395,039

Figure 4.16
The word "South" just under "Region" prints, even though that cell does not contain this word. It is one of the more amazing features of Excel.

Mark Totals with *

Checking this option will mark subtotals with an asterisk if the data is based on an OLAP data source and contains values where some of the data items are hidden. This option is designed to make you aware that there are data items that are not being calculated in the subtotals.

Page Layout

This option alters the orientation of your page area layout. Typically, multiple page fields are stacked going down a column, as shown in Figure 4.17.

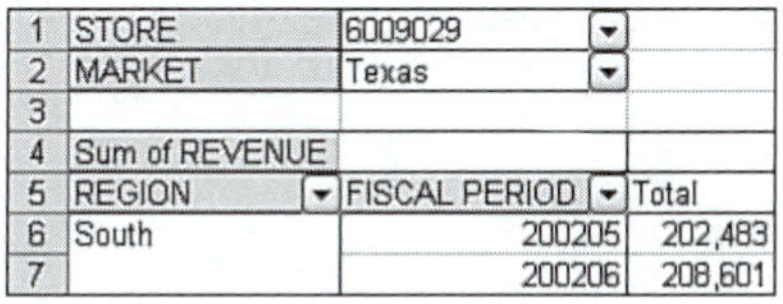

1	STORE	6009029	
2	MARKET	Texas	
3			
4	Sum of REVENUE		
5	REGION	FISCAL PERIOD	Total
6	South	200205	202,483
7		200206	208,601

Figure 4.17
This arrangement of page fields is due to selecting Down, Then Over from the Page Layout drop-down.

If you change the Page Layout drop-down to Over, Then Down, as shown in Figure 4.18, the page fields will stretch across a row.

It's important to note that setting the Page Layout alone to "Over, Then Down" will merely cause your page fields to line up across the same row. To get the correct effect, this setting should be used in conjunction with the Fields per Row setting shown in Figure 4.18. Figure 4.19 shows the results of the settings in Figure 4.18. The effect is that the page fields are rearranged to line up two per row, as Fields per Row is set to 2.

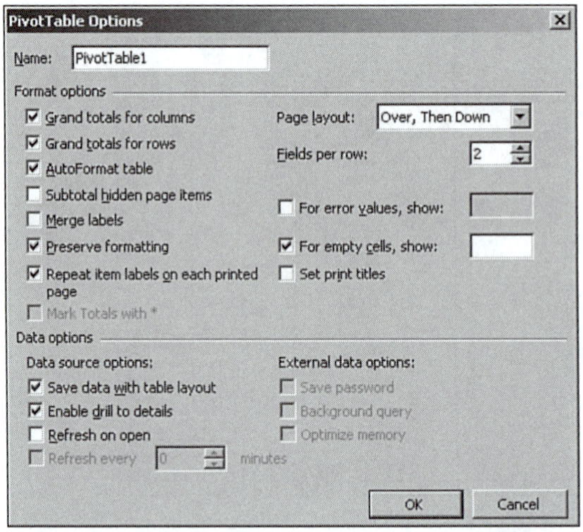

Figure 4.18
You can rearrange the page fields by selecting Over, Then Down from the Page Layout drop-down.

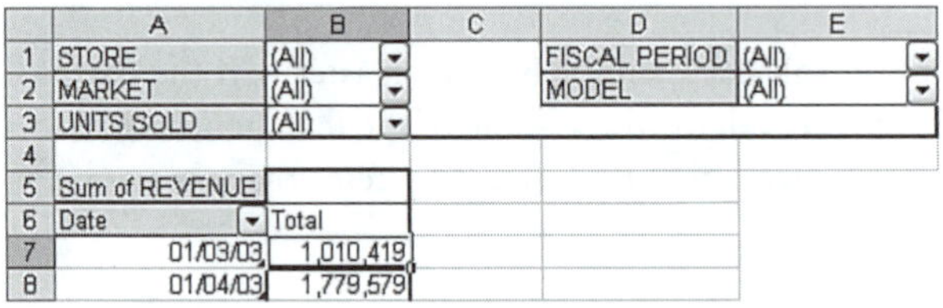

Figure 4.19
You can control how your page fields are displayed by using the Fields per Row setting in conjunction with the Page Layout setting.

For Error Values Show

When you check this option, you can replace the error values in your pivot table report with any character you specify. Error values are as follows: #####, #VALUE!, #DIV/0!, #NAME?, #N/A, #REF!, #NUM!, #NULL!.

For Empty Cells Show

This is one of the more annoying features of pivot tables. In Figure 4.20, cell B7 shows that there were no sales on January 5 for store 2004014. Excel shows this by leaving the cell blank. In Chapter 3, "Customizing Fields in a Pivot Table," you learned that having blank cells instead of numeric cells can cause Excel to erroneously choose to count instead of sum data. It seems that Microsoft is breaking its own rules by leaving these cells blank instead of putting a zero in them.

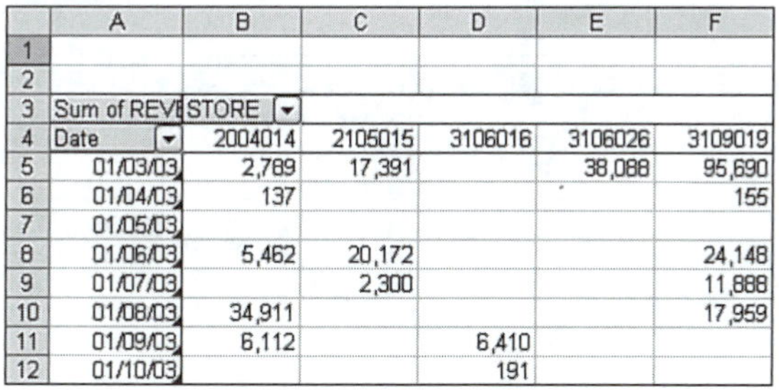

Figure 4.20

Excel leaves a cell blank if there are no records that show sales for a particular combination of date and store. If you would prefer to have a zero appear instead, use the For Empty Cells Show field.

	A	B	C	D	E	F
1						
2						
3	Sum of REVE	STORE ▾				
4	Date ▾	2004014	2105015	3106016	3106026	3109019
5	01/03/03	2,789	17,391		38,088	95,690
6	01/04/03	137				155
7	01/05/03					
8	01/06/03	5,462	20,172			24,148
9	01/07/03		2,300			11,888
10	01/08/03	34,911				17,959
11	01/09/03	6,112		6,410		
12	01/10/03			191		

By setting the For Empty Cells Show field to a zero, you can ensure that all the fields in the data section of your pivot table have a value.

Set Print Titles

If you want to show the row and column labels in your pivot table report on each printed page of your report, check this option.

4

CASE STUDY

Formatting a Pivot Table

You were emailed the pivot table report in Figure 4.21 and your goal is to make it easier to read and comprehend. You decide that all it needs is a few format adjustments. Here are the steps you will follow:

Figure 4.21
Your goal is to make this report easier to read.

	A	B	C	D	E	F	G	H	I	J	K	L	M
1	REGION	North											
2	STORE	(All)											
3													
4				MODEL									
5	MARKET	LINE OF BUSINESS	Data	2500C	2500P	3002C	3002P	4055T	4500C	4500P	5001C	5001P	Grand Total
6	Great Lakes	Copier Sale	UNITS SOLD	611									611
7			SERVICE PLANS SOLD										
8		Parts	UNITS SOLD										
9			SERVICE PLANS SOLD										
10		Printer Sale	UNITS SOLD		649								649
11			SERVICE PLANS SOLD										
12		Service Plan	UNITS SOLD										
13			SERVICE PLANS SOLD			1422	4479		5038	212	426	996	12573
14	Great Lakes UNITS SOLD			611	649								1260
15	Great Lakes SERVICE PLANS SOLD					1422	4479		5038	212	426	996	12573
16	New England	Copier Sale	UNITS SOLD	1820									1820
17			SERVICE PLANS SOLD										
18		Parts	UNITS SOLD										
19			SERVICE PLANS SOLD										
20		Printer Sale	UNITS SOLD		702								702
21			SERVICE PLANS SOLD										
22		Service Plan	UNITS SOLD										
23			SERVICE PLANS SOLD			1526	4526		4336	425	119	691	11623
24	New England UNITS SOLD			1820	702								2522
25	New England SERVICE PLANS SOLD					1526	4526		4336	425	119	691	11623
26	New York North	Copier Sale	UNITS SOLD	1274									1274
27			SERVICE PLANS SOLD										
28		Parts	UNITS SOLD										
29			SERVICE PLANS SOLD										
30		Printer Sale	UNITS SOLD		951								951
31			SERVICE PLANS SOLD										
32		Service Plan	UNITS SOLD										
33			SERVICE PLANS SOLD			1756	4618		5899	155	204	692	13324
34	New York North UNITS SOLD			1274	951								2225
35	New York North SERVICE PLANS SOLD					1756	4618		5899	155	204	692	13324

1. Select the Market field and then format the background color as blue and change the font color to bold white, as shown in Figure 4.22.

Figure 4.22
Remember to place the mouse pointer at the top edge of the Market field in order to select all Market cells.

	A	B	C	D	E	F	G	H	I	J	K	L	M
1	REGION	North											
2	STORE	(All)											
3													
4				MODEL									
5	MARKET	LINE OF BUSINESS	Data	2500C	2500P	3002C	3002P	4055T	4500C	4500P	5001C	5001P	Grand Total
6	Great Lakes	Copier Sale	UNITS SOLD	611									611
7			SERVICE PLANS SOLD										
8		Parts	UNITS SOLD										
9			SERVICE PLANS SOLD										
10		Printer Sale	UNITS SOLD		649								649
11			SERVICE PLANS SOLD										
12		Service Plan	UNITS SOLD										
13			SERVICE PLANS SOLD			1422	4479		5038	212	426	996	12573
14	Great Lakes UNITS SOLD			611	649								1260
15	Great Lakes SERVICE PLANS SOLD					1422	4479		5038	212	426	996	12573
16	New England	Copier Sale	UNITS SOLD	1820									1820
17			SERVICE PLANS SOLD										
18		Parts	UNITS SOLD										
19			SERVICE PLANS SOLD										
20		Printer Sale	UNITS SOLD		702								702
21			SERVICE PLANS SOLD										
22		Service Plan	UNITS SOLD										
23			SERVICE PLANS SOLD			1526	4526		4336	425	119	691	11623
24	New England UNITS SOLD			1820	702								2522
25	New England SERVICE PLANS SOLD					1526	4526		4336	425	119	691	11623
26	New York North	Copier Sale	UNITS SOLD	1274									1274
27			SERVICE PLANS SOLD										
28		Parts	UNITS SOLD										
29			SERVICE PLANS SOLD										
30		Printer Sale	UNITS SOLD		951								951
31			SERVICE PLANS SOLD										
32		Service Plan	UNITS SOLD										
33			SERVICE PLANS SOLD			1756	4618		5899	155	204	692	13324
34	New York North UNITS SOLD			1274	951								2225
35	New York North SERVICE PLANS SOLD					1756	4618		5899	155	204	692	13324

2. Select both subtotals for the Market field and make the font bold.

3. Select the Line of Business field and then format the background color as gray and format the font as bold, as shown in Figure 4.23.

Figure 4.23
Formatting the Line of Business cells.

4. Activate the PivotTable Options dialog box and make the following changes, as shown in Figure 4.24:

Figure 4.24
The PivotTable Options dialog box after making all the changes described in step 4.

4

- Remove the grand totals for columns.
- Remove the grand totals for rows.
- Disable the AutoFormat Table option.
- Change Page Layout to Over, Then Down.
- Check the For Empty Cells Show option and enter an underscore character (_).

With just a few clicks, you've improved the look of your pivot table report, eliminated conspicuous empty spaces, and made your report easier to read and comprehend. The resulting pivot table is shown in Figure 4.25.

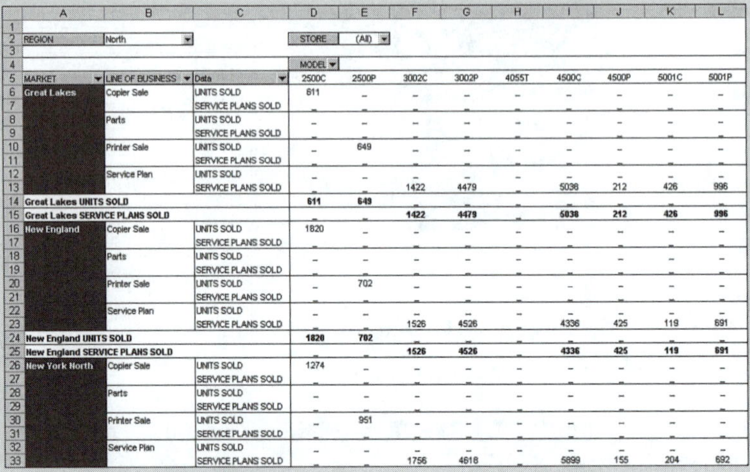

	A	B	C	D	E	F	G	H	I	J	K	L
1												
2	REGION	North		STORE	(All)							
3												
4				MODEL								
5	MARKET	LINE OF BUSINESS	Data	2500C	2500P	3002C	3002P	4055T	4500C	4500P	5001C	5001P
6	Great Lakes	Copier Sale	UNITS SOLD	611	_	_	_	_	_	_	_	_
7			SERVICE PLANS SOLD	_	_	_	_	_	_	_	_	_
8		Parts	UNITS SOLD	_	_	_	_	_	_	_	_	_
9			SERVICE PLANS SOLD	_	_	_	_	_	_	_	_	_
10		Printer Sale	UNITS SOLD	_	649	_	_	_	_	_	_	_
11			SERVICE PLANS SOLD	_	_	_	_	_	_	_	_	_
12		Service Plan	UNITS SOLD	_	_	_	_	_	_	_	_	_
13			SERVICE PLANS SOLD	_	_	1422	4479	_	5038	212	426	996
14	**Great Lakes UNITS SOLD**			**611**	**649**	_	_	_	_	_	_	_
15	**Great Lakes SERVICE PLANS SOLD**			_	_	**1422**	**4479**	_	**5038**	**212**	**426**	**996**
16	New England	Copier Sale	UNITS SOLD	1820	_	_	_	_	_	_	_	_
17			SERVICE PLANS SOLD	_	_	_	_	_	_	_	_	_
18		Parts	UNITS SOLD	_	_	_	_	_	_	_	_	_
19			SERVICE PLANS SOLD	_	_	_	_	_	_	_	_	_
20		Printer Sale	UNITS SOLD	_	702	_	_	_	_	_	_	_
21			SERVICE PLANS SOLD	_	_	_	_	_	_	_	_	_
22		Service Plan	UNITS SOLD	_	_	_	_	_	_	_	_	_
23			SERVICE PLANS SOLD	_	_	1526	4526	_	4336	425	119	691
24	**New England UNITS SOLD**			**1820**	**702**	_	_	_	_	_	_	_
25	**New England SERVICE PLANS SOLD**			_	_	**1526**	**4526**	_	**4336**	**425**	**119**	**691**
26	New York North	Copier Sale	UNITS SOLD	1274	_	_	_	_	_	_	_	_
27			SERVICE PLANS SOLD	_	_	_	_	_	_	_	_	_
28		Parts	UNITS SOLD	_	_	_	_	_	_	_	_	_
29			SERVICE PLANS SOLD	_	_	_	_	_	_	_	_	_
30		Printer Sale	UNITS SOLD	_	951	_	_	_	_	_	_	_
31			SERVICE PLANS SOLD	_	_	_	_	_	_	_	_	_
32		Service Plan	UNITS SOLD	_	_	_	_	_	_	_	_	_
33			SERVICE PLANS SOLD	_	_	1756	4618	_	5899	155	204	692

Figure 4.25
The final report.

Next Steps

In Chapter 5, "Controlling the Way You View Your Pivot Data," you will learn about the various tools you can use to alter the way you see your pivot data. You will become skilled at hiding data as well as grouping, sorting, ranking, and limiting data to the top or bottom values.

Controlling the Way You View Your Pivot Data

5

Showing and Hiding Options

By their nature, pivot tables will summarize and show the data from all records in your dataset. There may, however, be situations when you want to inhibit certain data items from being included in your pivot table summary. In these situations, you can choose to hide a data item.

The Basics of Hiding an Item

When you hide a data item, you are not only preventing the data item from being shown on the report, you are also preventing it from being factored into the summary calculation.

Figure 5.1 shows a pivot table with Market in the row area. Two numeric fields—Units Sold and Revenue—appear along the column area. Line of Business is in the page area and is currently set to Copier Sales.

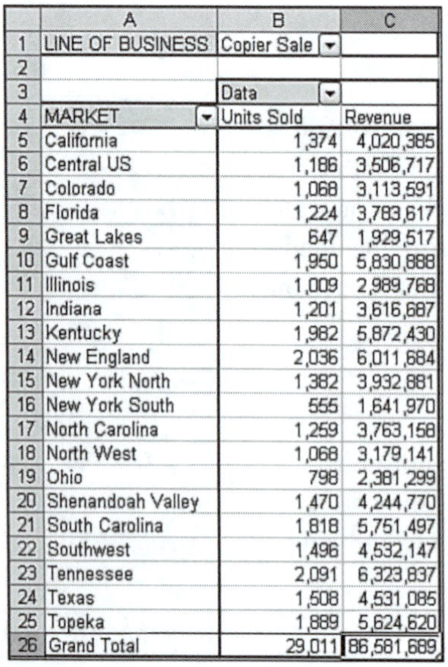

Figure 5.1

This pivot table summa-rizes all copier sales, and it reports $86 million in sales.

	A	B	C
1	LINE OF BUSINESS	Copier Sale ▼	
2			
3		Data ▼	
4	MARKET ▼	Units Sold	Revenue
5	California	1,374	4,020,385
6	Central US	1,186	3,506,717
7	Colorado	1,068	3,113,591
8	Florida	1,224	3,783,617
9	Great Lakes	647	1,929,517
10	Gulf Coast	1,950	5,830,888
11	Illinois	1,009	2,989,768
12	Indiana	1,201	3,616,687
13	Kentucky	1,982	5,872,430
14	New England	2,036	6,011,684
15	New York North	1,382	3,932,881
16	New York South	555	1,641,970
17	North Carolina	1,259	3,763,158
18	North West	1,068	3,179,141
19	Ohio	798	2,381,299
20	Shenandoah Valley	1,470	4,244,770
21	South Carolina	1,818	5,751,497
22	Southwest	1,496	4,532,147
23	Tennessee	2,091	6,323,837
24	Texas	1,508	4,531,085
25	Topeka	1,889	5,624,620
26	Grand Total	29,011	86,581,689

TIP

When you add two fields to the data area, Excel will default to showing the data fields as the last row field. To create the more useful view shown in Figure 5.1, drag the grey Data button from cell B3 to cell C3.

Note that the Market field contains a drop-down arrow on the right side of cell A4. If you select this drop-down, as shown in Figure 5.2, you will see a list of all the pivot items along the market dimension. By default, all the market items are selected.

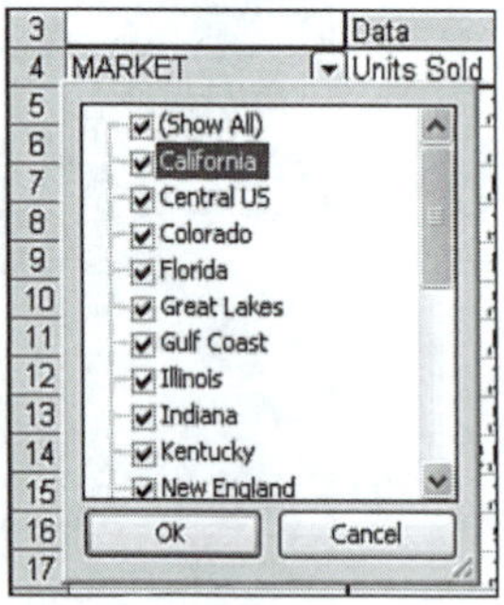

Figure 5.2

The Market drop-down contains a list of all the markets. By default, all are selected.

		Data
3		
4	MARKET ▼	Units Sold
5		☑ (Show All)
6		☑ California
7		☑ Central US
8		☑ Colorado
9		☑ Florida
10		☑ Great Lakes
11		☑ Gulf Coast
12		☑ Illinois
13		☑ Indiana
14		☑ Kentucky
15		☑ New England
16	OK	Cancel
17		

To hide one market, you can uncheck the check box for that item. If your manager needs a report of all markets except California, simply uncheck California.

After you click OK to close the selection box, the pivot table instantly recalculates, leaving out the California market. As shown in Figure 5.3, the total copier sales drops by $4 million to $82 million without California.

Figure 5.3

After California is removed, the report recalculates without California's $4 million in sales.

	A	B	C
1	LINE OF BUSINESS	Copier Sale ▾	
2			
3		Data ▾	
4	MARKET ▾	Units Sold	Revenue
5	Central US	1,186	3,506,717
6	Colorado	1,068	3,113,591
7	Florida	1,224	3,783,617
8	Great Lakes	647	1,929,517
9	Gulf Coast	1,950	5,830,888
10	Illinois	1,009	2,989,768
11	Indiana	1,201	3,616,687
12	Kentucky	1,982	5,872,430
13	New England	2,036	6,011,684
14	New York North	1,382	3,932,881
15	New York South	555	1,641,970
16	North Carolina	1,259	3,763,158
17	North West	1,068	3,179,141
18	Ohio	798	2,381,299
19	Shenandoah Valley	1,470	4,244,770
20	South Carolina	1,818	5,751,497
21	Southwest	1,496	4,532,147
22	Tennessee	2,091	6,323,837
23	Texas	1,508	4,531,085
24	Topeka	1,889	5,624,620
25	Grand Total	27,637	82,561,304

CAUTION

There is no outward sign that this report has been filtered to exclude California. Normally, you would expect Excel to change the arrow color of a filtered field to blue to indicate that some items are hidden. That functionality was not added to the pivot field arrows.

Showing All Items Again

You can just as quickly reinstate all hidden data items for a field with a few clicks. Select the drop-down arrow in the Market field and select the (Show All) selection. This will cause all unchecked items to reassume a checked state.

Showing or Hiding Most Items

In Excel 2002 and later, it is easy to produce a report that includes only two or three items along a dimension. If you need to produce a report of just Florida and the Gulf Coast, this will require only a few mouse clicks.

Select the Market drop-down. Unselect the (Show All) option, and all the markets will become unselected.

You can now select just Florida and Gulf Coast, as shown in Figure 5.4.

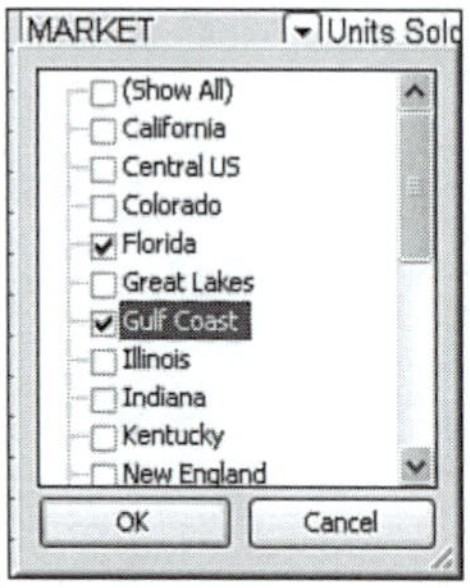

Figure 5.4
In Excel 2002 and later, it takes just three mouse clicks to unselect all markets and then to select two markets.

Figure 5.5 shows that Florida and the Gulf Coast accounted for $9.6 million of copier sales. This task is fairly easy in Excel 2002 and later.

Figure 5.5
This pivot table has all markets except two hidden.

	A	B	C
1	LINE OF BUSINESS	Copier Sale ▾	
2			
3		Data ▾	
4	MARKET ▾	Units Sold	Revenue
5	Florida	1,224	3,783,617
6	Gulf Coast	1,950	5,830,888
7	Grand Total	3,174	9,614,505

NOTE Excel 2000 does not offer the (Show All) option. This could present a significant problem if there were, for example, 200 customers and you needed to display only two of the customers. If you don't particularly feel like unchecking 198 items to get the view you need, an alternative solution would be to use the group method to create two or three groups of all the undesired markets. You could then easily uncheck these three groups. You will learn about the group method later in this chapter.

In Excel 97, you would have to double-click your field and then highlight the items to be hidden.

Hiding or Showing Items Without Data

By default, your pivot table will only show data items that have data. This inherent behavior may cause unintended problems for your data analysis. Look at Figure 5.6, which shows a pivot table with a date field in the page area. When the date field is set to (All), all 21 markets appear in the report.

Figure 5.6
A page field containing dates has been added to this pivot table.

	A	B	C
1	LINE OF BUSINESS	Copier Sale ▼	
2	IN BALANCE DATE	(All) ▼	
3			
4		Data ▼	
5	MARKET ▼	Units Sold	Revenue
6	California	1,374	4,020,385
7	Central US	1,186	3,506,717
8	Colorado	1,068	3,113,591
9	Florida	1,224	3,783,617
10	Great Lakes	647	1,929,517
11	Gulf Coast	1,950	5,830,888
12	Illinois	1,009	2,989,768
13	Indiana	1,201	3,616,687
14	Kentucky	1,982	5,872,430
15	New England	2,036	6,011,684
16	New York North	1,382	3,932,881
17	New York South	555	1,641,970
18	North Carolina	1,259	3,763,158
19	North West	1,068	3,179,141
20	Ohio	798	2,381,299
21	Shenandoah Valley	1,470	4,244,770
22	South Carolina	1,818	5,751,497
23	Southwest	1,496	4,532,147
24	Tennessee	2,091	6,323,837
25	Texas	1,508	4,531,085
26	Topeka	1,889	5,624,620
27	Grand Total	29,011	86,581,689

Select January 3 from the date page field, and the pivot report redraws to show only the three markets with copier sales on that day. Figure 5.7 shows that these markets happened to be Gulf Coast, Shenandoah Valley, and Southwest.

Figure 5.7
By default, a pivot table will hide the markets with no data for this combination of page field selections.

	A	B	C
1	LINE OF BUSINESS	Copier Sale ▼	
2	IN BALANCE DATE	01/03/06 ▼ ⓐ	
3			
4		Data ▼	
5	MARKET ▼	Units Sold	Revenue
6	Gulf Coast	2	3,703
7	Shenandoah Valley	6	12,968
8	Southwest	14	40,347
9	Grand Total	22	57,018

5

Select a different date from the date page field. The report will redraw to include the markets with sales on that day. Figure 5.8 shows that on January 6, there were five markets with copier sales.

Figure 5.8
Change the date in the page field, and a different set of markets will appear.

	A	B	C
1	LINE OF BUSINESS	Copier Sale ▼	
2	IN BALANCE DATE	01/06/06 ▼	
3			
4		Data ▼	
5	MARKET ▼	Units Sold	Revenue
6	California	8	26,822
7	Central US	5	22,296
8	New England	8	28,702
9	Southwest	9	32,441
10	Tennessee	7	22,011
11	Grand Total	37	132,272

The behavior of displaying only items with data makes for a very concise report, but it could be annoying if you later wish to compare snapshots of several days. In that case, you might wish that Excel would show you all 21 markets every time. To prevent Excel from hiding pivot items without data, double-click the Market field to display the PivotTable Field dialog box, as shown in Figure 5.9. In the lower-left corner, choose Show Items with No Data.

Figure 5.9
Double-click the Market field to display this dialog box. Choose the box in the lower-left corner to force all markets to display.

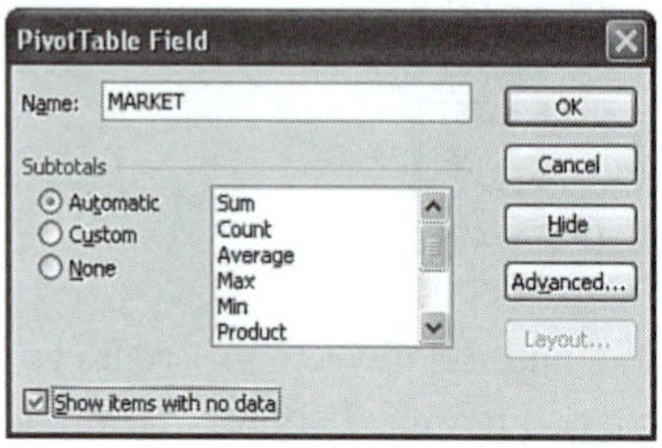

After you choose the Show Items with No Data option, all the markets will appear, regardless of whether they had sales that day, as shown in Figure 5.10.

Figure 5.10
It would be easier to compare a snapshot of this report with other days after all days contain the same list of markets.

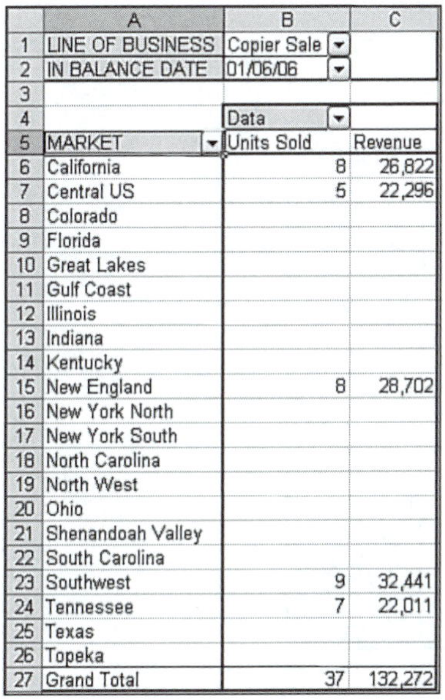

	A	B	C
1	LINE OF BUSINESS	Copier Sale	
2	IN BALANCE DATE	01/06/06	
3			
4		Data	
5	MARKET	Units Sold	Revenue
6	California	8	26,822
7	Central US	5	22,296
8	Colorado		
9	Florida		
10	Great Lakes		
11	Gulf Coast		
12	Illinois		
13	Indiana		
14	Kentucky		
15	New England	8	28,702
16	New York North		
17	New York South		
18	North Carolina		
19	North West		
20	Ohio		
21	Shenandoah Valley		
22	South Carolina		
23	Southwest	9	32,441
24	Tennessee	7	22,011
25	Texas		
26	Topeka		
27	Grand Total	37	132,272

Hiding or Showing Items in a Page Field

A page field typically includes either (All) or one pivot item. If you select the Line of Business drop-down, you can either select one single line of business or select the (All) option to see all lines of business. There does not appear to be a way to create a report with the total of copier sales and printer sales.

The solution is to drag the Line of Business field into either the row or the column area of your report. After it is there, use the Line of Business drop-down to select only printer and copier sales, as shown in Figure 5.11.

Figure 5.11
Temporarily drag the page field to the row area and then select the desired product lines.

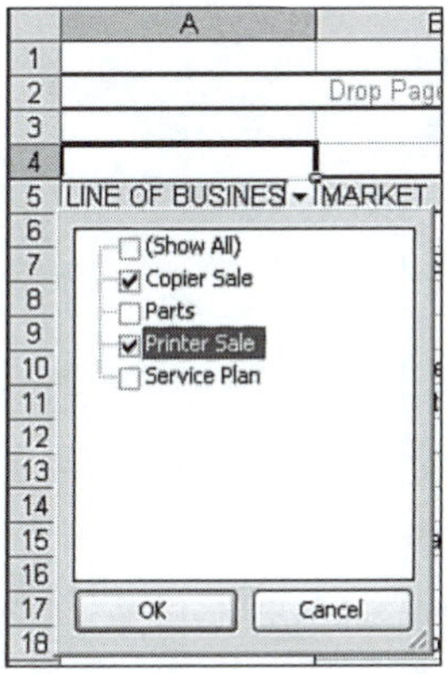

	A	B
1		
2		Drop Page
3		
4		
5	LINE OF BUSINES ▾	MARKET
6	☐ (Show All)	
7	☑ Copier Sale	
8	☐ Parts	
9	☑ Printer Sale	
10	☐ Service Plan	
11		
12		
13		
14		
15		
16		
17	OK Cancel	
18		

After choosing two items, drag the Line of Business field back to the page area of the report. Magically, a new option called (Multiple Items) will be selected in the page field, as shown in Figure 5.12.

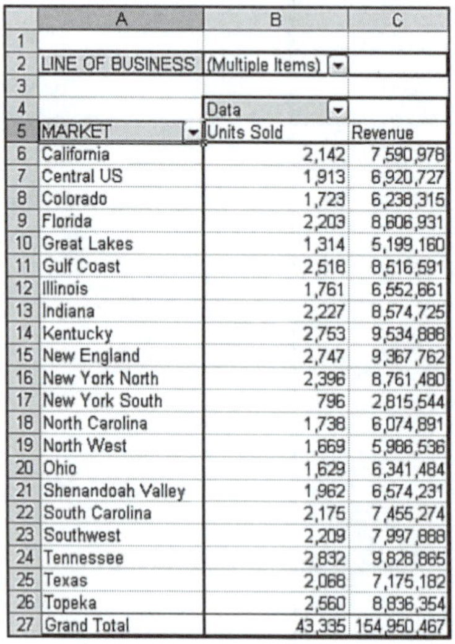

Figure 5.12
Drag the Line of Business field back to the page area, and the pivot table remembers the two lines selected in the previous step.

	A	B	C
1			
2	LINE OF BUSINESS	(Multiple Items) ▾	
3			
4		Data ▾	
5	MARKET ▾	Units Sold	Revenue
6	California	2,142	7,590,978
7	Central US	1,913	6,920,727
8	Colorado	1,723	6,238,315
9	Florida	2,203	8,606,931
10	Great Lakes	1,314	5,199,160
11	Gulf Coast	2,518	8,516,591
12	Illinois	1,761	6,552,661
13	Indiana	2,227	8,574,725
14	Kentucky	2,753	9,534,888
15	New England	2,747	9,367,762
16	New York North	2,396	8,761,480
17	New York South	796	2,815,544
18	North Carolina	1,738	6,074,891
19	North West	1,669	5,986,536
20	Ohio	1,629	6,341,484
21	Shenandoah Valley	1,962	6,574,231
22	South Carolina	2,175	7,455,274
23	Southwest	2,209	7,997,888
24	Tennessee	2,832	9,828,865
25	Texas	2,068	7,175,182
26	Topeka	2,560	8,836,354
27	Grand Total	43,335	154,950,467

> **CAUTION**
>
> After using this technique, you have no way to add hidden items back to the page field. You will have to drag the page field back to the row or column area to show the hidden items.

Showing or Hiding Items in a Data Field

In Excel 2000 and later, pivot reports with multiple fields in the data area of the report will include a gray data field with a drop-down. To remove the Units Sold field from the data area, you can use one of two methods. You can uncheck the item from the Data drop-down, as shown in Figure 5.13.

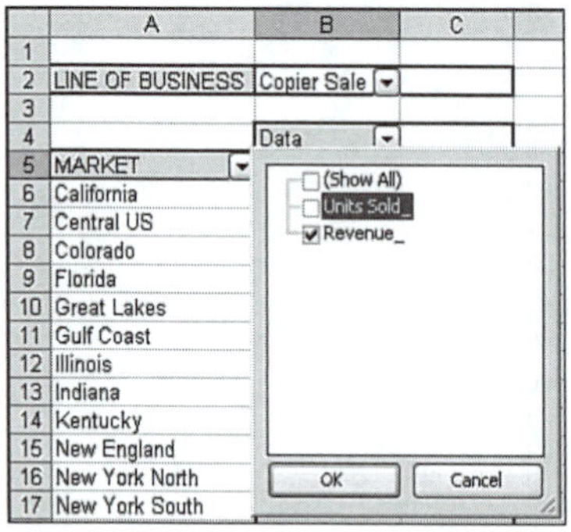

Figure 5.13
After you have multiple data fields, there is no way to drag one of the data fields from the report. You can use the Data drop-down to remove the field.

	A	B	C
1			
2	LINE OF BUSINESS	Copier Sale ▾	
3			
4		Data ▾	
5	MARKET ▾	☐ (Show All)	
6	California	☐ Units Sold	
7	Central US	☑ Revenue_	
8	Colorado		
9	Florida		
10	Great Lakes		
11	Gulf Coast		
12	Illinois		
13	Indiana		
14	Kentucky		
15	New England		
16	New York North	OK	Cancel
17	New York South		

Alternatively, you can right-click the Units heading and choose Hide, as shown in Figure 5.14.

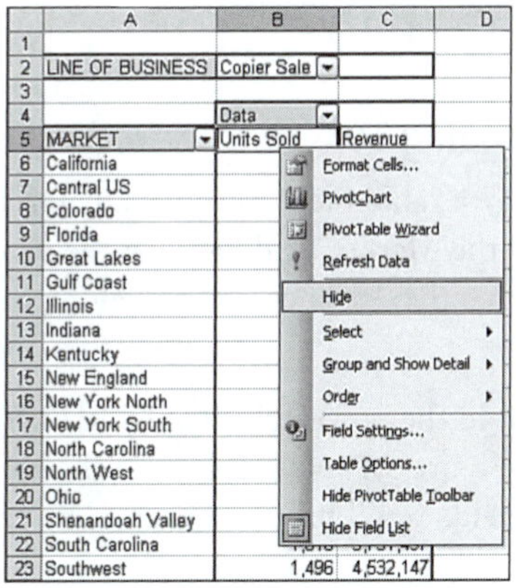

Figure 5.14
Alternatively, you can remove a data field by right-clicking the field name and choosing Hide.

	A	B	C	D
1				
2	LINE OF BUSINESS	Copier Sale ▾		
3				
4		Data ▾		
5	MARKET ▾	Units Sold	Revenue	
6	California			
7	Central US	🔲 Format Cells...		
8	Colorado	📊 PivotChart		
9	Florida	📄 PivotTable Wizard		
10	Great Lakes	⚡ Refresh Data		
11	Gulf Coast			
12	Illinois	Hide		
13	Indiana			
14	Kentucky	Select ▸		
15	New England	Group and Show Detail ▸		
16	New York North	Order ▸		
17	New York South			
18	North Carolina	🔲 Field Settings...		
19	North West	Table Options...		
20	Ohio			
21	Shenandoah Valley	Hide PivotTable Toolbar		
22	South Carolina	🔲 Hide Field List		
23	Southwest	1,496 4,532,147		

Sorting in a Pivot Table

By default, items in each pivot field are sorted in ascending sequence based on the item name. Figure 5.15 shows that the Market field is sorted alphabetically by market name.

Figure 5.15
By default, a pivot table is sorted alphabetically. In this default table, markets are presented in A–Z order.

	A	B	C
1			
2	LINE OF BUSINESS	Copier Sale ▾	
3			
4		Data ▾	
5	MARKET ▾	Units Sold	Revenue
6	California	1,374	4,020,385
7	Central US	1,186	3,506,717
8	Colorado	1,068	3,113,591
9	Florida	1,224	3,783,617
10	Great Lakes	647	1,929,517
11	Gulf Coast	1,950	5,830,888
12	Illinois	1,009	2,989,768
13	Indiana	1,201	3,616,687
14	Kentucky	1,982	5,872,430
15	New England	2,036	6,011,684
16	New York North	1,382	3,932,881
17	New York South	555	1,641,970
18	North Carolina	1,259	3,763,158
19	North West	1,068	3,179,141
20	Ohio	798	2,381,299
21	Shenandoah Valley	1,470	4,244,770
22	South Carolina	1,818	5,751,497
23	Southwest	1,496	4,532,147
24	Tennessee	2,091	6,323,837
25	Texas	1,508	4,531,085
26	Topeka	1,889	5,624,620
27	Grand Total	29,011	86,581,689

Excel gives you the freedom to sort your data fields to suit your needs. You can use one of three methods to apply sorting to your pivot table:

- Using the Advanced Options dialog box
- Using the manual method
- Using the sorting buttons on the standard toolbar

Sorting Using the Advanced Options Dialog Box

Sort options are controlled from the PivotTable Field Advanced dialog box. To get to this dialog box, you must first double-click the Market field name in the pivot table to display the PivotTable Field dialog box. Look for the Advanced button along the right side of this dialog box.

Clicking the Advanced button will lead to the powerful PivotTable Field Advanced Options dialog box. This dialog box, shown in Figure 5.16, controls both the sorting options for a field and the AutoShow options for a field. You'll have a chance to try out the AutoShow options later in this chapter.

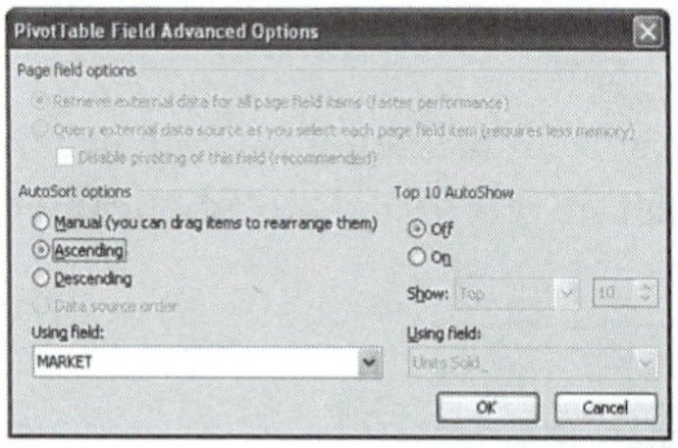

Figure 5.16
The Advanced Options dialog box contains the AutoSort and AutoShow features, which are really too powerful to be buried in an obscure place.

Figure 5.16 shows that the default sort for the Market field is to be sorted in ascending order using the Market field. To change the report to list the largest markets first, change the AutoSort option to Descending.

As shown in Figure 5.17, choose the drop-down for Using Field. Typically, your choices are to sort by the original field or by any of the data fields currently in the pivot table. In this example, your choices are to sort by descending units or to sort by descending revenue. Choose Revenue from the drop-down.

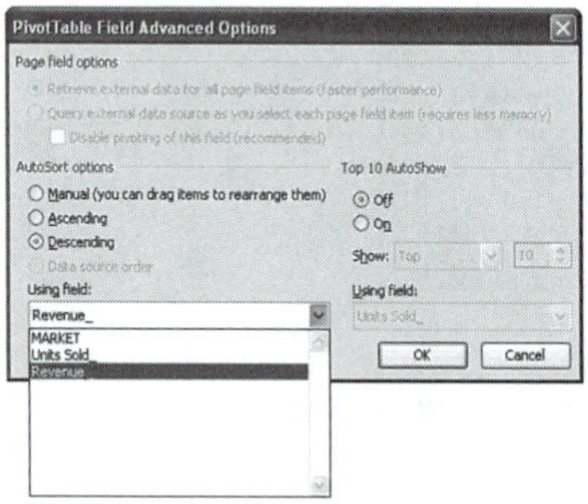

Figure 5.17
You can sort a column field by any of the data fields or by the column field itself.

After completing the Advanced Options dialog box, you must click OK twice—once to close the Advanced Options dialog box, and once to close the PivotTable Field dialog box.

As shown in Figure 5.18, the result will be that the pivot report is sorted by descending revenue. Tennessee was the top market for copier sales with $6.3 million.

Figure 5.18
The report is sorted with the largest market at the top.

	A	B	C
1			
2	LINE OF BUSINESS	Copier Sale ▼	
3			
4		Data ▼	
5	MARKET ▼	Units Sold	Revenue
6	Tennessee	2,091	6,323,837
7	New England	2,036	6,011,684
8	Kentucky	1,982	5,872,430
9	Gulf Coast	1,950	5,830,888
10	South Carolina	1,818	5,751,497
11	Topeka	1,889	5,624,620
12	Southwest	1,496	4,532,147
13	Texas	1,508	4,531,085
14	Shenandoah Valley	1,470	4,244,770
15	California	1,374	4,020,385
16	New York North	1,382	3,932,881
17	Florida	1,224	3,783,617
18	North Carolina	1,259	3,763,158
19	Indiana	1,201	3,616,687
20	Central US	1,186	3,506,717
21	North West	1,068	3,179,141
22	Colorado	1,068	3,113,591
23	Illinois	1,009	2,989,768
24	Ohio	798	2,381,299
25	Great Lakes	647	1,929,517
26	New York South	555	1,641,970
27	Grand Total	29,011	86,581,689

Although it may seem a bit labor intensive to navigate to the Advanced Options dialog box, this is by far the best method of all the sorting methods covered in this book. Sorting applied in this method persists no matter how you reshape the pivot report. This will prevent you from having to apply your sorting preferences repeatedly.

5

Note the Effect of Layout Changes on AutoSort

If you change the page field to show printer sales, the report will automatically re-sort. Figure 5.19 shows the report after Printer Sales has been selected from the Line of Business drop-down. The report automatically sorted to show that Indiana is the top market for printer sales with $4.9 million.

Figure 5.19

Change to a new page field value, and the markets re-sort to show which market is the largest in printer sales.

2	LINE OF BUSINESS	Printer Sale ⌄	
3			
4		Data ⌄	
5	MARKET ⌄	Units Sold	Revenue
6	Indiana	1,026	4,958,038
7	New York North	1,014	4,828,599
8	Florida	979	4,823,314
9	Ohio	831	3,960,185
10	Kentucky	771	3,662,458
11	California	768	3,570,593
12	Illinois	752	3,562,893
13	Tennessee	741	3,505,028
14	Southwest	713	3,465,741
15	Central US	727	3,414,010
16	New England	711	3,356,078
17	Great Lakes	667	3,269,643
18	Topeka	671	3,211,734
19	Colorado	655	3,124,724
20	North West	601	2,807,395
21	Gulf Coast	568	2,685,703
22	Texas	560	2,644,097
23	Shenandoah Valley	492	2,329,461
24	North Carolina	479	2,311,733
25	South Carolina	357	1,703,777
26	New York South	241	1,173,574
27	Grand Total	14,324	68,368,778

If you drop a new field on the report, the pivot table will remember the AutoSort option for the Market field and do its best to present the data in that order. This may not be in the spirit of your report focusing on the best markets. Figure 5.20 shows the report after the Region field was added as the outer row field. The Region field is sorted alphabetically by region name, but within each region, the markets are arranged in descending order by revenue.

Figure 5.20

After a Region field was added with the default sort, the report shows regions alphabetically, but within each region, the markets are reported by descending revenue.

2	LINE OF BUSINESS	Printer Sale	⌄	
3				
4			Data ⌄	
5	REGION ⌄	MARKET ⌄	Units Sold	Revenue
6	North	New York North	1,014	4,828,599
7		Ohio	831	3,960,185
8		New England	711	3,356,078
9		Great Lakes	667	3,269,643
10		Shenandoah Valley	492	2,329,461
11		South Carolina	357	1,703,777
12		New York South	241	1,173,574
13	North Total		4,313	20,621,317
14	South	Indiana	1,026	4,958,038
15		Florida	979	4,823,314
16		Kentucky	771	3,662,458
17		Illinois	752	3,562,893
18		Tennessee	741	3,505,028
19		Gulf Coast	568	2,685,703
20		Texas	560	2,644,097
21		North Carolina	479	2,311,733
22	South Total		5,876	28,153,264
23	West	California	768	3,570,593
24		Southwest	713	3,465,741
25		Central US	727	3,414,010
26		Topeka	671	3,211,734
27		Colorado	655	3,124,724
28		North West	601	2,807,395
29	West Total		4,135	19,594,197
30	Grand Total		14,324	68,368,778

You can choose to sort the Region field by descending revenue. In this case, the South region appears first because it produced $28 million of printer sales. Within the South region, markets are sorted in descending order by revenue, as shown in Figure 5.21. Although such a sort would be relatively simple in a regular Excel table, it requires two visits to the Advanced Options dialog box—once for the Region field and once for the Market field.

Figure 5.21

Set the AutoSort option for the Region field to sort descending based on Revenue.

2	LINE OF BUSINESS	Printer Sale		
3				
4	Revenue			
5	REGION		MARKET	Total
6	South		Indiana	4,958,038
7			Florida	4,823,314
8			Kentucky	3,662,458
9			Illinois	3,562,893
10			Tennessee	3,505,028
11			Gulf Coast	2,685,703
12			Texas	2,644,097
13			North Carolina	2,311,733
14	South Total			28,153,264
15	North		New York North	4,828,599
16			Ohio	3,960,185
17			New England	3,356,078
18			Great Lakes	3,269,643
19			Shenandoah Valley	2,329,461
20			South Carolina	1,703,777
21			New York South	1,173,574
22	North Total			20,621,317
23	West		California	3,570,593
24			Southwest	3,465,741
25			Central US	3,414,010
26			Topeka	3,211,734
27			Colorado	3,124,724
28			North West	2,807,395
29	West Total			19,594,197
30	Grand Total			68,368,778

Sorting Using the Manual Method

Figure 5.22 shows the default sequence of regions in a pivot table report. Alphabetically, the regions are shown in the sequence North, South, West. If this company is based in California, company traditions might dictate that the West region should be shown first, followed by North and South.

Figure 5.22

Company traditions might dictate that the Region field should be in West, North, South sequence instead.

4	Revenue		REGION			
5	LINE OF BUSINESS		North	South	West	Grand Total
6	Copier Sale		25,893,618	36,711,470	23,976,601	86,581,689
7	Parts		29,063,171	31,205,269	23,670,053	83,938,493
8	Printer Sale		20,621,317	28,153,264	19,594,197	68,368,778
9	Service Plan		201,414,511	223,750,307	149,341,261	574,506,079
10	Grand Total		276,992,617	319,820,310	216,582,112	813,395,039

On the face of it, there is no easy way to sort the Region field into this sequence. An ascending sort would cause the West region to be last. A descending sort would cause the West region to be first, but then the South and North regions would not be in the proper sequence to match the company's standard reporting.

5

You might try to convince your company to change a decade-long tradition of reporting in the West, North, South sequence, or even change the region names in order to accommodate sorting in your pivot table. Both of these concepts would be tough to sell and are not viable options. Luckily, Microsoft offers a very simple solution to this problem.

Move the cellpointer to cell B5 of the pivot table, or the cell that currently contains the heading for North. In cell B5, type the word "West" and press Enter. Remarkably, the pivot table will automatically resequence. The $216 million in sales for the West will automatically move from column D to column B. The remaining regions will move over to take the next columns. The result, shown in Figure 5.23, presents the report in the desired West, North, South sequence.

Figure 5.23
Simply typing "West" in cell B5 will resequence the report.

2	Drop Page Fields Here				
3					
4	Revenue	REGION			
5	LINE OF BUSINESS	West	North	South	Grand Total
6	Copier Sale	23,976,601	25,893,618	36,711,470	86,581,689
7	Parts	23,670,053	29,063,171	31,205,269	83,938,493
8	Printer Sale	19,594,197	20,621,317	28,153,264	68,368,778
9	Service Plan	149,341,261	201,414,511	223,750,307	574,506,079
10	Grand Total	216,582,112	276,992,617	319,820,310	813,395,039

Example of Adding a New Region

After using this technique, any new regions you add to the data source will be added at the end of the list. Figure 5.24 shows the pivot table after a region named Central is added. Because Excel does not know where to add Central, it automatically goes to the end of the list.

Figure 5.24
After you specify a manual sort, new regions are added at the end of the list.

2	Drop Page Fields Here					
3						
4	Revenue	REGION				
5	LINE OF BUSINESS	West	North	South	Central	Grand Total
6	Copier Sale	23,976,601	25,893,618	36,711,470		86,581,689
7	Parts	23,670,053	29,063,171	31,205,269		83,938,493
8	Printer Sale	19,594,197	20,621,317	28,153,264		68,368,778
9	Service Plan	149,341,261	201,414,511	223,731,090	19,217	574,506,079
10	Grand Total	216,582,112	276,992,617	319,801,093	19,217	813,395,039

5

The other solution to the West, North, South sequence problem is to set up a custom sort list. Custom sort lists are maintained on the Custom Lists tab of the Options dialog box. Choose Options from the Tools menu. Type "West, North, South" in the List Entries box and click the Add button.

As shown in Figure 5.25, the Custom Lists list box will show your new list of West, North, South.

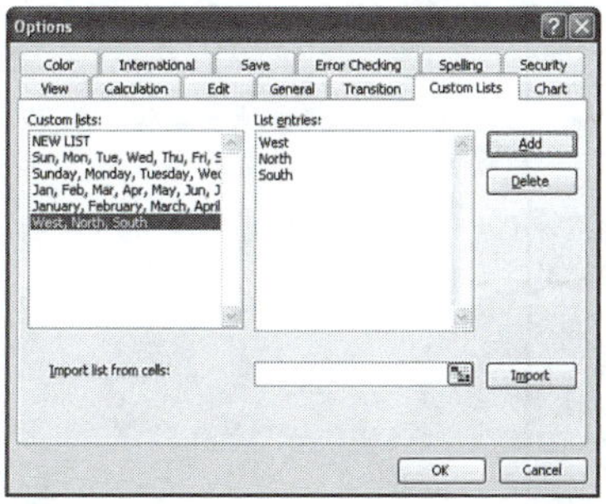

Figure 5.25
A custom list of West, North, South is now available.

After setting up a custom list, you can specify that the Region field should be sorted in ascending sequence. Excel's IntelliSense technology will realize that the items along the Region field match a custom list and will sort the report to match your custom list.

Sorting Using the Sorting Buttons on the Standard Toolbar

With a little practice, you can sort some pivot tables using the sorting buttons on the standard toolbar.

> **CAUTION**
>
> Doing any sort using the toolbar buttons will change the AutoSort option to Manual. The logic behind the sort will not be remembered as the layout of the report changes.

Sorting a pivot table using the toolbar buttons is a little different from sorting a regular dataset.

5

Select any cell from A5 through A26 in Figure 5.26 to sort the pivot table by market. Because this is a row field, you can select the Market heading or any of the individual market items before clicking the sort button.

Figure 5.26

Sort the Market field by selecting any cell in A5:A26 and clicking the A–Z sort button.

2	LINE OF BUSINESS	Copier Sale ▾
3		
4	Revenue	
5	MARKET ▾	Total
6	California	4,020,385
7	Central US	3,506,717
8	Colorado	3,113,591
9	Florida	3,783,617
10	Great Lakes	1,929,517
11	Gulf Coast	5,830,888
12	Illinois	2,989,768
13	Indiana	3,616,687
14	Kentucky	5,872,430
15	New England	6,011,684
16	New York North	3,932,881
17	New York South	1,641,970
18	North Carolina	3,763,158
19	North West	3,179,141
20	Ohio	2,381,299
21	Shenandoah Valley	4,244,770
22	South Carolina	5,751,497
23	Southwest	4,532,147
24	Tennessee	6,323,837
25	Texas	4,531,085
26	Topeka	5,624,620
27	Grand Total	86,581,689

To sort by revenue as shown in Figure 5.26, you must select one of the values from B6 through B26. If you select the heading in A4 or B4, Excel will report that it does not understand by which field to sort.

Figure 5.27 shows a pivot table with two data fields along the column area. Choosing a cell in A5:A26 and then clicking a sort icon will sort the report by market. Choosing a cell in B6:B26 will sort the report by revenue. Choosing a cell in C6:C26 will sort the report by units. Interestingly, choosing a cell in either B5 or C5 and then sorting will sort the Revenue and Units fields into ascending or descending order based on their heading names. Choosing a cell in either B27 or C27 will sort the Revenue and Unit columns based on their total values.

Figure 5.27

Sorting using the toolbar buttons becomes more complex as the report structure becomes more complex.

2	LINE OF BUSINESS	Copier Sale ▼	
3			
4		Data ▼	
5	MARKET ▼	Units	Revenue
6	New York South	555	1,641,970
7	Great Lakes	647	1,929,517
8	Ohio	798	2,381,299
9	Illinois	1009	2,989,768
10	Colorado	1068	3,113,591
11	North West	1068	3,179,141
12	Central US	1186	3,506,717
13	Indiana	1201	3,616,687
14	North Carolina	1259	3,763,158
15	Florida	1224	3,783,617
16	New York North	1382	3,932,881
17	California	1374	4,020,385
18	Shenandoah Valley	1470	4,244,770
19	Texas	1508	4,531,085
20	Southwest	1496	4,532,147
21	Topeka	1889	5,624,620
22	South Carolina	1818	5,751,497
23	Gulf Coast	1950	5,830,888
24	Kentucky	1982	5,872,430
25	New England	2036	6,011,684
26	Tennessee	2091	6,323,837
27	Grand Total	29011	86,581,689

It is critical to remember that any sort performed using the toolbar buttons is a one-time sort. The result will be the AutoSort option changing to Manual. The left side of Figure 5.28 shows a pivot table showing copier sales by market. The report was sorted in descending revenue by choosing cell B6 and clicking the Z–A toolbar icon. Although this appears equivalent to the more laborious process of setting up an AutoSort, the sort only applies to the current view of the table.

5

If you change the page field to show Printer Sales, the pivot table is not automatically re-sorted. As shown on the right side of Figure 5.28, the markets are reported in the same sequence as when the report was showing Copier Sales. Although there are instances when this is desirable, most of the time, you would want the report to automatically sort based on the new field.

Figure 5.28
Change to Printer Sales, and the report is not properly sorted. This is because sorts using the A–Z and Z–A toolbar icons result in a manual setting for the AutoSort feature.

2	LINE OF BUSINESS	Copier Sale ▼		2	LINE OF BUSINESS	Printer Sale ▼
3				3		
4	Revenue			4	Revenue	
5	MARKET ▼	Total		5	MARKET ▼	Total
6	Tennessee	6,323,837		6	Tennessee	3,505,028
7	New England	6,011,684		7	New England	3,356,078
8	Kentucky	5,872,430		8	Kentucky	3,662,458
9	Gulf Coast	5,830,888		9	Gulf Coast	2,685,703
10	South Carolina	5,751,497		10	South Carolina	1,703,777
11	Topeka	5,624,620		11	Topeka	3,211,734
12	Southwest	4,532,147		12	Southwest	3,465,741
13	Texas	4,531,085		13	Texas	2,644,097
14	Shenandoah Valley	4,244,770		14	Shenandoah Valley	2,329,461
15	California	4,020,385		15	California	3,570,593
16	New York North	3,932,881		16	New York North	4,828,599
17	Florida	3,783,617		17	Florida	4,823,314
18	North Carolina	3,763,158		18	North Carolina	2,311,733
19	Indiana	3,616,687		19	Indiana	4,958,038
20	Central US	3,506,717		20	Central US	3,414,010
21	North West	3,179,141		21	North West	2,807,395
22	Colorado	3,113,591		22	Colorado	3,124,724
23	Illinois	2,989,768		23	Illinois	3,562,893
24	Ohio	2,381,299		24	Ohio	3,960,185
25	Great Lakes	1,929,517		25	Great Lakes	3,269,643
26	New York South	1,641,970		26	New York South	1,173,574
27	Grand Total	86,581,689		27	Grand Total	68,368,778

Producing Top 10 Reports

The 80/20 rule often applies to a business dataset. Perhaps 80% of the revenue comes from 20% of the customers. You may find that beyond the top 10 or 20 customers, the report contains many tiny customers who are just buying a few dollars of repair parts. Your VP of Sales probably has the attention span to look at a one-page report of the top 20 customers, but may ignore a 10-page report with 500 customers on it.

Luckily, pivot tables make it easy to filter the report to the top 5, bottom 10, or any conceivable combination of top or bottom records.

Figure 5.29 shows a report of copier sales by store. There are 128 stores in the report.

Figure 5.29
This summary report will span four printed pages and contains too much detail for a high-level manager.

4	Revenue	
5	STORE	Total
6	2004014	756,874
7	2105015	447,881
8	3106016	273,005
9	3106026	185,772
10	3109019	1,756,864
11	6002012	80,777
12	6002022	456,509
13	6009029	738,131
14	7008018	404,117
15	7008048	791,971
16	12011011	361,180
17	12016016	1,608,904
18	12118018	599,319
19	12118048	663,694
20	12118068	118,406
21	12118088	260,551
22	13013013	1,455,229
23	13013023	846,695
24	13019019	1,518,424
25	13019029	858,136
26	13019049	681,536

Top 10 reports are controlled on the Advanced Options dialog box. Double-click on the Store field to display the PivotTable Field dialog box. Then click the Advanced button to display the PivotTable Field Advanced Options dialog box. The Top 10 AutoShow settings appear on the right side of this dialog box.

Initially, the AutoShow settings are disabled. After you choose the option button to turn on the AutoShow feature, the three controls are enabled. The Show drop-down allows you to choose Top or Bottom. The spin button allows you to select a number between 1 and 255. The Using Field control will be used to limit the Store field to the top 15 records using the Revenue field. Figure 5.30 shows the completed dialog box.

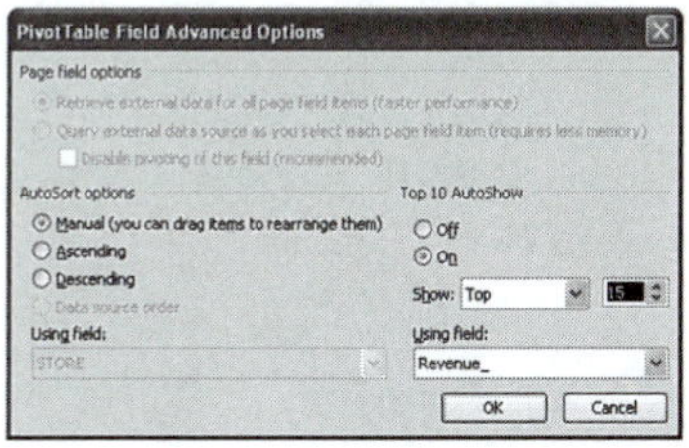

Figure 5.30
The Top 10 AutoShow settings allow you to limit a report to just the top or bottom records.

As you can see in Figure 5.31, the resulting report is now limited to the top 15 stores. The Store field is now shown in blue to indicate that the Store list has been filtered using the AutoShow feature. Note that using AutoShow does not automatically sort the report. You have to use the AutoSort feature in order to sort the report. Also, note that the grand total at the bottom of the report reflects the total for only the 15 customers shown.

Figure 5.31
Using the AutoShow option to produce a report of just the largest stores.

2	LINE OF BUSINESS	Copier Sale ▾
3		
4	Revenue	
5	STORE ▾	Total
6	3109019	1,756,864
7	12016016	1,608,904
8	13013013	1,455,229
9	13019019	1,518,424
10	33031021	1,323,914
11	47142012	1,434,231
12	63163013	1,217,881
13	67166016	1,647,569
14	72070010	1,589,312
15	73171011	2,659,817
16	74075025	1,241,201
17	83080010	1,908,104
18	85085025	1,998,514
19	94091011	1,177,528
20	96094014	1,477,754
21	Grand Total	24,015,246

As you change the page field, the list of top stores will automatically change.

A Bug Example in the AutoShow Logic

There is an apparent bug in the AutoShow logic. If you ask for 10 values and there is a tie for tenth place, Excel will show you all the tied records. As you drill further down into the report, there's a chance you will encounter a situation where you have asked for the top 10 records, but only nine or fewer records have nonzero sales. This then creates a massive tie at tenth place. The result will be a pivot table with far too many records reporting zero at the end, as shown in Figure 5.32.

Figure 5.32
This report violates the spirit of the AutoShow feature. The page fields are so narrow, only nine styles had nonzero records. Excel shows all the remaining records in an eight-way tie at zero.

	A	B
1	Group	Handbags ▾
2	Region	West ▾
3		
4	Sum of Sales	
5	Style ▾	Total
6	A103	980
7	A111	870
8	A117	777
9	A109	702
10	A107	662
11	A105	345
12	A101	281
13	A113	232
14	A115	86
15	A106	0
16	A110	0
17	A102	0
18	A112	0
19	A108	0
20	A114	0
21	A104	0
22	A116	0
23	Grand Total	4935

Remember that if you manually filtered the Store field and then moved it to the page field, the report would continue to be filtered for the matching stores. This technique does not work with fields filtered using AutoShow. Move the filtered Store field to the page area, and all the stores become selected again.

Grouping Pivot Fields

Although most of your summarization and calculation needs can be accomplished with standard pivot table settings, there are special situations where you might want your report to be summarized even further.

For example, transactional data is typically stored with a transaction date. It is common that you will want to report this data by month, quarter, or year. The Group option allows you to quickly and easily consolidate transactional dates into a larger group such as month or quarter. Then you can summarize the data in those groups just as you would with any other field in your pivot table.

As you will learn in the next section, grouping is not limited to date fields. You can also group nondate fields to consolidate specific pivot items into a single item.

Grouping Date Fields

Figure 5.33 shows a pivot report by date. With two years of transactional data, the report spans 700+ rows. Yes, 700 rows are a summary from the original 41,550 rows, but managers will often want detail by month instead of detail by day.

Figure 5.33
When reported by day, the summary report spans 700+ rows. It would be meaningful to report by month or year instead.

2	LINE OF BUSINESS	Copier Sale ▼
3		
4	Revenue	
5	IN BALANCE DATE ▼	Total
6	01/03/06	57,018
7	01/04/06	51,628
8	01/05/06	100,116
9	01/06/06	132,272
10	01/07/06	23,086
11	01/08/06	174,158
12	01/09/06	113,218
13	01/10/06	18,498
14	01/11/06	36,811
15	01/12/06	172,620
16	01/13/06	103,723
17	01/14/06	156,226
18	01/15/06	215,407
19	01/16/06	132,032
20	01/17/06	59,077
21	01/18/06	55,747
22	01/19/06	182,083
23	01/20/06	77,823
24	01/21/06	63,683

5

Excel makes it easy to group date fields. Right-click the date heading or any date item, choose Group and Show Detail, and then choose Group, as shown in Figure 5.34.

Figure 5.34
Right-click a field heading to access the Group menu.

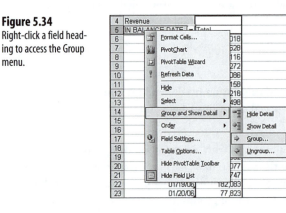

When your field contains date information, the Grouping dialog box, shown in Figure 5.35, will appear. By default, the Months option is selected. You have choices to group by Seconds, Minutes, Hours, Days, Months, Quarters, and Years. It is possible and usually advisable to select more than one field in the Grouping dialog box. In this case, you will want to select Months, Quarters, and Years.

Figure 5.35
Business users of Excel will usually group by months, quarters, and years.

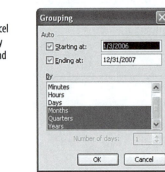

There are several interesting things to note about the resulting pivot table. First, notice that Quarters and Years have been added to your field list. Don't let this fool you—your source data is not changed to include these new fields; instead, these fields are now part of your pivot cache in memory. Another interesting thing to note is that, by default, the Years and Quarters fields are automatically added next to the original date field in the pivot table layout, as shown in Figure 5.36.

Figure 5.36
By default, Excel adds the new grouped date fields to your pivot table layout.

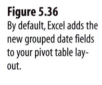

2	LINE OF BUSINESS	Copier Sale		
3				
4	Revenue			
5	Years	Quarters	IN BALANCE DATE	Total
6	2006	Qtr1	Jan	2,715,020
7			Feb	3,088,467
8			Mar	3,201,442
9		Qtr2	Apr	3,309,439
10			May	3,435,284
11			Jun	3,384,032
12		Qtr3	Jul	3,651,569
13			Aug	3,461,037
14			Sep	3,531,622
15		Qtr4	Oct	3,627,505
16			Nov	3,563,280
17			Dec	3,363,154
18	2007	Qtr1	Jan	3,331,228
19			Feb	3,560,179
20			Mar	3,950,904
21		Qtr2	Apr	3,895,744
22			May	3,879,592

PivotTable Field List
Drag items to the PivotTable report
- FISCAL PERIOD
- MODEL
- **LINE OF BUSINESS**
- **REVENUE**
- UNITS SOLD
- SERVICE PLANS SOLD
- DAYS IN PERIOD
- MarketRank
- **Quarters**
- **Years**

Add To   Row Area

When Grouping by Months, Include Years

Although this is not immediately obvious, it is important if you group a date field by month that you also include the year in the grouping.

Examine the pivot table shown in Figure 5.37. This table has a date field that has been grouped by month and year. The months in column A use the generic abbreviations Jan, Feb, and so on. The copier sales for January 2006 are $2.715 million.

Figure 5.37
This table has a date field that is grouped by both month and year.

2	LINE OF BUSINESS	Copier Sale		
3				
4	Revenue	Years		
5	IN BALANCE DATE	2006	2007	Grand Total
6	Jan	2,715,020	3,331,228	6,046,248
7	Feb	3,088,467	3,560,179	6,648,646
8	Mar	3,201,442	3,950,904	7,152,346
9	Apr	3,309,439	3,895,744	7,205,183
10	May	3,435,284	3,879,592	7,314,876
11	Jun	3,384,032	3,923,025	7,307,057
12	Jul	3,651,569	3,903,992	7,555,561
13	Aug	3,461,037	3,986,585	7,447,622
14	Sep	3,531,622	3,856,852	7,388,474
15	Oct	3,627,505	4,211,254	7,838,759
16	Nov	3,563,280	4,078,083	7,641,363
17	Dec	3,363,154	3,672,400	7,035,554
18	Grand Total	40,331,851	46,249,838	86,581,689

5

If, instead, you had chosen to group the date field only by month, Excel still continues to report the date field using the generic Jan abbreviation. The problem is that dates from January 2006 and January 2007 are both rolled up and reported together as "Jan." Having a report that totals Jan 2006 and Jan 2007 might only be useful if you are performing a seasonality analysis. Under any other circumstance, the report of $6 million in copier sales in January will be too ambiguous and will likely be interpreted wrong. To avoid ambiguous reports like the one shown in Figure 5.38, always include a year in the Group dialog box when you are grouping by month.

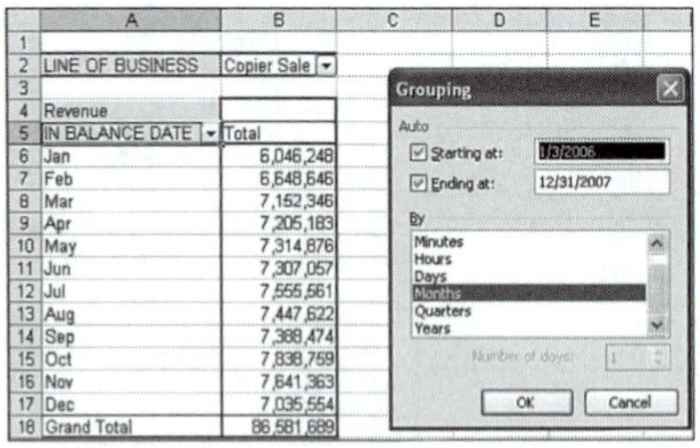

Figure 5.38
If you fail to include the Year field in the grouping, the report will mix sales from Jan 2006 and Jan 2007 in the same number.

Grouping Date Fields by Week

The Grouping dialog box offers the choices to group by second, minute, hour, day, month, quarter, or year. What if you need to group on a weekly or bi-weekly basis? This can be done.

The first step is to find an actual paper calendar for the year in question. Your data might start on January 3, 2006, so it is helpful to know that January 3 was a Tuesday in that year. You are going to have to decide if weeks should start on Sunday or Monday or any other day. Check the paper calendar to learn that the nearest starting Monday is January 2, 2006.

Right-click the date heading in your pivot table. Choose Group and Show Detail and then choose Group. In the Grouping dialog box, unselect all the By options and choose only the Days field. This will enable the spin button for Number of Days. To produce a report by week, increase the number of days from 1 to 7.

Finally, you have to set up the Starting At date. If you were to accept the default of starting at January 3, 2006, then all your weekly periods would run from Tuesday through Monday. By checking a calendar before you begin, you know that you want the first group to start on January 2, 2006. Change this as shown in Figure 5.39.

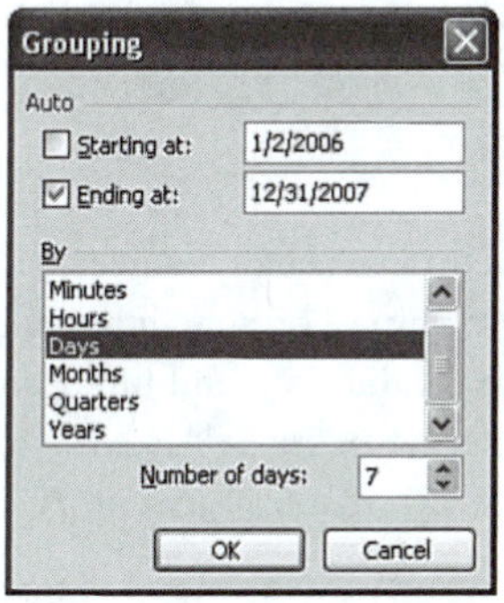

Figure 5.39
The key to being able to access the Number of Days spin button is to select Days and only Days from the By field.

The result will be a report showing sales by week, as shown in Figure 5.40.

Figure 5.40
You've produced a report showing sales by week.

	LINE OF BUSINESS	Copier Sale ▼
2		
3		
4	Revenue	
5	IN BALANCE DATE ▼	Total
6	1/2/2006 - 1/8/2006	538,278
7	1/9/2006 - 1/15/2006	816,503
8	1/16/2006 - 1/22/2006	632,411
9	1/23/2006 - 1/29/2006	487,928
10	1/30/2006 - 2/5/2006	705,964
11	2/6/2006 - 2/12/2006	698,789
12	2/13/2006 - 2/19/2006	636,649
13	2/20/2006 - 2/26/2006	879,789
14	2/27/2006 - 3/5/2006	1,211,616
15	3/6/2006 - 3/12/2006	621,595
16	3/13/2006 - 3/19/2006	647,396
17	3/20/2006 - 3/26/2006	686,309
18	3/27/2006 - 4/2/2006	549,539
19	4/3/2006 - 4/9/2006	771,229
20	4/10/2006 - 4/16/2006	725,350
21	4/17/2006 - 4/23/2006	840,719

CAUTION

If you choose to group by week, none of the other grouping options can be selected. You will not be able to group this or any other field by month or quarter.

Grouping Two Date Fields in One Report

When you group a date field by months and years, Excel repurposes the original date field to show months and adds a new field to show years. The new field is called Years. This is simple enough if you have only one date field in the report.

If you need to produce a report that has two date fields, and you attempt to group both date fields by months and years, Excel will arbitrarily name the first grouped field "Years" and the second grouped field "Years2." This inevitably leads to confusion. In this case, it is important to rename the fields with a meaningful name.

CASE STUDY

Order Lead-Time Report

The material schedulers at a manufacturing plant are usually concerned with the lead time from when an order arrives to when it needs to ship. The schedulers may know that it takes 60 business days to procure material, schedule production, and build the product. In a perfect world, if all their customers would order 61 or more days in advance, the manufacturing plant would not have to keep any excess raw material inventory on hand.

But, in the real world, orders always come in where the customer wants the product faster. In these cases, the manufacturing plant may purchase extra inventory of the components with the longest lead time in order to accommodate rush orders.

If your transactional data source includes a field for date shipped and another field for date ordered, you can easily produce a report showing the normal order lead time by product. This is a valuable report for the master schedulers in the manufacturing plant. Here are the steps to follow:

1. Build a report with "Ship Date" going down the row area of the report. You will ultimately want ship dates to go across the column area, but if your data has more than 253 dates, you cannot initially fit the report going across the worksheet.

2. Group the Ship Date field by month and year.

3. Drag the Ship Date field (now containing months) to the column area of the pivot table. Drag the Years field to the page area of the pivot table and select the first year.

4. Drag the Order Date field to the row area of the pivot table.

5. Group the Order Date field by months and years.

6. Excel will arbitrarily name the years field for Order Date as "Years2," so rename the field to be "Order Year."

7. Double-click the Revenue field. Choose the Options button and change the report to show % of Column.

8. While you are in the PivotTable Field Options dialog box, click the Number button. Give the Revenue field a custom number format of 0.0%;;. The semicolons will suppress the display of negative and zero values.

The resulting table is shown in Figure 5.41. Cell C12 indicates that 19.9% of the copier orders shipped in January 2006 were ordered during the month of January. Another 38.4% of those orders were received in December. This means that 58% of the copier sales from January were received within the manufacturing lead time. This fact dictates that your manufacturing facility will have to keep a whole lot of inventory on hand to meet these short lead-time orders.

Figure 5.41

The order lead-time report makes use of two fields grouped by month and year.

	A	B	C	D	E	F	G	H	I	J	K
1	Years	2006									
2	LINE OF BUSINESS	Copier Sale									
3											
4	Revenue		Ship Date								
5	Order Year	Order Date	Jan	Feb	Mar	Apr	May	Jun	Jul	Aug	Sep
6	2005	Jul	1.0%								
7		Aug	0.8%	0.6%							
8		Sep		0.6%	0.8%						
9		Oct	14.1%	2.0%							
10		Nov	25.9%	17.7%	0.3%	1.0%					
11		Dec	38.4%	36.1%	30.3%	2.5%		0.6%			
12	2006	Jan	19.9%	25.8%	30.5%	16.1%	1.7%		0.7%		
13		Feb		17.1%	28.2%	34.3%	16.9%		2.4%		
14		Mar			9.8%	29.0%	33.5%	14.9%	0.4%	0.9%	
15		Apr				17.1%	32.8%	39.9%	16.7%	1.7%	2.5%
16		May					15.1%	31.3%	35.4%	17.8%	1.1%
17		Jun						13.3%	31.9%	35.7%	12.4%
18		Jul							12.5%	24.7%	36.5%
19		Aug								19.2%	27.8%
20		Sep									19.7%
21		Oct									
22		Nov									
23		Dec									
24	Grand Total		100.0%	100.0%	100.0%	100.0%	100.0%	100.0%	100.0%	100.0%	100.0%

Grouping Numeric Fields

The Grouping dialog box for numeric fields allows you to group items into equal ranges. Specify a start number, an end number, and how many numbers should be in each group.

Grouping Text Fields

You get a call from the VP of Sales. Secretly, they are considering a massive reorganization of the sales regions. He would like to see a report showing sales for the last two years by the new proposed regions. You've been around long enough to know that the proposed regions will change several times before the reorganization happens, so you are not willing to change the Region field in your source data just yet.

5

First, build a report showing revenue by year and by market. The VP of Sales is proposing building a Southeast region composed of Texas, the Gulf Coast, Florida, the Carolinas, and the Shenandoah Valley. Using the Ctrl key, highlight the six markets that will make up the proposed Southeast region. Right-click one of the markets and choose to group those items. Figure 5.42 shows the pivot table before the first group is created.

Figure 5.42
Use the Ctrl key to select the noncontiguous cells that will make up the new Southeast region.

LINE OF BUSINESS	Copier Sale		
Revenue	Ship Date		
MARKET	2006	2007	Grand Total
California	1,945,645	2,074,740	4,020,385
Central US	1,765,979	1,740,738	3,506,717
Colorado	1,273,808	1,839,783	3,113,591
Florida		,057,032	3,783,617
Great Lakes		,043,161	1,929,517
Gulf Coast		909,904	5,830,888
Illinois		,486,388	2,989,768
Indiana		,868,886	3,616,687
Kentucky		,308,158	5,872,430
New England		,224,288	6,011,684
New York North		,171,906	3,932,881
New York South		898,975	1,641,970
North Carolina			58
North West			41
Ohio			99
Shenandoah V			70
South Carolina			97
Southwest			,747
Tennessee		355,517	6,323,837
Texas		,338,412	4,531,085
Topeka	2,657,004	2,967,616	5,624,620
Grand Total	40,331,851	46,249,838	86,581,689

(Right-click context menu: Format Cells..., PivotChart, PivotTable Wizard, Refresh Data, Hide, Select ▶, Group and Show Detail ▶ [Hide Detail, Show Detail, Group..., Ungroup...], Order ▶, Field Settings..., Table Options..., Hide PivotTable Toolbar, Hide Field List)

After the Group command, Excel will add a new field called MARKET2. The six selected cells will be sequenced together and belong to a MARKET2 grouping that is arbitrarily called Group1, as shown in Figure 5.43.

Figure 5.43
Excel arbitrarily calls the first grouping Group1.

LINE OF BUSINESS	Copier Sale			
Revenue		Ship Date		
MARKET2	MARKET	2006	2007	Grand Total
California	California	1,945,645	2,074,740	4,020,385
Central US	Central US	1,765,979	1,740,738	3,506,717
Colorado	Colorado	1,273,808	1,839,783	3,113,591
Group1	Florida	1,726,585	2,057,032	3,783,617
	Gulf Coast	2,920,984	2,909,904	5,830,888
	North Carolina	1,513,984	2,249,174	3,763,158
	Shenandoah Valley	1,994,123	2,250,647	4,244,770
	South Carolina	2,656,626	3,094,871	5,751,497
	Texas	2,192,673	2,338,412	4,531,085
Great Lakes	Great Lakes	886,356	1,043,161	1,929,517
Illinois	Illinois	1,503,380	1,486,388	2,989,768
Indiana	Indiana	1,747,801	1,868,886	3,616,687
Kentucky	Kentucky	2,564,272	3,308,158	5,872,430
New England	New England	2,787,396	3,224,288	6,011,684
New York North	New York North	1,760,975	2,171,906	3,932,881
New York South	New York South	742,995	898,975	1,641,970
North West	North West	1,443,962	1,735,179	3,179,141
Ohio	Ohio	1,104,104	1,277,195	2,381,299
Southwest	Southwest	2,174,879	2,357,268	4,532,147
Tennessee	Tennessee	2,968,320	3,355,517	6,323,837
Topeka	Topeka	2,657,004	2,967,616	5,624,620
Grand Total		40,331,851	46,249,838	86,581,689

Double-click the MARKET2 field and give it a name such as New Region. Click in cell A9 and type a meaningful name instead of Group1.

As you repeat these steps to build other regions, Excel will continue to assign names such as Group2, Group3, and so on. After creating each region, simply type a meaningful name over the cell containing the arbitrary group name.

You will find that the New Region field is a real field. Use the AutoSort feature to sequence it alphabetically.

By default, Excel does not add subtotals for the New Region field. You can easily access the PivotTable Field dialog box for New Region to add subtotals.

Figure 5.44 shows the report as it is ready for the VP of Sales. You can probably already predict that they will need to shuffle markets to the Northeast region in order to balance the regions.

Figure 5.44

After you group all the markets into new regions, the report is ready for review.

2	LINE OF BUSINESS	Copier Sale	▼			
3						
4	Revenue			Ship Date ▼		
5	New Region ▼	MARKET ▼		2006	2007	Grand Total
6	West	California		1,945,645	2,074,740	4,020,385
7		Colorado		1,273,808	1,839,783	3,113,591
8		North West		1,443,962	1,735,179	3,179,141
9		Southwest		2,174,879	2,357,268	4,532,147
10		Topeka		2,657,004	2,967,616	5,624,620
11	West Sum			9,495,298	10,974,586	20,469,884
12	Midwest	Central US		1,765,979	1,740,738	3,506,717
13		Great Lakes		886,356	1,043,161	1,929,517
14		Illinois		1,503,380	1,486,388	2,989,768
15		Indiana		1,747,801	1,868,886	3,616,687
16		Kentucky		2,564,272	3,308,158	5,872,430
17		Ohio		1,104,104	1,277,195	2,381,299
18		Tennessee		2,968,320	3,355,517	6,323,837
19	Midwest Sum			12,540,212	14,080,043	26,620,255
20	Northeast	New England		2,787,396	3,224,288	6,011,684
21		New York North		1,760,975	2,171,906	3,932,881
22		New York South		742,995	898,975	1,641,970
23	Northeast Sum			5,291,366	6,295,169	11,586,535
24	Southeast	Florida		1,726,585	2,057,032	3,783,617
25		Gulf Coast		2,920,984	2,909,904	5,830,888
26		North Carolina		1,513,984	2,249,174	3,763,158
27		Shenandoah Valley		1,994,123	2,250,647	4,244,770
28		South Carolina		2,656,626	3,094,871	5,751,497
29		Texas		2,192,673	2,338,412	4,531,085
30	Southeast Sum			13,004,975	14,900,040	27,905,015
31	Grand Total			40,331,851	46,249,838	86,581,689

Grouping and Ungrouping

After you have established groups, you can hide or show detail using the Hide Detail and Show Detail menu items under Group and Show Detail on the right-click menu. Figure 5.45 shows the pivot table from Figure 5.44 with the detail hidden.

Figure 5.45

With text groups, you can hide or show detail. This view has the market detail hidden.

2	LINE OF BUSINESS	Copier Sale ▼				
3						
4	Revenue			Ship Date ▼		
5	New Region ▼	MARKET ▼		2006	2007	Grand Total
6	West			9,495,298	10,974,586	20,469,884
7	Midwest			12,540,212	14,080,043	26,620,255
8	Northeast			5,291,366	6,295,169	11,586,535
9	Southeast			13,004,975	14,900,040	27,905,015
10	Grand Total			40,331,851	46,249,838	86,581,689

Next Steps

Excel is fantastic at doing calculations, and Microsoft has added two types of calculations to pivot tables. You can add a new item along an existing dimension, or you can add a completely new field altogether. In the next chapter, you will learn how to fully utilize calculated fields and calculated items.

5

Performing Calculations Within Your Pivot Tables

6

Introducing Calculated Fields and Calculated Items

When analyzing data with pivot tables, you will often find the need to expand your analysis to include data based on calculations that are not in your original dataset. Excel provides a way to perform calculations within your pivot table through calculated fields and calculated items.

A *calculated field* is a data field you create by executing a calculation against existing fields in the pivot table. Think of a calculated field as adding a virtual column to your dataset. This column takes up no space in your source data, contains the data you define with a formula, and interacts with your pivot data as a field—just like all the other fields in your pivot table.

A *calculated item* is a data item you create by executing a calculation against existing items within a data field. Think of a calculated item as adding a virtual row of data to your dataset. This virtual row takes up no space in your source data and contains summarized values based on calculations performed on other rows in the same field. Calculated items interact with your pivot data as a data item, just like all the other items in your pivot table.

With calculated fields and calculated items, you can insert a formula into your pivot table in order to create your own custom field or data item. Your newly created data becomes a part of your pivot table, interacting with other pivot data, recalculating when you refresh and supplying you with a calculated metric that does not exist in your source data.

The example in Figure 6.1 demonstrates how a basic calculated field can add another perspective to your data.

Figure 6.1
Average Revenue per Unit is a calculated field that adds another perspective to your data analysis.

			Data		
LINE OF BUSINESS	REGION		REVENUE	UNITS SOLD	Average Revenue per Unit
Copier Sale	North		$25,893,618	8,706	2,974
	South		$36,711,470	12,224	3,003
	West		$23,976,601	8,081	2,967
Copier Sale Total			$86,581,689	29,011	2,984
Printer Sale	North		$20,621,317	4,313	4,781
	South		$28,153,264	5,876	4,791
	West		$19,594,197	4,135	4,739
Printer Sale Total			$68,368,778	14,324	4,773
Service Plan	North		$201,414,511	103,595	1,944
	South		$223,750,307	115,742	1,933
	West		$149,341,261	76,954	1,941
Service Plan Total			$574,506,079	296,291	1,939
Grand Total			$729,456,546	339,626	2,148

Your pivot table shows revenue and number of units sold by region and line of business. A calculated field that shows you average revenue per unit enhances this analysis and adds another dimension to your data.

Now you may look at Figure 6.1 and ask yourself, "Why go through all the trouble of creating calculated fields or calculated items? Why not just use formulas in surrounding cells or even add your calculation directly into the source table in order to get the information you need?"

To answer these questions, look at the different methods you could use to create the calculated field in Figure 6.1.

Method 1: Manually Add the Calculated Field to Your Data Source

You can manually add a calculated field to your data source, as shown in Figure 6.2, allowing the pivot table to pick the field up as a regular data field.

Figure 6.2
Precalculating calculated fields in your data source is both cumbersome and impractical.

	A	B	C	D	E	F	G
							Added Field
					Units	Days in	Average Revenue per
	Region	Market	Line of Business	Revenue	Sold	Period	Unit
1	North	Great Lakes	Parts	$3,454	1	19.0	$3,454
2	North	Shenandoah Valley	Printer Sale	$15,682	2	19.0	$7,841
3	North	Shenandoah Valley	Copier Sale	$12,968	6	19.0	$2,161
4	North	New England	Parts	$2,789	1	19.0	$2,789
5	North	New England	Service Plan	$32,605	23	19.0	$1,418
6	North	New England	Service Plan	$52,437	30	19.0	$1,748
7	North	New England	Printer Sale	$17,391	2	19.0	$8,696
8	North	New England	Parts	$2,468	1	19.0	$2,468
9	North	New England	Parts	$375	1	19.0	$375
10	North	New York South	Service Plan	$67,592	30	19.0	$2,253
11	North	New York South	Service Plan	$21,454	15	19.0	$1,430
12	North	Ohio	Parts	$979	1	19.0	$979

On the surface, it looks like a simple option, but this method of precalculating metrics and incorporating them into your data source is impractical on several levels.

Besides the fact that you increase the chance for errors by calculating and managing data with formulas, you limit your flexibility when requirements change.

If the definitions of your calculated fields change, you will have to go back to the data source, recalculate the metric for each row, and refresh your pivot table. If you have to add a metric, you will have go back to the data source, add a new calculated field, and then change the range of your pivot table to capture the new field.

Method 2: Use a Formula Outside of Your Pivot Table to Create the Calculated Field

You can add a calculated field by performing the calculation in an external cell with a formula. In the example in Figure 6.3, each cell in the Average Revenue per Unit column is made up of a formula that references the pivot table.

Figure 6.3
Typing a formula next to your pivot table will essentially give you a calculated field that refreshes when your pivot table is refreshed.

2			Data		ADDED FIELD
3	Region	Line of Business	Revenue	Units Sold	Average Revenue Per Unit
4	North	Copier Sale	$25,893,618	8,706	$2,974
5		Printer Sale	$20,621,317	4,313	$4,781
6		Service Plan	$201,414,511	103,595	$1,944
7	**North Total**		**$247,929,446**	**116,614**	$2,126
8	South	Copier Sale	$36,711,470	12,224	$3,003
9		Printer Sale	$28,153,264	5,876	$4,791
10		Service Plan	$223,750,307	115,742	$1,933
11	**South Total**		**$288,615,041**	**113,842**	$2,535
12	West	Copier Sale	$23,976,601	8,081	$2,967
13		Printer Sale	$19,594,197	4,135	$4,739
14		Service Plan	$149,341,261	76,954	$1,941
15	**West Total**		**$192,912,059**	**89,170**	$2,163
16	Grand Total		$729,456,546	339,626	$2,148

Although this method will give you a calculated field that updates when your pivot table is refreshed, as you can see in Figure 6.4, any changes in the structure of your pivot table have the potential of rendering your formula useless.

Figure 6.4
Moving the Region field to the page area changes the structure of your pivot table, exposing the weakness of makeshift calculated fields that use external formulas.

	A	B	C	D	E
1	Region	(All)			
2					ADDED FIELD
3		Data			Average Revenue Per Unit
4	Line of Business	Sum of Revenue	Sum of Units Sold		#VALUE!
5	Copier Sale	$86,581,689	29,011		#DIV/0!
6	Printer Sale	$68,368,778	14,324		#DIV/0!
7	Service Plan	$574,506,079	296,291		#DIV/0!
8	Grand Total	$729,456,546	339,626		#DIV/0!
9					#DIV/0!
10					#DIV/0!
11					#DIV/0!
12					#DIV/0!
13					#DIV/0!
14					#DIV/0!
15					#DIV/0!
16					#DIV/0!

Method 3: Insert a Calculated Field Directly into Your Pivot Table

Inserting the calculated field directly into your pivot table is the best option. This eliminates the need to manage formulas, provides for scalability when your data source grows or changes, and allows for flexibility in the event that your metric definitions change.

Another huge advantage of this method is that you can alter your pivot table's structure and even measure different data fields against your calculated field without worrying about errors in your formulas or losing cell references.

6

The pivot table report shown in Figure 6.5 is the same pivot table you see in Figure 6.1, except it has been restructured so that you get the average revenue per unit by market.

Figure 6.5
Your calculated field remains viable even when your pivot table's structure changes to measure average revenue per unit for every market.

	A	B	C	D
1				
2		Data		
3	MARKET	REVENUE	UNITS SOLD	Average Revenue per Unit
4	California	$61,636,732	24,785	2,487
5	Central	$30,503,842	12,940	2,357
6	Colorado	$26,217,201	11,020	2,379
7	Florida	$47,362,461	19,372	2,445
8	Great Lakes	$36,992,638	15,903	2,326
9	Gulf Coast	$45,159,185	18,555	2,434
10	Illinois	$42,101,421	18,390	2,289
11	Indiana	$41,043,454	17,416	2,357
12	Kentucky	$37,363,632	15,448	2,419
13	New England	$37,341,224	15,315	2,438
14	New York North	$41,493,673	16,908	2,454
15	New York South	$29,482,893	12,955	2,276

The bottom line is that there are significant benefits to integrating your custom calculations into your pivot table. These benefits include the following:

■ The elimination of potential formula and cell reference errors

■ The ability to add and remove data from your pivot table without affecting your calculations

■ The ability to auto-recalculate when your pivot table is changed or refreshed

■ The flexibility to change calculations easily when your metric definitions change

■ The ability to manage and maintain your calculations effectively

Creating Your First Calculated Field

To create a calculated field, first activate the Insert Calculated Field dialog box shown in Figure 6.6. To call up this dialog box, place your cursor anywhere in your pivot table, click the PivotTable icon in the PivotTable toolbar, and then select Formulas, Calculated Field.

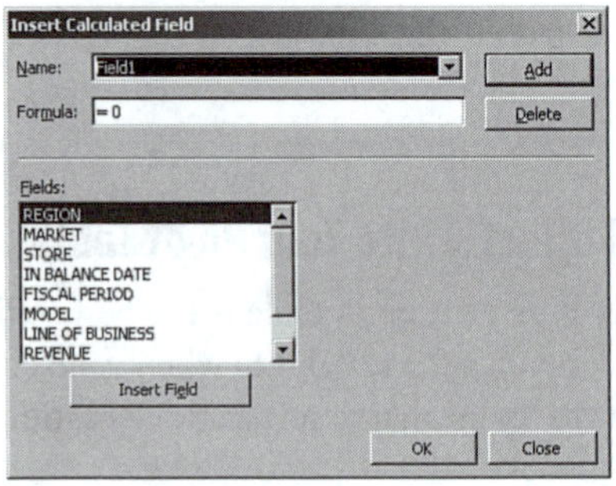

Figure 6.6
The Insert Calculated Field dialog box will assist you in creating a calculated field in your pivot table.

> **NOTE**
> Within Office 2000, right-click on your pivot table and select Formulas, Calculated Field to get to the Insert Calculation Field dialog box.

If your PivotTable toolbar is active, you can click anywhere inside your pivot table and press Alt+P to see all the menu items under the PivotTable icon selection.

You will notice the two input boxes at the top of the dialog box shown in Figure 6.7: Name and Formula. The objective here is to give your calculated field a name and then build the formula by selecting the combination of data fields and mathematical operators that will provide you the metric you are looking for. In this example, you will first name your calculated field "Avg Revenue per Unit."

Figure 6.7
Give your calculated field a descriptive name.

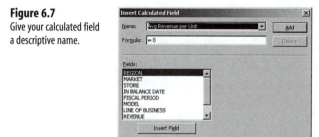

Next, you will go to the Fields list, as shown in Figure 6.8, and double-click on the Revenue field. Then enter a slash (/) to let Excel know you will be dividing the Revenue field by something.

CAUTION

By default, the Formula input box in the Insert Calculated Field dialog box contains "= 0." Ensure that you delete the zero before continuing with your formula.

Figure 6.8
Start your formula with = Revenue /.

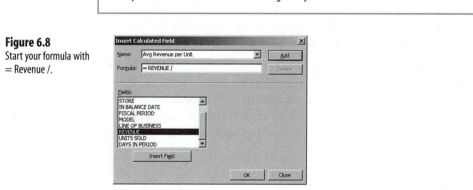

6

Finish your formula by double-clicking on the Units Sold field. Your finished formula is shown in Figure 6.9.

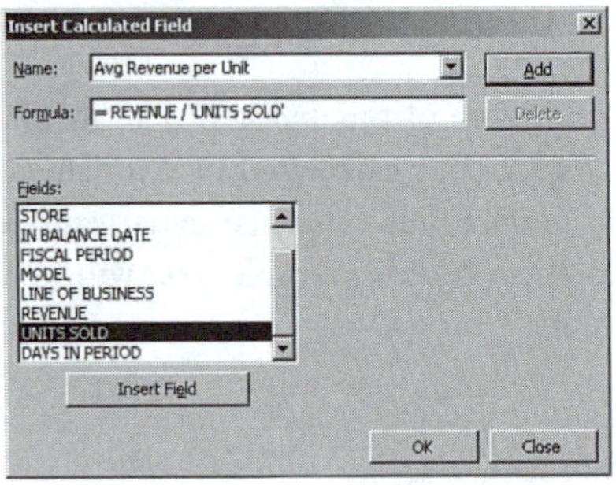

Figure 6.9
The full formula, = Revenue / 'Units Sold', will give you the calculated field you need.

Click the Add button and then click OK to activate your new calculated field. As you can see in Figure 6.10, the result of your efforts is a calculated field within your pivot table.

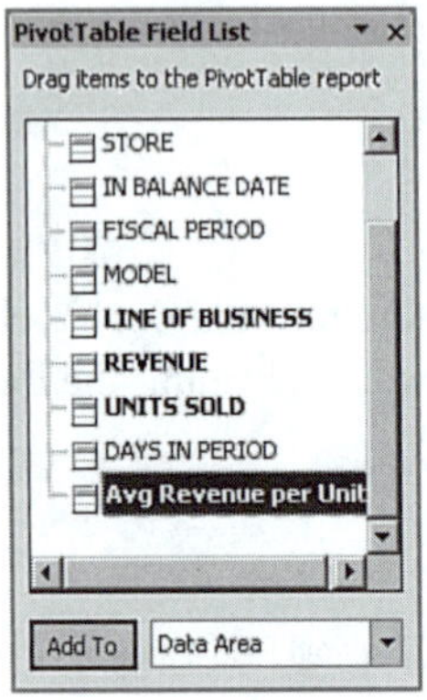

Figure 6.10
You have successfully added a calculated field to your pivot table. You may now change the settings on this new field just as you would any other field (for example, you could change the field name, the number format, or the color).

Notice that not only did your pivot table create a new field called Sum of Avg Revenue per Unit, but your field list now includes your new calculated field.

Does this mean you have just added a column to your data source? The answer is no. Calculated fields are similar to the pivot table's default Subtotal and Grand Total calculations in that they are all mathematical functions that recalculate when the pivot table changes or is refreshed. Calculated fields merely mimic the hard fields in your data source, allowing you to drag them, change field settings, and use them with other calculated fields.

Take a moment to look at Figure 6.9 closely. Notice the formula you entered is similar in format to those used in the standard Excel formula bar. The obvious difference is that instead of using hard numbers or cell references, you are referencing pivot data fields to define the arguments used in this calculation. If you have worked with formulas in Excel before, you will quickly grasp the concept of creating calculated fields.

CASE STUDY

Summarizing Next Year's Forecast

Each store in your company has submitted its initial revenue forecast for next year. Your task is to take the first-pass numbers the stores submitted and create a summary report showing the following:

- Total revenue forecast by region and market
- Total percentage growth over last year
- Total contribution margin by region and market

Because these numbers are first-pass submissions and you know they will change over the course of the next two weeks, you decide to use a pivot table to create the requested forecast summary from the source data shown in Figure 6.11.

Figure 6.11
Using a pivot table will give you the flexibility to update your summary report without re-creating it.

	A	B	C	D	E	F
1	REGION	MARKET	STORE	Revenue Last Year	Forecast Next Year	Variable Cost Next Year
2	North	New England	2004014	$1,825,142	$1,788,639	($249,225)
3	North	New England	2105015	$955,797	$1,099,167	($226,284)
4	South	Gulf Coast	3106016	$1,878,608	$1,963,145	($669,394)
5	South	Gulf Coast	3106026	$1,558,607	$1,479,621	($275,185)
6	South	Kentucky	3109019	$1,611,371	$1,524,357	($212,783)
7	South	Texas	6002012	$1,400,037	$1,491,039	($348,657)
8	South	Texas	6002022	$501,892	$577,176	($126,406)
9	South	Texas	6009029	$299,320	$336,735	($248,154)
10	West	Southwest	7008018	$2,870,867	$2,776,586	($418,324)
11	West	Southwest	7008048	$1,202,129	$1,396,111	($327,184)
12	North	New England	12011011	$880,242	$528,145	($294,655)
13	North	Shenandoah Valley	12016016	$1,396,617	$1,326,786	($145,957)
14	North	Shenandoah Valley	12016026	$583,542	$886,984	($669,590)
15	North	New York South	12118018	$1,021,388	$1,235,879	($345,886)
16	North	New York South	12118048	$1,350,657	$1,229,098	($235,106)
17	North	New York South	12118058	$420,054	$483,062	($56,281)
18	North	New York South	12118068	$347,789	$424,303	($83,887)
19	North	New York South	12118088	$158,536	$206,097	($114,644)

Create the initial pivot table to include the fields Revenue Last Year and Forecast Next Year for each region and market.

As you can see in Figure 6.12, by virtue of adding the Forecast Next Year field in the data area, you have met your first requirement—to show the total revenue forecast by region and market.

Figure 6.12
The initial pivot table is basic, but it provides the data for your first requirement—to show the total revenue forecast by region and market.

	A	B	C	D
1			Data	
2	REGION	MARKET	Revenue Last Year	Forecast Next Year
3	North	Great Lakes	3,195,710	3,584,517
4		New England	4,931,119	4,795,652
5		New York North	3,682,182	3,906,225
6		New York South	3,298,424	3,578,439
7		Ohio	3,424,208	3,689,359
8		Shenandoah Valley	3,555,032	4,036,888
9		South Carolina	5,795,378	6,135,018
10	North Total		27,882,053	29,725,897
11	South	Florida	6,211,824	6,401,397
12		Gulf Coast	5,736,364	6,116,796
13		Illinois	2,833,555	2,795,029
14		Indiana	4,123,062	4,417,918
15		Kentucky	4,008,095	4,211,045

6

The next metric you need is percentage growth over last year. To get this data, you will need to add a calculated field that uses the following formula:

(Forecast Next Year - Revenue Last Year) / 'Revenue Last Year'

Click the PivotTable icon in the PivotTable toolbar and then select Formulas, Calculated Field. When you have activated the Insert Calculated Field dialog box, name your new field Percent Growth.

Activate the Insert Calculated Field dialog box and name your new field Percent Growth.

Delete the zero that appears in the Formula input box and then follow these steps:

1. Enter an opening parenthesis [(].
2. Double-click on the Forecast Next Year field.
3. Enter a minus sign (-).
4. Double-click on the Revenue Last Year field.
5. Enter a closing parenthesis [)].
6. Enter a division sign (/).
7. Double-click on the Revenue Last Year field.

At this point, your dialog box should look similar to the one shown in Figure 6.13. With your formula typed in, you can now click OK to add your new field.

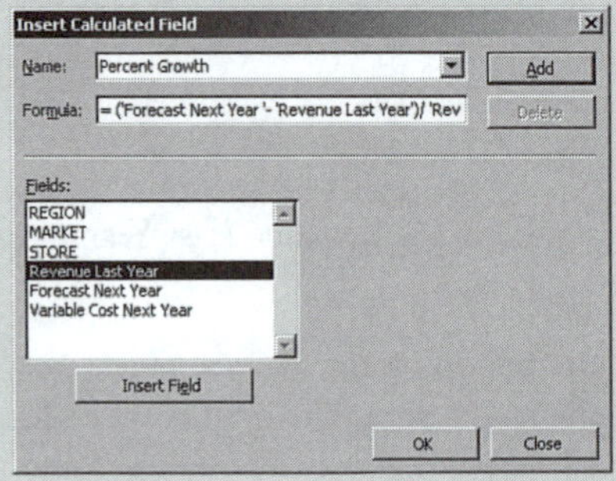

Figure 6.13
With just a few clicks, you have created your percentage growth formula.

As you can see in Figure 6.14, the default format of your calculated field makes it look like there is zero growth across the board. You will often find that it is necessary to format your newly calculated fields to present your data properly. In this case, you will have to go into your new field's settings and format it to show your data as percentages.

Figure 6.14
Some formatting is needed to show data correctly.

	A	B	C	D	E
1			Data		
2	REGION	MARKET	Revenue Last Year	Forecast Next Year	Sum of Percent Growth
3	North	Great Lakes	3,195,710	3,584,517	0
4		New England	4,931,119	4,795,652	0
5		New York North	3,682,182	3,906,225	0
6		New York South	3,298,424	3,578,439	0
7		Ohio	3,424,208	3,689,359	0
8		Shenandoah Valley	3,555,032	4,036,688	0
9		South Carolina	5,795,378	6,135,018	0
10	North Total		27,882,053	29,725,897	0
11	South	Florida	6,211,824	6,401,397	0
12		Gulf Coast	5,736,364	6,116,796	0
13		Illinois	2,833,555	2,795,029	0
14		Indiana	4,123,062	4,417,918	0
15		Kentucky	4,008,095	4,211,045	0
16		North Carolina	5,536,547	5,802,912	0

After you have formatted your calculated field, your pivot table should look similar to the one shown in Figure 6.15. With your new calculated field in place, you can easily see that the New England market and the Illinois market will have to resubmit their forecasts to reflect a positive growth over last year.

Figure 6.15
You can already discern some information from your calculated field, identifying New England and Illinois as problem markets.

	A	B	C	D	E
1			Data		
2	REGION	MARKET	Revenue Last Year	Forecast Next Year	Percent Growth
3	North	Great Lakes	3,195,710	3,584,517	12.2%
4		New England	4,931,119	4,795,652	-2.7%
5		New York North	3,682,182	3,906,225	6.1%
6		New York South	3,298,424	3,578,439	8.5%
7		Ohio	3,424,208	3,689,359	7.7%
8		Shenandoah Valley	3,555,032	4,036,688	13.5%
9		South Carolina	5,795,378	6,135,018	5.9%
10	North Total		27,882,053	29,725,897	6.6%
11	South	Florida	6,211,824	6,401,397	3.1%
12		Gulf Coast	5,736,364	6,116,796	6.6%
13		Illinois	2,833,555	2,795,029	-1.4%
14		Indiana	4,123,062	4,417,918	7.2%
15		Kentucky	4,008,095	4,211,045	5.1%
16		North Carolina	5,536,547	5,802,912	4.8%

Now that you show total revenue forecast by region and market as well as the total percentage growth over last year, it's time to focus on your last requirement—to show the total contribution margin by region and market.

To get this data, you will need to add a calculated field that uses the following formula:

Forecast Next Year + Variable Cost Next Year

NOTE

By looking at Figure 6.15, you can see that Variable Cost Next Year is not in your pivot table report. Your calculated field can use fields that are not visible in your pivot table.

6

Activate the Insert Calculated Field dialog box and then name your new field Contribution Margin.

Delete the zero that appears in the Formula input box and then follow these steps:

1. Double-click on the Forecast Next Year field.
2. Enter a plus sign (+).
3. Double-click on the Variable Cost Next Year field.

At this point, your dialog box should look similar to the one shown in Figure 6.16.

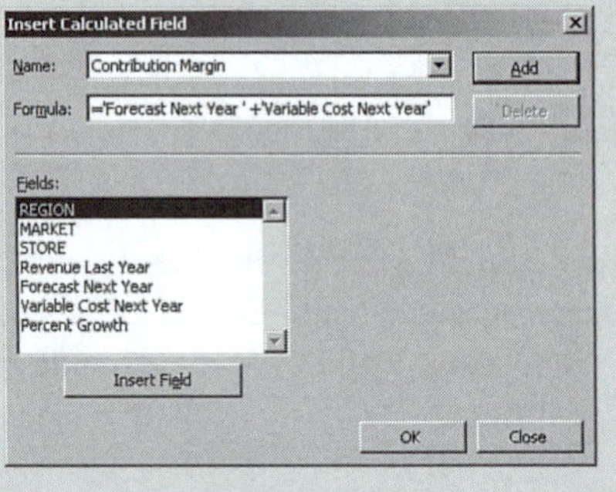

Figure 6.16
With just a few clicks, you have created your contribution margin formula.

With the creation of the contribution margin, your pivot table report should look similar to the one shown in Figure 6.17. This report is ready to be delivered.

Figure 6.17
Contribution margin is now a data field in your pivot table report thanks to your calculated field.

	A	B	C	D	E	F
1			Data			
2	REGION	MARKET	Revenue Last Year	Forecast Next Year	Percent Growth	Contribution Margin
3	North	Great Lakes	3,195,710	3,584,517	12.2%	2,765,802
4		New England	4,931,119	4,795,652	-2.7%	3,664,958
5		New York North	3,682,182	3,906,225	6.1%	2,919,377
6		New York South	3,298,424	3,578,439	8.5%	2,743,035
7		Ohio	3,424,208	3,689,359	7.7%	2,647,732
8		Shenandoah Valley	3,555,032	4,036,688	13.5%	2,865,439
9		South Carolina	5,795,378	6,135,016	5.9%	4,941,832
10	North Total		27,882,053	29,725,897	6.6%	22,548,177
11	South	Florida	6,211,824	6,401,397	3.1%	4,774,773
12		Gulf Coast	5,736,364	6,116,796	6.6%	4,193,780
13		Illinois	2,833,555	2,795,029	-1.4%	2,197,804
14		Indiana	4,123,062	4,417,918	7.2%	3,328,858
15		Kentucky	4,008,095	4,211,045	5.1%	2,973,512
16		North Carolina	5,536,547	5,802,912	4.8%	4,331,500
17		Tennessee	5,788,209	6,113,491	5.6%	4,613,075
18		Texas	2,934,707	3,175,691	8.2%	2,211,415

Now that your pivot table report is built, any new forecast submissions can easily be analyzed by refreshing your report with the new updates.

Creating Your First Calculated Item

As you learned at the beginning of this chapter, a calculated item is essentially a row of data you add by performing a calculation on the other rows in the same field. Therefore, it makes sense that you must first select the field where you want to add your calculated item.

> **NOTE**
>
> As you go through this section, keep in mind that grouping items can give you an effect similar to that of creating a calculated item. Indeed, in many cases, grouping would be a great alternative to using calculated items. Chapter 5, "Controlling the Way You View Your Pivot Data," covers grouping in detail.

In the pivot table shown in Figure 6.18, you see totals for copier sales and printer sales under the Line of Business field. You need to group both of these data items into a calculated item called Equipment.

Figure 6.18
You want to add a new data item called Equipment that will represent the sum of copier sales and printer sales.

Place your cursor on any data item with the Line of Business field, click the PivotTable icon in the PivotTable toolbar, and select Formulas, Calculated Item. This activates the Insert Calculated Item dialog box shown in Figure 6.19.

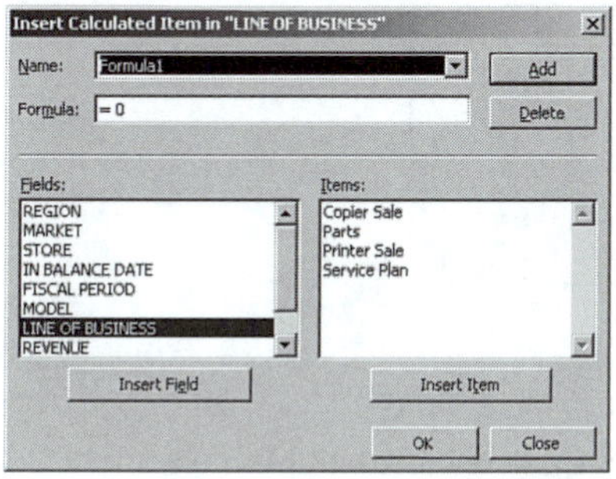

Figure 6.19
The Insert Calculated Item dialog box will assist you in creating your calculated item.

6

Notice that the top of the dialog box identifies which field you are working with. In this case, it is the Line of Business field. Also, notice the list box that contains all the items in the Line of Business field. Your goal is to give your calculated item a name and then build its formula by selecting the combination of data items and operators that will provide you the metric you are looking for.

As you can see in Figure 6.20, you will first name your calculated item Equipment.

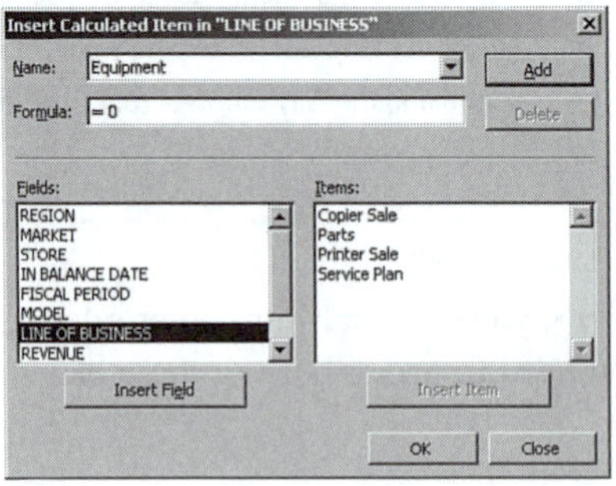

Figure 6.20
Give your calculated item a descriptive name.

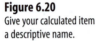

As mentioned before, the formula input box contains "= 0" by default. Ensure that you delete the zero before continuing with your formula.

Next, go to the Items list and double-click on the Copier Sale item. Then enter a plus sign (+) to signify that you will be adding this item to something. Finish your formula by double-clicking on the Printer Sale item in the Items list box.

At this point, your dialog box should look similar to the one shown in Figure 6.21. Here's your full formula:

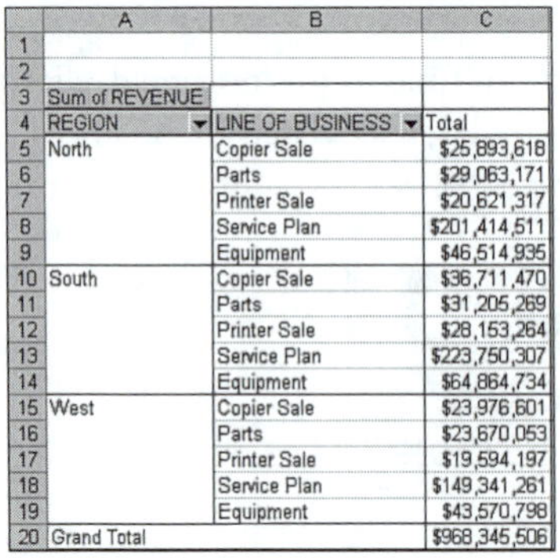

Figure 6.21
You have successfully added a calculated item to your pivot table.

	A	B	C
1			
2			
3	Sum of REVENUE		
4	REGION	LINE OF BUSINESS	Total
5	North	Copier Sale	$25,893,618
6		Parts	$29,063,171
7		Printer Sale	$20,621,317
8		Service Plan	$201,414,511
9		Equipment	$46,514,935
10	South	Copier Sale	$36,711,470
11		Parts	$31,205,269
12		Printer Sale	$28,153,264
13		Service Plan	$223,750,307
14		Equipment	$64,864,734
15	West	Copier Sale	$23,976,601
16		Parts	$23,670,053
17		Printer Sale	$19,594,197
18		Service Plan	$149,341,261
19		Equipment	$43,570,798
20	Grand Total		$968,345,506

= 'Copier Sale' + 'Printer Sale'

This will give you the calculated item you need. Click OK to activate your new calculated item.

Now you can hide Copier Sale and Printer Sale, leaving the three distinct pivot items shown in Figure 6.22. Keep in mind that you can also change the settings on this new data item just as you would any other (for example, you can change the format or the color).

Figure 6.22
Hiding the Copier Sale and Printer Sale items gives you three distinct items and corrects the grand total.

3	Sum of REVENUE		
4	REGION ▾	LINE OF BUSINESS ▾	Total
5	North	Parts	$29,063,171
6		Service Plan	$201,414,511
7		Equipment	$46,514,935
8	South	Parts	$31,205,269
9		Service Plan	$223,750,307
10		Equipment	$64,864,734
11	West	Parts	$23,670,053
12		Service Plan	$149,341,261
13		Equipment	$43,570,798
14	Grand Total		$813,395,039

CAUTION

If you don't hide the data items you used to create your calculated item, your grand totals and subtotals may double-count your units of measure (revenue, gallons, and so on). Compare the grand total in Figure 6.21 to the one in Figure 6.22.

CASE STUDY

Creating a Mini-Dashboard

You need to create a mini-dashboard that shows two key variances for each store:

- The current fiscal period versus the same period last year
- The last three fiscal period averages versus the same three last year

Figure 6.23 shows the data source you will be working with. Given the amount of data in your source table and the possibility that this will be a recurring exercise, you decide to build the dashboard with a pivot table.

Figure 6.23
Using a pivot table will give you the flexibility to update your dashboard report without re-creating it.

	A	B	C	D	E	F	G	H	I	J
1	REGION	MARKET	STORE	IN BALANCE DATE	FISCAL PERIOD	MODEL	LINE OF BUSINESS	REVENUE	Units Sold	DAYS IN PERIOD
2	North	Great Lakes	65061011	01/03/03	200205	4055T	Parts	$3,454	0	19.0
3	North	Shenandoah Valley	62067017	01/03/03	200205	2500P	Printer Sale	$15,682	2	19.0
4	North	Shenandoah Valley	32139049	01/03/03	200205	2500C	Copier Sale	$12,968	6	19.0
5	North	New England	2004014	01/03/03	200205	4055T	Parts	$2,789	0	19.0
6	North	New England	72074014	01/03/03	200205	4500C	Service Plan	$32,605	23	19.0
7	North	New England	12011011	01/03/03	200205	3002P	Service Plan	$52,437	30	19.0
8	North	New England	2105015	01/03/03	200205	2500P	Printer Sale	$17,391	2	19.0
9	North	New England	22022012	01/03/03	200205	4055T	Parts	$2,468	0	19.0
10	North	New England	22022012	01/03/03	200205	3002C	Parts	$375	0	19.0
11	North	New York South	12118068	01/03/03	200205	4500C	Service Plan	$67,592	30	19.0
12	North	New York South	12118068	01/03/03	200205	3002C	Service Plan	$21,454	15	19.0
13	North	Ohio	44040030	01/03/03	200205	3002C	Parts	$979	0	19.0
14	North	Ohio	44040020	01/03/03	200205	4055T	Parts	$4,539	0	19.0
15	North	Ohio	44040020	01/03/03	200205	3002P	Parts	$3,209	0	19.0
16	North	Ohio	34037017	01/03/03	200205	3002P	Parts	$34,612	0	19.0
17	North	South Carolina	53154014	01/03/03	200205	3002C	Service Plan	$14,051	9	19.0

Create the initial pivot table as shown in Figure 6.24 by placing the Fiscal Period field in the row area and Revenue field in the data area.

Figure 6.24
The initial pivot table is basic, showing you revenue by fiscal period.

	A	B
1	Sum of REVENUE	
2	FISCAL PERIOD ▼	Total
3	200205	32684448
4	200206	34090824
5	200207	34648991
6	200208	33958920
7	200209	35112864
8	200210	33704405
9	200211	33133608
10	200212	32991065
11	200301	32305497
12	200302	34445448
13	200303	33744529
14	200304	33051136
15	200305	33742628

The first metric you need is the current fiscal period versus the same period last year. You will need to add a calculated item that uses the following formula:

Fiscal Period 200404 – Fiscal Period 200304

Place your cursor on any data item under the Fiscal Period field and then click the PivotTable icon in the PivotTable toolbar. Next, select Formulas, Calculated Item. This activates the Insert Calculated Item dialog box. Name your new item Current PD vs. Last PD.

Delete the zero that appears in the Formula input box and then follow these steps:

1. Double-click on the 200404 item.
2. Enter a division sign (/).
3. Double-click on the 200304 item.
4. Enter -1.

At this point, your dialog box should look similar to the one shown in Figure 6.25. You can now click OK to add your new item.

6

Figure 6.25
You have successfully created the formula for your first metric (the current fiscal period versus the same period last year).

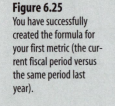

Next, you need to create a calculated item for the last three fiscal period averages versus the same three averages last year. The calculation for this metric is as follows:

Average('200404','200403','200402') / Average('200304','200303','200302') - 1

Place your cursor on any data item under the Fiscal Year field and activate the Insert Calculated Item dialog box. Then name your new item Last 3 PD Avg vs. Same PDS Last Year.

Delete the zero that appears in the Formula input box and then follow these steps:

1. Enter =Average(.

2. Double-click on the 200404 item and then enter a comma.

3. Double-click on the 200403 item and then enter a comma.

4. Double-click on the 200402 item.

5. Enter)/Average(.

6. Double-click on the 200304 item and then enter a comma.

7. Double-click on the 200303 item and then enter a comma.

8. Double-click on the 200302 item.

9. Enter)-1.

Figure 6.26 gives you a good idea how this formula will look in your dialog box.

Figure 6.26
Your second formula uses six data items and two Average functions.

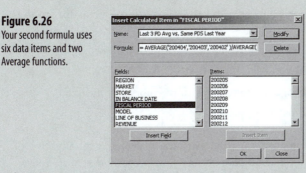

NOTE

Notice that you are using the Average function in this example. When building formulas in calculated fields or calculated items, you can use any worksheet function that does not require cell references or defined names as arguments.

6

Now hide all the data items in the Fiscal Year field except for the two calculated items you just created. Then change the calculated item values to percentage format. At this point, your pivot table should look like the one shown in Figure 6.27.

Figure 6.27

After hiding the data items you don't need and formatting the data in percentage format, you can see your dashboard starting to come together.

	A	B
1	Sum of REVENUE	
2	FISCAL PERIOD ▼	Total
3	Current PD vs. Same PD Last Year	0.0%
4	Last 3 PD Avg vs. Same PDS Last Year	2.7%
5	Grand Total	2.7%

Add the Store field to the row field of your pivot table and drag Fiscal Period on top of Total, as shown in Figure 6.28.

Figure 6.28

Add the Store field and change the orientation of your calculated items to columnar.

	A	B	C
1			
2	Sum of REVENUE		
3	STORE ▼	FISCAL PERIOD ▼	Total
4	2004014	Current PD vs. Last PD	7.4%
5		Last 3 PD Avg vs. Same PDS Last Year	16.5%
6	2105015	Current PD vs. Last PD	-16.3%
7		Last 3 PD Avg vs. Same PDS Last Year	3.8%

The last step in creating your mini-dashboard is to apply conditional formatting to your pivot table. Follow these steps:

1. Select all the cells that contain your data area and apply conditional formatting to those cells.

2. Go up to the application menu bar and select Format, Conditional Formatting.

3. Set your condition to show: Cell Value is, less than, 0.

4. Click the Format button and change the font and pattern colors to your liking.

5. Click OK to apply your new format.

As you can see in Figure 6.29, conditional formatting provides for dynamic highlighting of problem areas, which adds another level of functionality to your pivot table report. Your mini-dashboard is ready for distribution!

Figure 6.29

You have successfully created your dashboard!

	A	B	C
1	REGION	(All) ▼	
2	MARKET	(All) ▼	
3			
4	Sum of REVENUE	FISCAL PERIO ▼	
5	STORE ▼	Current PD vs. Last PD	Last 3 PD Avg vs. Same PDS Last Year
6	2004014	7.4%	16.5%
7	2105015	-16.3%	3.8%
8	3106016	-12.8%	-4.4%
9	3106026	-22.9%	-6.8%
10	3109019	3.3%	2.2%
11	6002012	-17.1%	-4.5%
12	6002022	8.0%	21.8%
13	6009029	-31.8%	-19.6%
14	7008018	-19.9%	2.0%
15	7008048	-3.8%	-28.1%
16	12011011	49.1%	67.4%

If you need to see this same dashboard next fiscal period, all you have to do is slightly alter your formulas and refresh your pivot table.

Rules and Shortcomings of Pivot Table Calculations

Although there is no better way to integrate your calculations into a pivot table than using calculated fields and calculated items, they do come with their own set of drawbacks. It's important you understand what goes on behind the scenes when you use pivot table calculations, and even more important to be aware of the boundaries and limitations of calculated fields and calculated items in order to avoid potential errors in your data analysis.

This section will highlight the rules concerning calculated fields and calculated items that you will most likely encounter when working with pivot table calculations.

Order of Operator Precedence

Calculations in pivot tables follow the order of operator precedence—that is, the defined order that Excel evaluates and performs calculations. It is important to understand the order of operations in Excel in order to avoid miscalculating your data.

Just as in a spreadsheet, you can use any operator in your calculation formulas, meaning any symbol that represents a calculation to perform (+, -, *, /, %, ^, and so on). When you perform a calculation that combines several operators, as in (2+3)*4/50%, Excel evaluates and performs the calculation in a specific order. The order of operations for Excel is as follows:

- Evaluate items in parentheses.
- Evaluate ranges (:).
- Evaluate intersections (spaces).
- Evaluate unions (,).
- Perform negation (-).
- Convert percentages (%). (For example, turn 50% to .50.)
- Perform exponentiation (^).
- Perform multiplication (*) and division (/). These operations are of equal precedence.
- Perform addition (+) and subtraction (-). These operations are of equal precedence.
- Evaluate text operator (&). This is known as *concatenation*.
- Perform comparisons (=, <>, <=, >=).
- Finally, operations that are equal in precedence will be performed from left to right.

Consider this basic example: The correct answer to (2+3)*4 is 20. However, if you leave out the parentheses, as in 2+3*4, Excel will perform the calculation like this:

3*4 = 12 + 2 = 14

6

The order of operator precedence mandates that Excel perform multiplication before subtraction. Entering 2+3*4 will give you the wrong answer. Because Excel evaluates and performs all calculations in parentheses first, placing 2+3 inside parentheses ensures the correct answer.

Here is another widely demonstrated example: If you enter 10^2, which represents the exponent 10 to the 2nd power, as a formula, Excel will return 100 as the answer. If you enter -10^2, you would expect -100 to be the result. Instead, Excel will return 100 yet again. The reason is that Excel performs negation before exponentiation, meaning Excel is converting 10 to -10 before the exponentiation, effectively calculating -10*-10, which indeed equals 100. Using parentheses in the formula, –(10^2), will ensure that Excel calculates the exponent before negating the answer, giving you -100.

Cell References and Named Ranges

You cannot use cell references or named ranges in your calculation formulas, because when you create calculations in a pivot table, you are essentially working in a vacuum. The only data available to you is the data that exists in the pivot cache. Therefore, you cannot reach outside the confines of the pivot cache to reference cells or named ranges in your formula.

Worksheet Functions

You can use any worksheet function that does not require cell references or defined names as an argument. In effect, this means you can use any worksheet function that does not require cell references or defined names to work. Some of the many functions that fall into this category include COUNT, AVERAGE, IF, AND, NOT, and OR.

Constants

You may use any constant in your pivot table calculations. Constants are static values that do not change. For example, 5 is a constant in the following formula:

[Units Sold]*5

Though the value of Units Sold may change based on the available data, 5 will always have the same value.

Referencing Totals

Your calculation formulas cannot reference a pivot table's subtotals or grand total. In other words, you cannot use the result of a subtotal or grand total as a variable or argument in your calculated field.

Rules Specific to Calculated Fields

Calculated field calculations are always performed against totals as opposed to individual data items. In basic terms, Excel will always calculate data fields, subtotals, and grand totals before evaluating your calculated field. This means that your calculated field is always applied to the sum of the underlying data.

The example shown in Figure 6.30 demonstrates how this can adversely affect your data analysis.

Figure 6.30
Although the calculated field is correct for the individual data items in your pivot table, the subtotal is mathematically incorrect.

	A	B	C	D	E	F G	H	I
1			Data					
2	Qtr	Product	Number of Units	Price	CalcField Unit*Price			
3	Q1	A	10	22	$220			
4		B	5	30	$150			
5		C	5	44	$220			
6		D	11	54	$594			
7	Q1 Total		31	150	$4,650	$1,184 <<Real Q1 Sub Total		

In each quarter, you need to get the total revenue for every product by multiplying the number of units sold by the price. If you look at Q1 first, you will immediately see the problem. Instead of returning the sum of 220+150+220+594, which would give you $1,184, the subtotal is multiplying the sum of number of units by the sum of the price, which returns the wrong answer.

As you can see in Figure 6.31, including the whole year in your analysis compounds the problem.

Figure 6.31
The grand total for the year as a whole is completely wrong.

	A	B	C	D	E	F G	H	I
1			Data					
2	Qtr	Product	Number of Units	Price	CalcField Unit*Price			
3	Q1	A	10	22	$220			
4		B	5	30	$150			
5		C	5	44	$220			
6		D	11	54	$594			
7	Q1 Total		31	150	$4,650	$1,184 <<Real Q1 Sub Total		
8	Q2	A	7	19	$133			
9		B	12	25	$300			
10		C	9	39	$351			
11		D	5	52	$260			
12	Q2 Total		33	135	$4,455	$1,044 <<Real Q2 Sub Total		
13	Q3	A	6	17	$102			
14		B	8	21	$168			
15		C	6	40	$240			
16		D	7	55	$385			
17	Q3 Total		27	133	$3,591	$895 <<Real Q3 Sub Total		
18	Q4	A	8	22	$176			
19		B	7	31	$217			
20		C	6	35	$210			
21		D	10	49	$490			
22	Q4 Total		31	137	$4,247	$1,093 <<Real Q4 SubTotal		
23	Grand Total		122	555	$67,710	$4,216 <<Real Grand Total		

Unfortunately, there is no solution to this problem, but there is a workaround. In worst-case scenarios, you can configure your settings to eliminate subtotals and grand totals and then calculate your own totals. Figure 6.32 shows an example of this scenario.

Figure 6.32
Calculating your own totals can avoid reporting incorrect data.

	A	B	C	D	E
1			Data		
2	Qtr	Product	Number of Units	Price	CalcField Unit*Price
3	Q1	A	10	22	$220
4		B	5	30	$150
5		C	5	44	$220
6		D	11	54	$594
7	Q2	A	7	19	$133
8		B	12	25	$300
9		C	9	39	$351
10		D	5	52	$260
11	Q3	A	6	17	$102
12		B	8	21	$168
13		C	6	40	$240
14		D	7	55	$385
15	Q4	A	8	22	$176
16		B	7	31	$217
17		C	6	35	$210
18		D	10	49	$490
19					
20				Total	$4,216

6

Rules Specific to Calculated Items

You cannot use calculated items in a pivot table that uses averages, standard deviations, or variances. Conversely, you cannot use averages, standard deviations, or variances in a pivot table that contains a calculated item.

You cannot use a page field to create a calculated item, nor can you move any calculated item to the page area.

You cannot add a calculated item to a report that has a grouped field, nor can you group any field in a pivot table that contains a calculated item.

When building your calculated item formula, you cannot reference items from a field other than the one you are working with.

As you think about the section you have just read, don't be put off by these shortcomings. Despite the clear limitations highlighted, the ability to create custom calculations directly into your pivot table remains a powerful and practical feature that can enhance your data analysis. Now that you are aware of the inner workings of pivot table calculations and understand the limitations of calculated fields and items, you can avoid the pitfalls and use these features with confidence.

Managing and Maintaining Your Pivot Table Calculations

In your dealings with pivot tables, there will be times when you won't keep a pivot table for more than the time it takes to say, "Copy, Paste Special, Values." There will be other times, however, when it will be more cost-effective to keep your pivot table and all its functionality intact. When you do find yourself maintaining and managing your pivot table through changing requirements and growing data, you may find need to maintain and manage your calculated fields and calculated items as well.

Editing and Deleting Your Pivot Table Calculations

When your calculation's parameters change or you no longer need your calculated field or calculated item, you can activate the appropriate dialog box to edit or remove the calculation.

Simply activate the Insert Calculated Field dialog box or the Insert Calculated Item dialog box and select the Name drop-down, as shown in Figure 6.33.

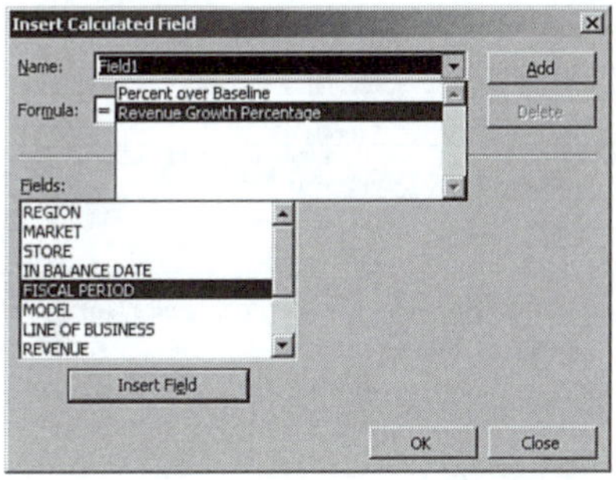

Figure 6.33
Opening the Name drop-down list reveals all the calculated fields or items in the pivot table.

Figure 6.33
Opening the Name drop-down list reveals all the calculated fields or items in the pivot table.

After you select a calculated field or item, you will have the option of deleting the calculation or modifying the formula.

Changing the Solve Order or Your Calculated Items

If the value of a cell in your pivot table is dependent on the results of two or more calculated items, you will have the option of changing the solve order of the calculated items. That is, you can specify the order in which the individual calculations are performed.

To get to the Calculated Item Solve Order dialog box shown in Figure 6.34, place your cursor anywhere in the pivot table and click the PivotTable icon in the PivotTable toolbar. Then select Formulas, Solve Order. Select any of the calculated items you see listed in order to enable the Move Up, Move Down, and Delete command buttons.

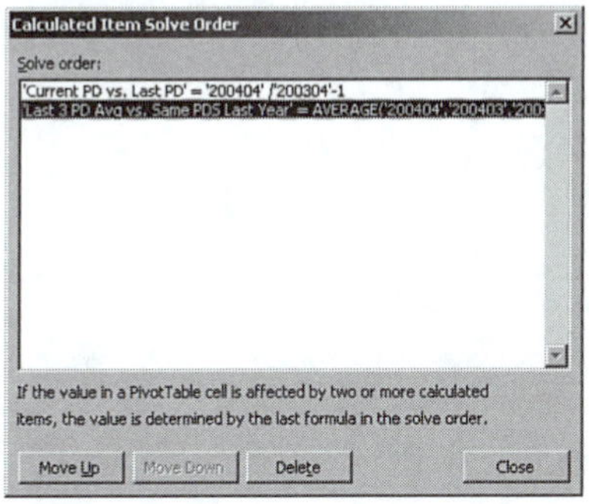

Figure 6.34
After you identify the calculated item you're working with, simply move the item up or down to change the solve order. You also have the option of deleting the item in this dialog box.

Documenting Your Formulas

Excel provides you a nice little function that lists the calculated fields and calculated items used in your pivot table, along with details on the solve order and formulas. This feature comes in especially handy if you're ever analyzing someone else's pivot table and you need to quickly determine what calculations are being applied and which fields and items they affect.

As you can see in Figure 6.35, in order to list your pivot table calculations, simply place your cursor anywhere in the pivot table and click the PivotTable icon in the PivotTable toolbar. Then select Formulas, List Formulas.

Figure 6.35

List Formulas allows you to document the details of your pivot table calculations quickly and easily.

	A	B	C
1	Calculated Field		
2	Solve Order	Field	Formula
3	1	Percent over Baseline	=REVENUE-'DAYS IN PERIOD'
4	2	Revenue Growth Percentage	=REVENUE/'Units Sold'
5			
6	Calculated Item		
7	Solve Order	Item	Formula
8	1	'Current PD vs. Last PD'	='200404'/'200304'-1
9	2	'Last 3 PD Avg vs. Same PDS Last Year'	=AVERAGE('200404','200403','200402')/AVERAGE('200304','20
10			
11			
12	Note:	When a cell is updated by more than one formula,	
13		the value is set by the formula with the last solve order.	
14			
15		To change formula solve orders,	
16		use the Solve Order command on the PivotTable command bar.	

Next Steps

In Chapter 7, "Creating and Using Pivot Charts," you will learn the fundamentals of pivot charts and the basics of representing your pivot data graphically. You will also get a firm understanding of the limitations of pivot charts and alternatives to using pivot charts.

Creating and Using Pivot Charts

7

What Is a Pivot Chart Really?

A common definition of *pivot chart* is a graphical representation of the data in your pivot table. Although this definition is technically correct, it somehow misses the mark on what a pivot chart truly does.

When you create a standard chart from data that is not in a pivot table, you feed the chart a range made up of individual cells holding individual pieces of data. Each cell is an individual object with its own piece of data, so your chart treats each cell as an individual data point, charting each one separately.

However, the data in your pivot table is part of a larger object. The pieces of data you see inside your pivot table are not individual pieces of data that occupy individual cells. Rather, they are items inside a larger pivot table object that is occupying space on your worksheet.

When you create a chart from your pivot table, you are not feeding it individual pieces of data inside individual cells; instead, you are feeding it the entire pivot table layout. Indeed, a true definition of *pivot chart* is a chart that uses a PivotLayout object to view and control the data in your pivot table.

Using the PivotLayout object allows you to interactively add, remove, filter, and refresh data fields inside the pivot chart, just like in your pivot table. The final result of all this action is a graphical representation of the data you see in your pivot table.

Creating Your First Pivot Chart

With all the complexity behind the make up of a pivot chart, you may get the impression that it is difficult to create one. The reality is that it's quite a simple task.

To demonstrate how simple it is to create a pivot chart, look at the pivot table shown in Figure 7.1.

This pivot table provides for a simple view of revenue by region. The Line of Business field in the page area lets you parse out revenue by line of business.

Figure 7.1
This basic pivot table shows revenue by region and allows for filtering by line of business.

	A	B
1	LINE OF BUSINESS	(All) ▾
2		
3	Sum of REVENUE	
4	REGION ▾	Total
5	North	276,992,617
6	South	319,820,310
7	West	216,582,112
8	Grand Total	813,395,039

The data in this pivot table would be easier to absorb if it were represented in a pie chart. Creating a pivot chart would allow you to chart this data without losing the ability to filter out line of business.

To start this process, simply right-click anywhere in the pivot table and select PivotChart.

You have just created your first pivot chart. However, as you can see in Figure 7.2, the resulting pivot chart is not a pie chart. You will have to carry out some additional formatting to get the effect you need.

Figure 7.2
Although you have created your first pivot chart, you will now have to format your chart in order to get the effect you are looking for.

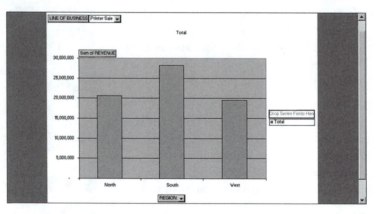

To transform this chart into a pie chart, simply right-click anywhere inside the chart and select Chart Type to display the dialog box shown in Figure 7.3.

Figure 7.3
Right-clicking on the chart and selecting Chart Type will allow you to change the type of chart your pivot data is shown through.

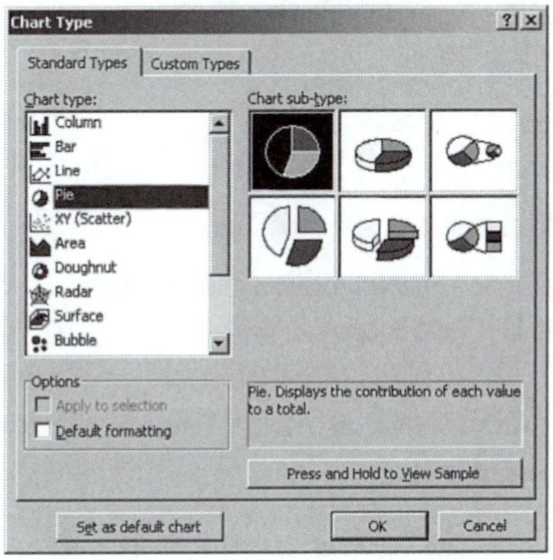

NOTE

Out of the box, Excel's default chart type is a stacked column chart. This is why when you create a chart automatically by pressing F11 or by creating a pivot chart, your chart is generated in a stacked column. You can change this setting to any chart type you would like.

In the example in Figure 7.3, if you wanted to set a pie chart as your default chart type, simply click the Set as Default Chart button you see on the lower-left corner of the dialog box. After your new default is set, all subsequent pivot charts you create will be created as a pie chart.

As shown in Figure 7.4, you now have an interactive pie chart that allows you not only to see revenue by region, but to filter on line of business as well.

Figure 7.4
Your final pie chart allows you to filter on line of business and to refresh your data, just as you would in your pivot table.

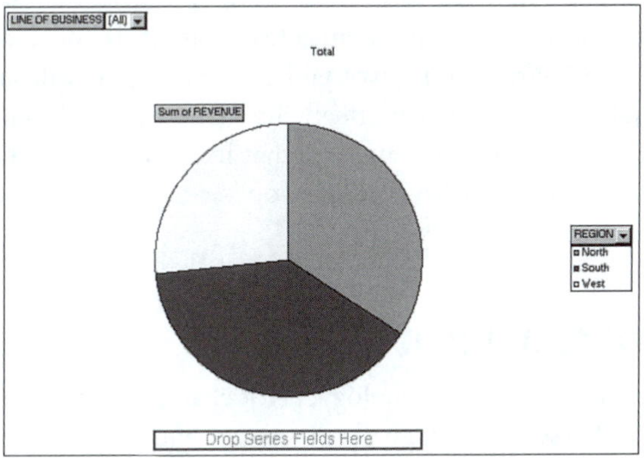

Pivot Chart Embedded on a Worksheet

You will notice that, by default, Excel created your pivot chart on its own chart sheet. For a more interesting effect where your pivot chart is on the same worksheet as your pivot table, follow these steps:

1. Place your cursor in a cell outside your pivot table.

2. Launch Excel's Chart Wizard.

3. In step 1 of the wizard, select the Pie Chart option.

4. In step 2 of the wizard, click on your pivot table and then click Finish.

5. Inside your newly created chart, you will see field buttons. Right-click on any of the field buttons and select Hide PivotChart Field Buttons.

Your reward is a pie chart on the same sheet as your pivot table. As shown in Figure 7.5, this new chart responds to filtering and other actions performed through your pivot table.

Figure 7.5
By following the steps, you have created a chart adjacent to the pivot table that will respond to changes in the pivot table.

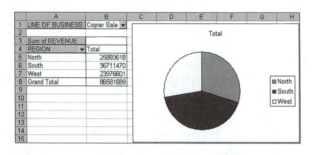

As you wrap up the walkthrough in the preceding sidebar, don't lose sight of the real power behind pivot charts. Pivot charts use the same pivot cache and pivot layout as their corresponding pivot table.

This means that if you add a new line of business to the pivot table shown earlier in Figure 7.1, your newly created pie chart will automatically capture it. If you add or remove data from your data source and refresh your pivot table, your pie chart will show the same data that your pivot table shows. This, in effect, eliminates the need to manage two sets of data—one that feeds your pivot table and one that feeds your pivot chart. As you can imagine, this fundamental functionality can save you headaches galore when trying to transform your data into visual reports.

Rules and Limitations of Pivot Charts

As with other aspects of pivot table technology, pivot charts do come with their own set of rules and limitations. This section will give you a better understanding of the boundaries and restrictions of pivot charts.

7

Pivot Chart Layout Optimization

The pivot table shown in Figure 7.6 is very easy to read and comprehend. The structure chosen shows Fiscal Periods in the column area and Line of Business in the page area. This structure works fine in the pivot table view.

Figure 7.6

The placement of your data fields here works for a pivot table view, making your data easy to read.

	A	B	C	D	E
1					
2	Sum of REVENUE	FISCAL PERIOD ▾			
3	LINE OF BUSINESS ▾	200205	200206	200207	200208
4	Copier Sale	2,715,020	3,088,467	3,201,442	3,309,439
5	Parts	3,186,930	3,567,109	3,695,256	3,511,314
6	Printer Sale	2,200,015	2,784,058	2,868,807	2,939,111
7	Service Plan	24,582,483	24,651,190	24,883,486	24,199,056
8	Grand Total	32,684,448	34,090,824	34,648,991	33,958,920

You decide to create a pivot chart from this pivot table, fully expecting to see fiscal periods across the X axis and lines of business along the Y axis.

However, if you right-click anywhere inside your pivot table and select PivotChart, you get a chart that does not make sense, such as the one shown in Figure 7.7.

Figure 7.7

Creating a pivot chart from your nicely structured pivot table does not yield the results you were expecting.

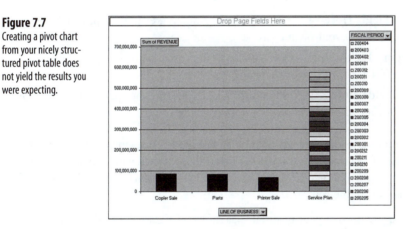

So why does the structure in your pivot table not translate to a clean pivot chart? It has to do with how pivot charts handle the different areas of your pivot table.

In a pivot chart, there are three areas where you can place fields, as shown in Figure 7.8. Each one of these areas corresponds to an area in your pivot table:

Figure 7.8
Each area in a pivot chart corresponds to an area in the matching pivot table.

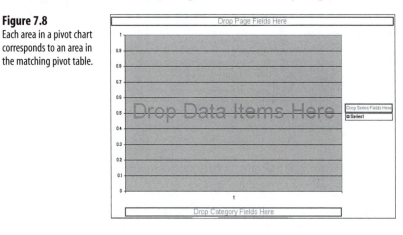

- **Drop Series Fields Here**—Corresponds to the column area in your pivot table and makes up the Y axis of your pivot chart
- **Drop Category Fields Here**—Corresponds to the row area in your pivot table and makes up the X axis of your pivot chart
- **Drop Page Fields Here**—Corresponds to the page area in your pivot table and allows for filtering in your pivot chart

Given this new information, look at the pivot table in Figure 7.6 again. When we translate this to a pivot chart, this structure says that the Fiscal Periods field will be treated as the Y axis because it is in the column area. Meanwhile, the Line of Business field will be treated as the X axis because it is in the row area.

Now reformat the structure of your pivot table as shown in Figure 7.9 to show fiscal periods in the row area and lines of business in the column area.

Figure 7.9
This format makes for slightly more difficult reading in a pivot table view, but it will allow your pivot chart to give you the effect you are looking for.

	Sum of REVENUE	LINE OF BUSINESS				
	FISCAL PERIOD	Copier Sale	Parts	Printer Sale	Service Plan	Grand Total
4	200205	2,715,020	3,186,930	2,200,015	24,582,483	32,684,448
5	200206	3,088,467	3,567,109	2,784,058	24,651,190	34,090,824
6	200207	3,201,442	3,695,256	2,868,807	24,883,486	34,648,991
7	200208	3,309,439	3,511,314	2,939,111	24,199,056	33,958,920
8	200209	3,435,284	3,612,557	2,899,422	25,165,601	35,112,864
9	200210	3,384,032	3,679,970	2,845,073	23,795,330	33,704,405
10	200211	3,651,569	3,711,185	2,735,472	23,035,382	33,133,608
11	200212	3,461,037	3,649,892	2,992,224	22,887,912	32,991,065
12	200301	3,531,622	3,585,369	2,878,685	22,309,821	32,305,497
13	200302	3,627,505	3,585,846	2,991,786	24,240,511	34,445,448
14	200303	3,563,280	3,446,154	2,918,143	23,816,952	33,744,529
15	200304	3,363,154	3,360,100	2,611,099	23,716,783	33,051,136
16	200305	3,331,228	3,489,508	2,642,837	24,279,055	33,742,628

When you right-click inside your newly formatted pivot table and select PivotChart, you will generate a pivot chart that makes sense, such as the one shown in Figure 7.10.

Figure 7.10
With the new structure in your pivot table, your pivot chart now makes sense.

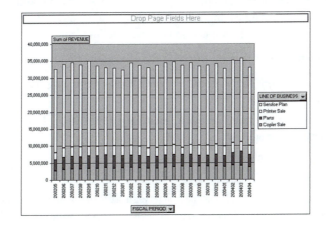

Scatter, Bubble, and Stock Charts Off Limits

By default, Excel generates your pivot chart as a stacked column chart. You may alter your chart type by going up to the application toolbar and activating the Chart Wizard while you are in your pivot chart. You can use any of the chart types available through the Chart Wizard except for XY (Scatter), Bubble, and Stock.

Limitations on Element Size and Location

You will find that formatting a pivot chart is very similar to formatting a standard chart. You will also realize however, there are some formatting options unavailable to you when working with a pivot chart:

- You cannot move or resize axes' titles.
- You cannot move or resize the chart title.
- You cannot move or resize the plot area.
- You cannot move or resize the value axis display.

Certain Customizations Aren't Permanent

Changing your pivot table will remove certain formatting customizations that you have made in a pivot chart. The customizations can be lost if you refresh a pivot table, move a field, add a field, remove a field, hide a data item, show a data item, or apply a filter. In any of these situations, you will lose the formatting changes you made to your data series and data points. The reason is that when you refresh or change the layout of your pivot table,

7

you initiate a kind of reset process where your pivot table recalculates and redefines your data fields and data items. Because your data fields and data items feed your pivot chart, making up your data series and data points, your data series and data points also go through a redefinition. Any formatting having to do with data series and data points gets lost because formatting does not persist to be applied to your new definition.

Here are the format options that are lost with the changing of your pivot charts:

- Any formatting options found in the Format Data Series dialog box, except for those found in the Options tab.

- Any formatting options found in the Format Data Point dialog box, except for those found in the Options tab.

- Any trend lines you have added.

> **TIP**
>
> If you regularly lose the formatting changes you make to your pivot chart, you can record a macro to capture the formatting changes you make and then run the macro to reapply the formatting as necessary.
>
> Before formatting your pivot chart, select Macro from the Tools menu and then select Record Macro. Name your macro and then start formatting your pivot chart. Excel will record all your actions. After you have completed formatting your pivot chart, select Macro from the Tools menu and then select Stop Recording.
>
> Now you have a macro that you can run when you need to reapply formatting changes.

CASE STUDY

Create a Dynamic Year-Over-Year Chart

You have been asked to provide all levels of management a way to quickly and easily see year-over-year revenue trends. Your solution needs to give managers the flexibility to filter out a particular line of business if needed.

Given the amount of data in your source table (shown in Figure 7.11) and the possibility that this will be a recurring exercise, you decide to use a pivot chart.

Figure 7.11
Using a pivot chart will give you the flexibility to update your report without re-creating it.

	A	B	C	D	E	F	G	H	I	J
1	REGION	MARKET	STORE	IN BALANCE DATE	FISCAL PERIOD	MODEL	LINE OF BUSINESS	REVENUE	Units Sold	DAYS IN PERIOD
2	North	Great Lakes	65061011	01/03/03	200205	405ST	Parts	$3,454	0	19.0
3	North	Shenandoah Valley	62067017	01/03/03	200205	2500P	Printer Sale	$15,682	2	19.0
4	North	Shenandoah Valley	32139049	01/03/03	200205	2500C	Copier Sale	$12,968	6	19.0
5	North	New England	2004014	01/03/03	200205	405ST	Parts	$2,789	0	19.0
6	North	New England	72074014	01/03/03	200205	4500C	Service Plan	$32,605	23	19.0
7	North	New England	12011011	01/03/03	200205	3002P	Service Plan	$52,437	30	19.0
8	North	New England	2105015	01/03/03	200205	2500P	Printer Sale	$17,391	2	19.0
9	North	New England	22022012	01/03/03	200205	405ST	Parts	$2,468	0	19.0
10	North	New England	22022012	01/03/03	200205	3002C	Parts	$375	0	19.0
11	North	New York South	12118068	01/03/03	200205	4500C	Service Plan	$67,592	30	19.0
12	North	New York South	12118068	01/03/03	200205	3002C	Service Plan	$21,454	15	19.0
13	North	Ohio	44040030	01/03/03	200205	3002C	Parts	$979	0	19.0
14	North	Ohio	44040020	01/03/03	200205	405ST	Parts	$4,539	0	19.0
15	North	Ohio	44040020	01/03/03	200205	3002P	Parts	$3,209	0	19.0
16	North	Ohio	34037017	01/03/03	200205	3002P	Parts	$34,612	0	19.0
17	North	South Carolina	53154014	01/03/03	200205	3002C	Service Plan	$14,051	9	19.0
18	South	North Carolina	63064014	01/03/03	200205	5001P	Parts	$249	0	19.0
19	South	North Carolina	73179019	01/03/03	200205	5001P	Service Plan	$3,951	1	19.0
20	South	Florida	33130010	01/03/03	200205	3002P	Service Plan	$157,434	68	19.0

Create the initial pivot table like the one shown in Figure 7.12 to include revenue for each in-balance date.

Figure 7.12

The initial pivot table is basic, showing you revenue by in-balance date.

	A	B
1		
2		
3	Sum of REVENUE	
4	IN BALANCE DATE ▼	Total
5	01/03/03	$1,010,419
6	01/04/03	$1,779,579
7	01/05/03	$1,372,001
8	01/06/03	$1,095,282
9	01/07/03	$1,190,391
10	01/08/03	$1,829,667
11	01/09/03	$1,614,830
12	01/10/03	$948,480
13	01/11/03	$648,668
14	01/12/03	$1,324,763
15	01/13/03	$829,600

The first thing you will need to do is group the In Balance Date field into years and months in order to be able to compare revenues year over year. The result is shown in Figure 7.13.

Figure 7.13

Group your In Balance Date field into years and months.

2			
3	Sum of REVENUE		
4	Years ▼	IN BALANCE DATE ▼	Total
5	2003	Jan	$32,684,448
6		Feb	$34,090,824
7		Mar	$34,648,991
8		Apr	$33,958,920
9		May	$35,112,864
10		Jun	$33,704,405
11		Jul	$33,133,608
12		Aug	$32,991,065
13		Sep	$32,305,497
14		Oct	$34,445,448
15		Nov	$33,744,529
16		Dec	$33,051,136
17	2004	Jan	$33,742,628
18		Feb	$34,528,629
19		Mar	$34,795,505
20		Apr	$33,710,396

For more on grouping, see "Grouping Pivot Fields" in Chapter 5, "Controlling the Way You View Your Pivot Data."

The plan is for you to have your months on the Y axis of your pivot chart and your months on the X axis. That means your years will have to appear in the column area of your pivot table and your months will have to be in the row area of your pivot table.

7

Because the months are already in correct placement, move the Years field into the column area, as shown in Figure 7.14.

Figure 7.14
Placing the years in the column area will ensure that your pivot chart picks up years as a Y-axis data series.

Sum of REVENUE	Years		
IN BALANCE DATE	2003	2004	Grand Total
Jan	$32,684,448	$33,742,628	$66,427,076
Feb	$34,090,824	$34,528,629	$68,619,453
Mar	$34,648,991	$34,795,505	$69,444,496
Apr	$33,958,920	$33,710,396	$67,669,316
May	$35,112,864	$34,459,211	$69,572,075
Jun	$33,704,405	$33,491,815	$67,196,220
Jul	$33,133,608	$33,751,163	$66,884,771
Aug	$32,991,065	$34,228,547	$67,219,612
Sep	$32,305,497	$32,835,603	$65,141,100
Oct	$34,445,448	$35,218,982	$69,664,430
Nov	$33,744,529	$35,704,439	$69,448,968
Dec	$33,051,136	$33,056,386	$66,107,522
Grand Total	$403,871,735	$409,523,304	$813,395,039

Finally, place Region, Market, Store, Line of Business, and Model into the page area of your pivot table to allow for filtering, as shown in Figure 7.15.

Figure 7.15
Fill the page area with the fields that hold the details your managers will want to filter by (Region, Market, Store, Line of Business, and Model).

	A	B	C	D
1	REGION	(All)		
2	MARKET	(All)		
3	STORE	(All)		
4	LINE OF BUSINESS	(All)		
5	MODEL	(All)		
6				
7	Sum of REVENUE	Years		
8	IN BALANCE DATE	2003	2004	Grand Total
9	Jan	$32,684,448	$33,742,628	$66,427,076
10	Feb	$34,090,824	$34,528,629	$68,619,453
11	Mar	$34,648,991	$34,795,505	$69,444,496
12	Apr	$33,958,920	$33,710,396	$67,669,316
13	May	$35,112,864	$34,459,211	$69,572,075
14	Jun	$33,704,405	$33,491,815	$67,196,220
15	Jul	$33,133,608	$33,751,163	$66,884,771
16	Aug	$32,991,065	$34,228,547	$67,219,612
17	Sep	$32,305,497	$32,835,603	$65,141,100
18	Oct	$34,445,448	$35,218,982	$69,664,430
19	Nov	$33,744,529	$35,704,439	$69,448,968
20	Dec	$33,051,136	$33,056,386	$66,107,522
21	Grand Total	$403,871,735	$409,523,304	$813,395,039

Now that you have prepared your pivot table, right click on your pivot table and select PivotChart. As you can see in Figure 7.16, the resulting pivot chart is a stacked column chart. In order to get the year-over-year effect you need, you will have to change the chart type.

Figure 7.16
Your resulting pivot chart gets you close to what you need, but you will have to change the chart type in order to get the year-over-year effect you are looking for.

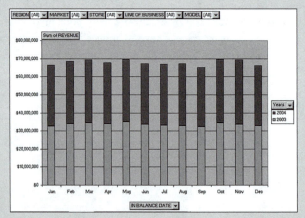

Right-click inside the chart and select Chart Type. You can now change the chart type to a line chart with markers, as shown in Figure 7.17.

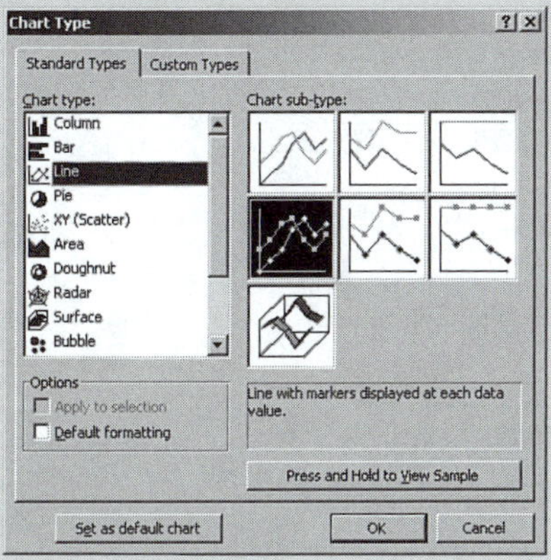

Figure 7.17
Change the chart type to a line chart.

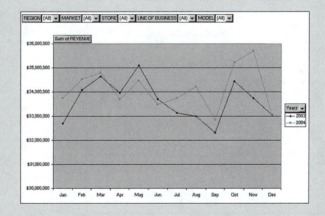

Your report is almost complete, as shown in Figure 7.18. There is one final formatting feature you can add in order to enhance your pivot chart. A data table will show your audience the figures that make up the data points right on the chart. This way, they won't have to go back and forth between the pivot chart and pivot table.

Figure 7.18
Your report is shaping up! You can now add a data table to your pivot chart so your audience won't have to go back and forth between the pivot chart and pivot table to see the figures that make up the data points in your chart.

7

Right-click on your pivot chart, select Chart Options, and then select the Data Table tab. Once on the Data Table tab, as shown in Figure 7.19, place a check inside the Show Data Table check box.

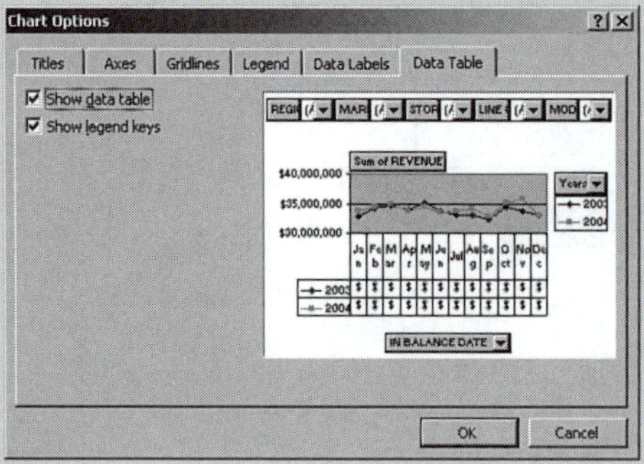

Figure 7.19

Right-click on your pivot chart, select Chart Options, and then select the Data Table tab. Place a check inside the Show Data Table check box and then click OK to activate your data table.

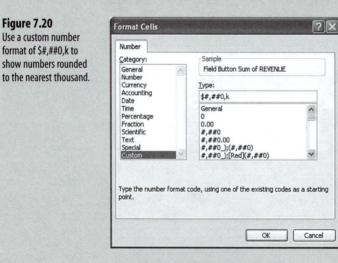

In order to see the revenues properly, you will have to show revenues in thousands. Right-click on the Sum of Revenue field in your pivot chart and select Format PivotChart Field. This will open the PivotTable Field dialog box. Select Number and change the format to Custom. Then type in "$#,##0,k" in the Type input box, as shown in Figure 7.20.

Figure 7.20

Use a custom number format of $#,##0,k to show numbers rounded to the nearest thousand.

You now have a year-over-year revenue trending report that provides two years' worth of revenue reporting that can be filtered by multiple criteria, as shown in Figure 7.21.

Figure 7.21
Your final report provides two years of revenue reporting that can be filtered by multiple criteria.

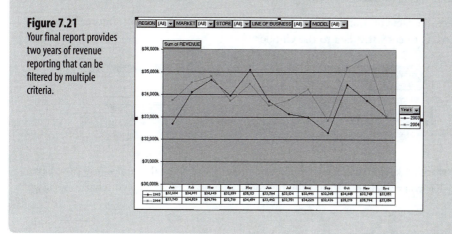

Alternatives to Using Pivot Charts

There are generally two reasons why you would need an alternative to using pivot charts. First, you do not want the overhead that comes with a pivot chart. Second, you want to avoid the formatting limitations of pivot charts.

Avoiding Overhead

There may be times when you create a pivot table simply to summarize and shape your data in preparation for charting. In these situations, you don't plan on keeping your source data, and you definitely don't want a pivot cache taking up memory and file space.

In the example in Figure 7.22, you see a pivot table that summarizes revenue by quarter for each line of business.

Figure 7.22
This pivot table was created to summarize and chart revenue by quarter for each line of business.

	A	B	C	D	E
1	REGION	(All)			
2	MARKET	(All)			
3					
4	Sum of REVENUE	IN BALANCE DATE			
5	LINE OF BUSINESS	Qtr1	Qtr2	Qtr3	Qtr4
6	Copier Sale	$19,847,240	$21,827,116	$22,391,657	$22,515,676
7	Parts	$20,923,077	$20,773,707	$20,867,813	$21,573,696
8	Printer Sale	$16,368,698	$16,975,476	$17,609,516	$17,415,088
9					

7

The issue is that you only created this pivot table in order to summarize and shape your data for charting. You don't want to keep the source data, nor do you want to keep the pivot table with all its overhead. The alternative here is to turn your pivot data into hard values and then create a chart from the values.

You can select the data you want to copy from the pivot table, as shown in Figure 7.23. Then use Ctrl+C to copy the data to the Clipboard.

Figure 7.23
Copy the data you need out of your pivot table.

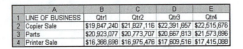

	A	B	C	D	E
1	REGION	(All) ▼			
2	MARKET	(All) ▼			
3					
4	Sum of REVENUE	IN BALANCE DATE ▼			
5	LINE OF BUSINESS ▼	Qtr1	Qtr2	Qtr3	Qtr4
6	Copier Sale	$19,847,240	$21,827,116	$22,391,657	$22,515,676
7	Parts	$20,923,077	$20,773,707	$20,667,813	$21,573,896
8	Printer Sale	$16,368,698	$16,975,476	$17,609,516	$17,415,088

Start a new workbook, right-click anywhere, and select Paste Special, Values. You now have hard values that you can chart without the overhead of a pivot table or pivot chart, as shown in Figure 7.24.

Figure 7.24
Pasting values to a new workbook allows you to base a chart on the summarized data without the overhead of a large pivot cache.

	A	B	C	D	E
1	LINE OF BUSINESS	Qtr1	Qtr2	Qtr3	Qtr4
2	Copier Sale	$19,847,240	$21,827,116	$22,391,657	$22,515,676
3	Parts	$20,923,077	$20,773,707	$20,667,813	$21,573,896
4	Printer Sale	$16,368,698	$16,975,476	$17,609,516	$17,415,088

> **NOTE**
> Use Paste Special, Values when you are pasting to a new worksheet in the existing workbook. If you are pasting to a completely new workbook, you can use Paste without having the pivot cache pasted along with the data.

Avoid the Formatting Limitations of Pivot Charts

Formatting is undoubtedly the Achilles heal of pivot charts. Many Excel users shy away from using pivot charts solely based on the formatting restrictions and issues they encounter when working with them. Oftentimes these users give up the functionality of a pivot table to avoid the limitations of pivot charts.

However, if you want to retain key functionality in your pivot table, such as page filters and a top 10 ranking, there is a way to link a standard chart to your pivot table without creating a pivot chart.

In the example in Figure 7.25, you have a pivot table that shows you the top 10 markets and their total revenue. You will notice that the page area allows you to filter by model, so you can see the top 10 markets by model.

Figure 7.25

This pivot table allows you to see the top 10 markets and their total revenue. In addition, the page area allows for the filtering of model numbers to get top 10 markets by model number.

	A	B
1	MODEL	(All)
2		
3	Sum of REVENUE	
4	MARKET	Total
5	California	$61,636,732
6	Shenandoah Valley	$56,233,581
7	Florida	$47,362,461
8	Gulf Coast	$45,159,185
9	Ohio	$42,703,718
10	Illinois	$42,101,421
11	New York North	$41,493,673
12	Indiana	$41,043,454
13	Topeka	$39,975,907
14	Texas	$39,143,422

The issue here is that you need to keep the functionality of being able to filter out 10 records by model number, but creating a chart from this pivot table will create a pivot chart. This will not do because we want to avoid the formatting limitations that plague pivot charts. The alternative solution is to use the cells around the pivot table to link back to the data you need and then chart those cells.

As shown in Figure 7.26, click your cursor in a cell next to your pivot table and reference the first data item that you will need to create the range you will feed your standard chart. The idea is to build a mini-dataset that will feed your standard chart. The trick is that this dataset links back to the data items in your pivot table.

Figure 7.26

Start your linked dataset by referencing the first data item you need to capture.

	A	B	C	D
1	MODEL	(All)		
2				
3	Sum of REVENUE			
4	MARKET	Total		
5	California	$61,636,732		=A5
6	Shenandoah Valley	$56,233,581		
7	Florida	$47,362,461		
8	Gulf Coast	$45,159,185		
9	Ohio	$42,703,718		
10	Illinois	$42,101,421		
11	New York North	$41,493,673		
12	Indiana	$41,043,454		
13	Topeka	$39,975,907		
14	Texas	$39,143,422		

Now copy the formula you just entered and paste that formula down and across in order to create your complete dataset, as shown in Figure 7.27.

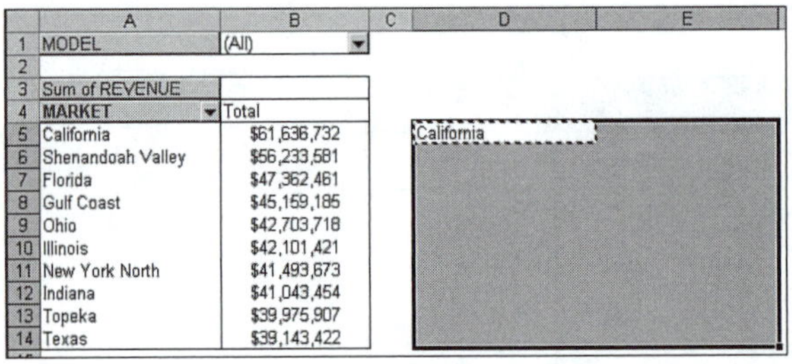

Figure 7.27
Copy the formula and paste it down and across to create your complete dataset.

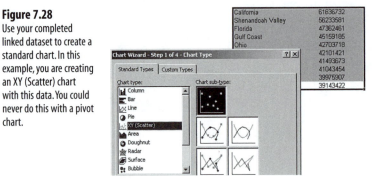

Disable GetPivotData

If you are working with Excel 2002 or a later version, you will find that Excel has an annoying default setting that revolves around the GETPIVOTDATA function. Excel automatically inserts the GETPIVOTDATA function into any cell where you are trying to enter a formula referencing your pivot data. The issue is that the GETPIVOTDATA function automatically references the cells in your pivot table as absolute references, effectively making it impossible to simply copy your formulas down and get the right answer.

Here's how to turn off this default setting:

1. Go to the application menu bar and select Tools, Customize.

2. In the Commands tab, select Data.

3. Find Generate GetPivotData and drag it to any one of your toolbars.

4. Click Close.

5. Now you can click the Generate GetPivotData button to turn this feature off.

After your linked dataset is complete, you can use it to create a standard chart that is linked to your pivot table, as shown in Figure 7.28.

Figure 7.28
Use your completed linked dataset to create a standard chart. In this example, you are creating an XY (Scatter) chart with this data. You could never do this with a pivot chart.

The final chart is shown in Figure 7.29. With this arrangement, you have the best of both worlds. You have kept the ability to filter out a model number using the page field, meanwhile you have all the formatting freedom of a standard chart without any issues related to losing formatting as you would have using a pivot chart.

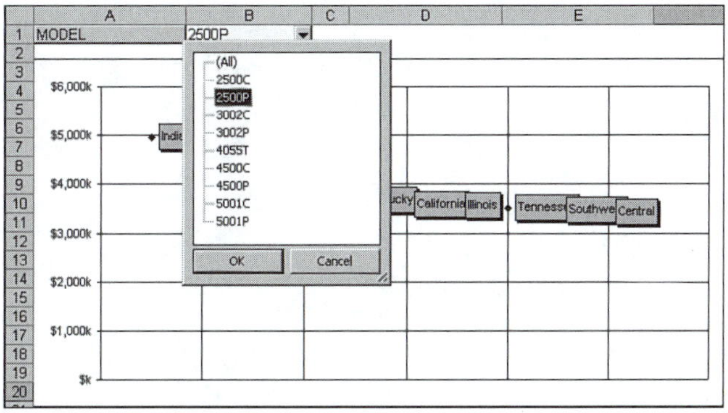

Figure 7.29
This solution allows you to continue using the functionality of your pivot table without any of the formatting limitations you would have with a pivot chart.

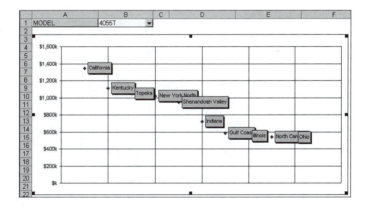

You can format your chart to hide the pivot table and the linked cells that feed the chart, as shown in Figure 7.30.

Figure 7.30
With some basic formatting, you can hide your pivot table and the linked cells that feed your chart, leaving only the pivot table's page area visible.

Next Steps

In Chapter 8, "Using Disparate Data Sources for Your Pivot Table," you will learn how to bring together disparate data sources into one pivot table. You will create a pivot table from multiple datasets, and you will learn the basics of creating pivot tables from other pivot tables.

7

Using Disparate Data Sources for Your Pivot Table

8

Working with Disparate Data Sources

Until this point, you have been working with one local table located in the worksheet within which you are operating. Indeed, it would be wonderful if every dataset you came across were neatly packed in one easy-to-use Excel table. Unfortunately, the business of data analysis does not always work out that way.

The reality is that some of the data you will encounter will come from *disparate* data sources—meaning sets of data that are from separate systems, stored in different locations, and saved in a variety of formats. In an Excel environment, disparate data sources generally fall into one of two categories: external data or multiple ranges.

External data is exactly what it sounds like—data that is not located in the Excel workbook in which you are operating. Some examples of external data sources are text files, Access tables, SQL Server tables, and other Excel workbooks.

Multiple ranges are separate datasets that are located in the same workbook, but separated either by blank cells or by different worksheets. For example, if your workbook has three tables on three different worksheets, each of your datasets covers a range of cells. You are therefore working with multiple ranges.

A pivot table can be an effective tool when you need to summarize data that is not neatly packed into one table. With a pivot table, you can quickly bring together either data found in an external source or data found in multiple tables within your workbook.

You may have noticed that when you initiate the creation of a pivot table, the PivotTable Wizard starts the process with the dialog box shown in Figure 8.1. In this dialog box, the first question you have to answer is, "Where is the data that you want to analyze?" Until this point, you have been working with a single dataset located in your local workbook. But as you can see, there are other options.

You can choose to work with a dataset from an external data source, you can choose to work with multiple ranges within your workbook, or you can choose to work with data already in a pivot table.

Figure 8.1
Until this point, you have been working with a single dataset located in your local workbook. However, as you can see, there are other options.

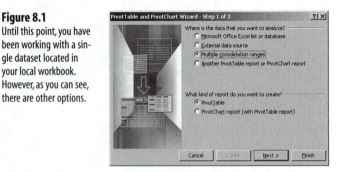

We will cover working with external data sources in the next chapter. As for now, we will concentrate on creating pivot tables from multiple ranges and other pivot tables.

Using Multiple Consolidation Ranges

If you need to analyze data dispersed in multiple ranges, your options are somewhat limited. For example, the data in Figure 8.2 shows you three ranges that you need to bring together to analyze as a group.

Figure 8.2
Someone passed you a file that has three ranges of data. You need to bring the three ranges together so you can analyze them as a group.

	A	B	C	D	E	F	G	H
1	NORTH							
2	Line of Business	Lob Manager	Jan	Feb	Mar	Apr	May	Ju
3	Copier Sale	Jim Graham	$1,670,642	$1,908,785	$2,185,037	$2,239,371	$2,121,648	$2,13
4	Parts	Mike Alexander	$2,378,240	$2,372,974	$2,537,793	$2,429,561	$2,419,169	$2,27
5	Printer Sale	Allan Howe	$1,443,106	$1,628,517	$1,745,271	$1,545,072	$1,808,141	$1,78
6	Service Plan	Kelly Richardson	$17,098,331	$17,045,471	$17,497,027	$16,903,477	$17,157,864	$16,42
7								
8	SOUTH							
9	Line of Business	Lob Manager	Jan	Feb	Mar	Apr	May	Ju
10	Copier Sale	Jim Graham	$2,703,264	$2,923,311	$2,869,761	$2,892,764	$3,203,760	$3,19
11	Parts	Mike Alexander	$2,457,824	$2,658,591	$2,736,089	$2,493,456	$2,583,428	$2,57
12	Printer Sale	Allan Howe	$2,016,462	$2,378,109	$2,467,409	$2,089,987	$2,351,109	$2,48
13	Service Plan	Kelly Richardson	$18,922,385	$19,240,187	$19,100,783	$19,072,738	$19,193,191	$18,40
14								
15	WEST							
16	Line of Business	Lob Manager	Jan	Feb	Mar	Apr	May	Ju
17	Copier Sale	Jim Graham	$1,672,342	$1,913,201	$2,000,897	$2,073,048	$1,989,468	$1,98
18	Parts	Mike Alexander	$1,840,374	$2,041,408	$1,899,784	$2,028,641	$2,031,725	$1,94
19	Printer Sale	Allan Howe	$1,383,284	$1,630,537	$1,676,003	$1,495,751	$1,700,226	$1,71
20	Service Plan	Kelly Richardson	$12,840,822	$12,878,362	$12,726,642	$12,405,450	$13,012,346	$12,29

You essentially have three paths you can take to get to the point where you can analyze all three ranges together:

- You can obtain the original data used to create this summary. This seems like a good choice, but in most cases, you could find another solution by the time it took you to obtain the original data—if you have access to it at all.

- You can manually shape the data into a proper tabular dataset and then do your analysis. In reality, this option would be the best one if you had the time to spare or you were planning to use this data on an on-going basis. However, if this is a one-time analysis or if you are in a crunch, you would not want to spend the time to manually format this data.

- You can create a pivot table using multiple consolidation ranges. With this pivot table option, you can quickly and easily consolidate all the data from your selected ranges into a single pivot table. This is the best option if you only need to perform a one-time analysis on multiple ranges or if you need to analyze multiple ranges in a hurry.

To start the process of bringing this data together with a pivot table, initiate the PivotTable Wizard shown in Figure 8.3 and select the Multiple Consolidation Ranges option.

Figure 8.3
Start the PivotTable Wizard and select Multiple Consolidation Ranges. Click Next to move to the next step.

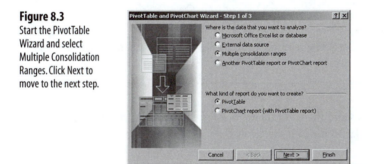

Figure 8.4 shows the next step, where you will specify whether you want Excel to create one page field for you or whether you would like to create your own. You will find that the page fields that Excel creates are, more often than not, ambiguous and of no value. Therefore, in almost all cases, you will want to select the option of creating your own page fields.

Figure 8.4
Specify that you want to create your own page fields and then click Next.

Next, you need to point Excel to each of your individual datasets, one by one. As you can see in Figure 8.5, you simply enter the entire range of your first dataset into the Range input field. After your range has been defined, click Add.

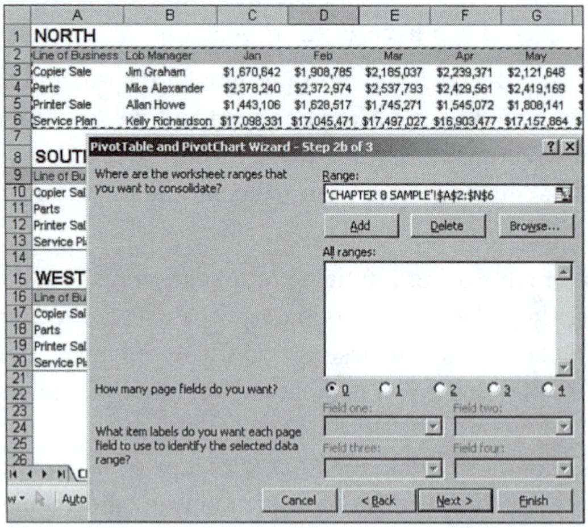

Figure 8.5
Select the entire range of your first dataset and click Add.

CAUTION

In order for your pivot table to generate properly, the first line of each range must include column labels.

Select the rest of your ranges and then add them your list of ranges. At this point, your dialog box should look similar to the one shown in Figure 8.6.

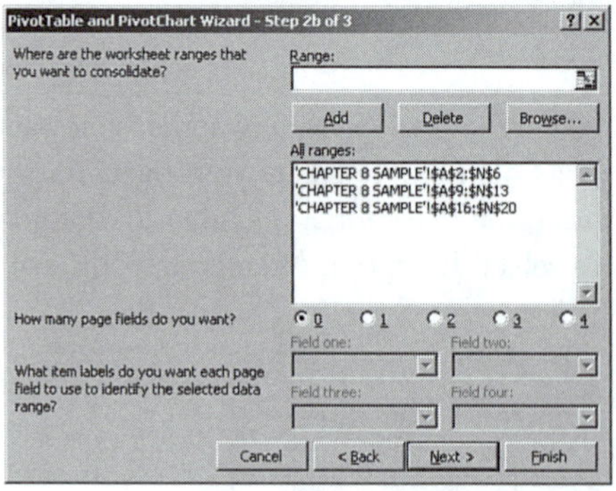

Figure 8.6
Add the other two dataset ranges to your range list.

You will notice that each of your datasets belong to a region (North, South, or West). When your pivot table brings your three datasets together, you will need a way to parse out each region again.

To ensure you will have that capability, you need to tag each range in your list of ranges with a name identifying which dataset that range came from. The result will be the creation of a page field that allows you to filter each region as needed.

The first thing you will have to do in order to create your Region page field is specify how many page fields you want to create. In Figure 8.7, you only want to create one page field for your region identifier, so simply click on the radio button next to the number 1. This action will enable the Field One input box. As you can see, you can create up to four page fields.

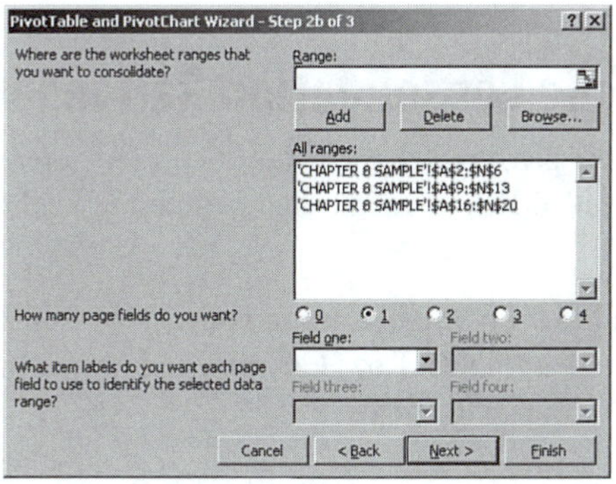

Figure 8.7
Click on the radio button next to the number 1. This action will enable the Field One input box.

In the next step, shown in Figure 8.8, you will have to tag each range one by one, so click on the first range in your range list to highlight it. Enter the region name into the Field One input box.

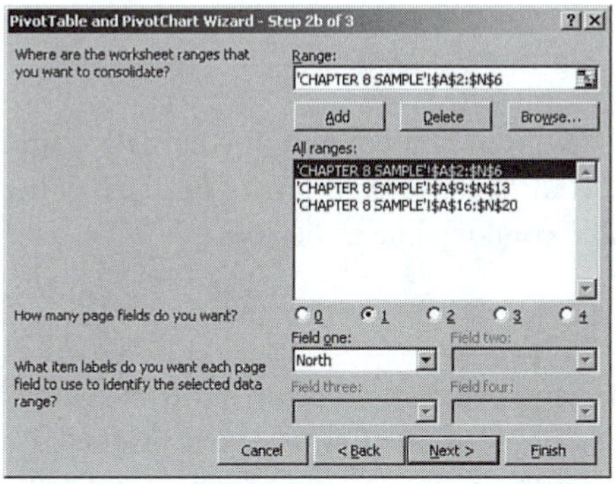

Figure 8.8
Select the first range that represents the dataset for the North region and enter the word "North" into the page field.

Repeat the process for the other regions. When you are done, click Next and then click Finish.

You have successfully brought three data sources together into one pivot table! At first glance, your final pivot table, shown in Figure 8.9, looks just like any other pivot table. However, a closer look will reveal that this pivot table has some strange default labels.

Figure 8.9
You now have a pivot table that contains data from three data sources.

	A	B	C	D	E	F	G
1	Page1	(All)					
2							
3	Count of Value	Column					
4	Row	Lob Manager	Jan	Feb	Mar	Apr	May
5	Copier Sale	3	3	3	3	3	
6	Parts	3	3	3	3	3	
7	Printer Sale	3	3	3	3	3	
8	Service Plan	3	3	3	3	3	
9	Grand Total	12	12	12	12	12	

The Anatomy of a Multiple Consolidation Range Pivot Table

After closer analysis of your new pivot table, you will notice a few interesting things. First, your field list includes a field called Row, a field called Column, a field called Value, and a Field called Page1.

It is important to keep in mind that pivot tables using multiple consolidation ranges as their data source can only have three base fields: Row, Column, and Value. In addition to these base fields, you can create up to four page fields.

> **TIP**
>
> You will notice that the fields generated with your pivot table have fairly generic names (Row, Column, Value, Page). You can customize the field settings for these fields to rename and format them in order to better suit your needs. See Chapter 3, "Customizing Fields in a Pivot Table," for a more detailed look at customizing field settings.

The Row Field

The Row field is always made up of the first column in your data source. Note that in Figure 8.2, the first column in your data source is line of business. Therefore, the Row field in your newly created pivot table contains line of business.

The Column Field

The Column field contains the remaining columns in your data source. Pivot tables that use multiple consolidation ranges combine all the fields in your original datasets (minus the first column, which is used for the Row field) into a kind of super field called the Column field. The fields in your original datasets become data items under the Column field.

As you will notice in Figure 8.10, your pivot table initially applies Count to your Column field. If you change the field setting of the Column field to Sum, all the data items under the Column field are affected.

Figure 8.10
The data items under the Column field are treated as one entity. When you change the calculation of the Column field from Count to Sum, the change applies to all items under the Column field.

	A	B	C	D	E	F	G
1	Page1	(All)					
2							
3	Sum of Value	Column					
4	Row	Lob Manager	Jan	Feb	Mar	Apr	May
5	Copier Sale	0	6,046,248	6,745,297	7,055,695	7,205,183	7,31
6	Parts	0	6,676,438	7,072,973	7,173,666	6,951,658	7,03
7	Printer Sale	0	4,842,852	5,637,163	5,888,683	5,130,810	5,88
8	Service Plan	0	48,861,538	49,164,020	49,326,452	48,381,665	49,36
9	Grand Total	0	66,427,076	68,619,453	69,444,496	67,669,316	69,57

The Value Field

The Value field contains the value for all data items under the Column field. Notice that even fields that were originally text fields in your dataset are treated as numerical values. An example is Lob Manager, shown in Figure 8.10. Although this field contained manager names in the original dataset, it is now treated as a number in your pivot table.

As mentioned before, pivot tables that use multiple consolidation ranges merge the fields in your original datasets (minus the first field), making them data items in the Column field. Therefore, although you may recognize fields such as Lob Manager as text fields that contain their own individual data items, they no longer hold data of their own. They have been transformed into data items themselves—data items with a value.

The net effect of this behavior is that fields originally holding text or dates show up in your pivot table as a meaningless numerical value. It's usually a good idea to simply hide these fields to avoid confusion. See Chapter 5, "Controlling the Way You View Your Pivot Data," for a more detailed look at hiding fields.

The Page Fields

Page fields are the only fields in a multiple consolidation range pivot tables that you have direct control over. You can create and define up to four page fields. The useful thing about these fields is that you can drag them to the row area or column area to add layers to your pivot table.

The Page1 field shown in the pivot table in Figure 8.10 was created to be able to filter by region. However, as you can see in Figure 8.11, if you drag the Page1 field to the row area of your pivot table, you can create a one-shot view of all your data by region.

	A	B	C	D	E	F	G	H
1								
2								
3	Sum of Value		Column					
4	Page1	Row	Jan	Feb	Mar	Apr	May	Jun
5	North	Copier Sale	1,670,642	1,908,785	2,185,037	2,239,371	2,121,648	2,133
6		Parts	2,378,240	2,372,974	2,537,793	2,429,561	2,419,169	2,271
7		Printer Sale	1,443,106	1,628,517	1,745,271	1,545,072	1,808,141	1,785
8		Service Plan	17,098,331	17,045,471	17,497,027	16,903,477	17,157,864	16,422
9	North Total		22,590,319	22,955,747	23,965,128	23,117,481	23,506,822	22,612
10	South	Copier Sale	2,703,264	2,923,311	2,869,761	2,892,764	3,203,760	3,192
11		Parts	2,457,824	2,658,591	2,736,089	2,493,456	2,583,428	2,572
12		Printer Sale	2,016,462	2,378,109	2,467,409	2,089,987	2,351,109	2,480
13		Service Plan	18,922,385	19,240,187	19,100,783	19,072,738	19,193,191	18,400
14	South Total		26,099,935	27,200,198	27,174,042	26,548,945	27,331,488	26,646
15	West	Copier Sale	1,672,342	1,913,201	2,000,897	2,073,048	1,989,468	1,981
16		Parts	1,840,374	2,041,408	1,899,784	2,028,641	2,031,725	1,943
17		Printer Sale	1,383,284	1,630,537	1,676,003	1,495,751	1,700,226	1,718
18		Service Plan	12,840,822	12,878,362	12,728,642	12,405,450	13,012,346	12,293
19	West Total		17,736,822	18,463,508	18,305,326	18,002,890	18,733,765	17,937
20	Grand Total		66,427,076	68,619,453	69,444,496	67,669,316	69,572,075	67,196

Figure 8.11
Dragging the Page1 field to the row area adds a layer to your pivot table report, giving you a one-shot view of all your data by region.

Redefining Your Pivot Table

You may run into a situation where you need to redefine your pivot table—that is, add a data range, remove a data range, or redefine your page fields. To redefine your pivot table, simply right-click anywhere inside your pivot table, select PivotTable Wizard, and then click the Back button until you get to the dialog box you need.

CASE STUDY

Consolidate and Analyze Eight Datasets

Your manager has forwarded you the spreadsheet shown in Figure 8.12 and has asked you to extract a two-year average revenue by quarter for each model number. Your manager requires these figures for a meeting that starts in 15 minutes, so you have very little time to organize and summarize this data.

	A	B	C	D	E	F	G	H	I	J	K
1	FY 2003										
2	MODEL	Q1		MODEL	Q2		MODEL	Q3		MODEL	Q4
3	2500C	$32,591		2500C	$18,498		2500C	$1,000		2500C	$14,771
4	2500P	$32,525		3002C	$1,590		3002C	$39,262		2500P	$34,608
5	3002C	$118,246		3002P	$217,856		3002P	$460,715		3002C	$21,924
6	3002P	$473,102		4055T	$19,499		4055T	$6,006		3002P	$18,327
7	4055T	$7,772		4500C	$148,565		4500C	$139,655		4500C	$68,413
8	4500C	$89,780		4500P	$16,842		4500P	$6,305		5001C	$12,634
9	4500P	$19,294		5001C	$13,191		5001C	$11,929		5001P	$65,902
10	5001C	$2,373		5001P	$27,192		5001P	$16,161			
11	5001P	$85,746									
12											
13	FY 2004										
14	MODEL	Q1		MODEL	Q2		MODEL	Q3		MODEL	Q4
15	2500C	$17,220		2500C	$63,379		2500C	$16,079		3002C	$54,884
16	2500P	$23,407		3002C	$89,463		2500P	$37,926		4055T	$29,892
17	3002C	$103,650		3002P	$324,679		3002C	$4,925		4500C	$324,957
18	3002P	$160,783		4055T	$22,789		3002P	$141,799		4500P	$33,904
19	4055T	$21,231		4500C	$44,398		4500P	$4,227		5001C	$4,687
20	4500P	$17,645		4500P	$12,797		5001C	$1,803		5001P	$33,282
21	5001C	$12,424		5001C	$3,242		5001P	$5,758			
22	5001P	$53,344		5001P	$18,144						
23											

Figure 8.12
You need to analyze the data in this spreadsheet and quickly extract the two-year average revenue by quarter for each model number.

Given that this is a one-time analysis that needs to be completed quickly, you decide to use a pivot table. Here are the steps you will follow:

1. Start the PivotTable Wizard and select Multiple Consolidation Ranges as your data source. Click Next.

2. Select the I Will Create the Page Fields option and then click Next.

3. Add your first data range and then select the radio button next to the number 1 to activate the Field One input box. Enter "2003" into the input box.

   At this point, your dialog box should look like Figure 8.13.

Figure 8.13
After you add your first data range, your dialog box should look like this.

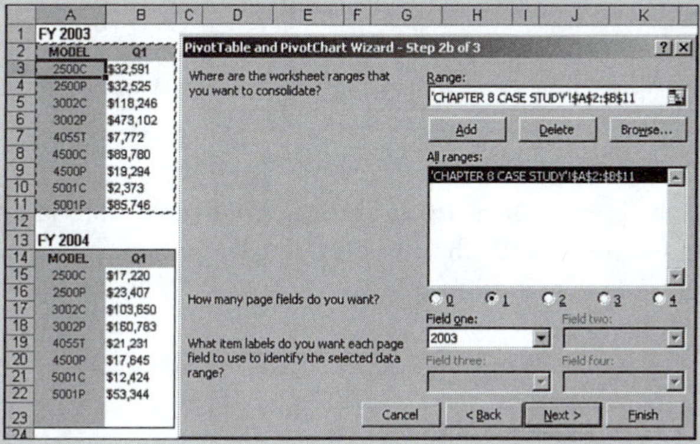

4. Add your second data range and enter "2003" into the input box.

5. Repeat step 4 for each of your datasets until you have added all your data ranges. Be sure to enter "2004" for all the datasets that are under FY 2004.

   At this point, your dialog box should look like Figure 8.14.

Figure 8.14
After all your data ranges have been added, click Finish to finalize your pivot table.

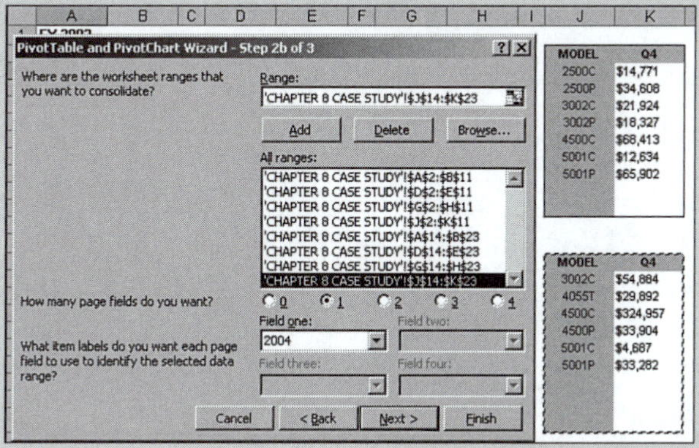

8

You have successfully consolidated your data into one pivot table! However, as you can see in Figure 8.15, you will have to change the field settings on your Value fields to calculate Average instead of Count. In addition, you will want to rename the fields in your pivot table to better define your data.

Figure 8.15

After your pivot table has been generated, you will need to change the field settings on your Value fields to calculate Average instead of Count.

	A	B	C	D	E	F	G	H	I	J
1	Page1	(All) ▼								
2										
3	Count of Value	Column ▼								
4	Row ▼	Q1	Q2	Q3	Q4	Grand Total				
5	2500C	2	2	2	1	7				
6	2500P	2		1	1	4				
7	3002C	2	2	2	2	8				
8	3002P	2	2	2	1	7				
9	4055T	2	2	1	1	6				
10	4500C	1	2	1	2	6				
11	4500P	2	2	2	1	7				
12	5001C	2	2	2	2	8				
13	5001P	2	2	2	2	8				
14	(blank)									
15	Grand Total	17	16	15	13	61				

PivotTable Field List ▼ ✕
Drag items to the PivotTable report

☐ Row
☐ Column
☐ Value
☐ Page1

Add To | Row Area ▼

After you apply the necessary formatting changes, your pivot table should look similar to the one shown in Figure 8.16. With this streamlined structure, you are showing the optimal amount of data in an easy-to-read format.

Figure 8.16

With your reorganized pivot table report, you have provided your manager with a report that shows the average revenue for each model number by quarter, by year, and as a two-year average.

	A	B	C	D	E	F	G
1	Average of Value		Quarter ▼				
2	Model ▼	Year ▼	Q1	Q2	Q3	Q4	Grand Total
3	2500C	2003	32,591	18,498	1,000	14,771	16,715
4		2004	17,220	63,379	16,079	0	32,226
5	2500C Total		24,906	40,939	8,540	14,771	23,363
6	2500P	2003	32,525	0	0	34,608	33,567
7		2004	23,407	0	37,926	0	30,667
8	2500P Total		27,966	0	37,926	34,608	32,117
9	3002C	2003	118,246	1,590	39,262	21,924	45,256
10		2004	103,650	89,463	4,925	54,884	63,231
11	3002C Total		110,948	45,527	22,094	38,404	54,243
12	3002P	2003	473,102	217,856	460,715	18,327	292,500
13		2004	160,783	324,679	141,799	0	209,087
14	3002P Total		316,943	271,268	301,257	18,327	256,752
15	4055T	2003	7,772	19,499	6,006	0	11,092
16		2004	21,231	22,789	0	29,892	24,637
17	4055T Total		14,502	21,144	6,006	29,892	17,865
18	4500C	2003	89,760	148,565	139,655	68,413	111,603
19		2004	0	44,398	0	324,957	184,678

Creating a Pivot Table from an Existing Pivot Table

If your workbook already contains one or more pivot tables, you will be given the option of using another pivot table as your data source. This means that the PivotTable Wizard dialog box, shown in Figure 8.17, will enable the Another PivotTable or PivotChart Report selection.

Figure 8.17
You have the option of using another pivot table as the data source when your workbook contains one or more pivot tables.

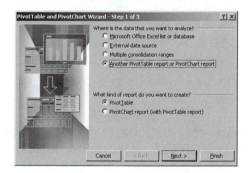

Unfortunately, the PivotTable Wizard does not adequately explain what this means exactly.

When you create a pivot table, you are storing a snapshot of your entire dataset in a pivot cache, or a memory subsystem in which your data source is duplicated for quick access. Each pivot table report you create from a separate data source will create its own pivot cache. The issue is that every pivot cache that is created increases your memory usage and file size.

If your workbook already contains a pivot table, Excel tries to save you memory and disk space by giving you the option of using the existing pivot cache. When you select the option of using another pivot table as your data source, as shown in Figure 8.17, you are telling Excel not to create a separate pivot cache for your new pivot table. Instead, Excel will use the existing one in order to save memory and disk space.

PivotTable Wizard Oddity

Suppose your workbook contains a pivot table. If you activate the PivotTable Wizard and immediately click Next, without changing and settings, you will get the message shown in Figure 8.18.

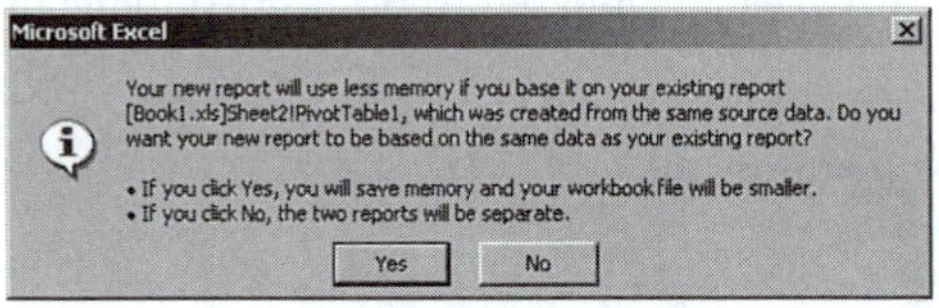

Figure 8.18

This message warns you about the file size implications of creating another pivot table from the same data source and asks if you want to use the same pivot cache in order to save memory and disk space.

However, if you activate the PivotTable Wizard and immediately click Finish without changing any settings, you will not get the warning shown in Figure 8.18. Instead, Excel will create a separate pivot cache for your new pivot table automatically.

By using the same pivot cache for multiple pivot tables, you gain a certain level of efficiency when it comes to memory usage and file size. However, there are some side effects to going this route.

Certain pivot table actions alter the content of the pivot cache. This means if you have two pivot tables using the same pivot cache, certain actions will affect both pivot tables. These include the following:

- **Refreshing your data**—You will not be able to refresh one pivot table and not the other. Refreshing affects both tables.

- **Adding a calculated field**—If you create a calculated field in one pivot table, your newly created calculated field will show up in the other pivot table's field list.

- **Adding a calculated item**—If you create a calculated item in one pivot table, it will show in the other as well.

- **Grouping or ungrouping fields**—Any grouping or ungrouping you perform will affect both pivot tables. For example, suppose you group a date field in one pivot table to show months. The same date field in the other pivot table will also be grouped to show months.

Although none of these side effects are critical flaws in the concept of sharing a pivot cache, it is important to keep them in mind when determining whether using a pivot table as your data source is the best option for your situation.

Next Steps

In Chapter 9, "Using External Data Sources for Your Pivot Table," you will learn the process of getting to external data with MS Query and how to use external data in your pivot tables. You'll learn how to use external data to avoid some of Excel's row limitations, as well as how to create dynamic pivot table reporting systems.

Using External Data Sources for Your Pivot Table

Building a Pivot Table Using External Data Sources

The general idea behind building your pivot table using an external data source is that you can create and use a pivot cache from a set of data that is not located in your Excel workbook. This means you can create a pivot table without one cell of data in your Excel workbook! Although there are many ways you can apply external data sources, one of the main benefits from this functionality is the ability to work around Excel's data management limitations.

Working Around Excel's Data Management Limitations

There is no argument that Excel is very good at processing and analyzing data. In fact, pivot tables themselves are a testament to the analytical power of Excel. However, with all its strengths comes one noticeable weakness. Excel makes for a poor data management platform—primarily for three reasons:

- The 65,536 row limitation alone makes it impossible to store large amounts of data easily.

- The lack of a relational data structure forces the use of flat tables that promote redundant data and increases the chance for errors.

- There is no way to index data fields in Excel to optimize performance when attempting to retrieve large amounts of data.

This is why in smart organizations, the task of data management is not performed by Excel; rather, it is primarily performed by databases such as Microsoft Access and SQL Server. These databases are used to store millions of records that can be rapidly searched and retrieved.

The effect of this separation in tasks is that you have a data management layer (your database) and a presentation layer (Excel). The trick is to find the best way to get information from your data management layer to your presentation layer for use by your pivot table.

Under normal circumstances, you would simply import or paste data from your database directly into an Excel spreadsheet as a standalone dataset. From there you could use it as a local data source for your pivot table (*local* meaning in the spreadsheet within which you are working).

However, there are a few situations where creating a local data source in Excel is just not practical:

- If the dataset you need to analyze contains more than 65,536 rows, you would not be able to create a local data source for your pivot table without splitting up your data into several spreadsheets.

- If your data is in a relational database, the fields you need for your data source may be in multiple tables, making it difficult to bring in one dataset.

Using an external data source in a pivot table would provide a way to avoid these problems.

About MS Query

Outside the realm of VBA, Excel cannot, in and of itself, link to external data sources. Rather, it gets its ability to link to external data sources from a little-known supplementary program called MS Query. MS Query is a standalone program, installed with the Office suite, that can be used through Excel or on its own. You will normally find this program under C:\Program Files\Microsoft Office\Office**\MSQRY32.exe (where the ** is the version of office you have installed) .

> **CAUTION**
>
> MS Query may or may not be installed on your system, based on how you performed your Office installation. Keep in mind that if you do not have the MSQRY32.exe program installed on your system, you will not be able to link to external data sources in Excel.
>
> To install MS Query you will need your Microsoft Office installation disc. Start the Microsoft Office Setup and choose to customize your installation. While you are customizing your installation, look for Office Tools. You will find an entry called Microsoft Query under Office Tools. Make sure you set it to Run from My Computer and then complete the installation.

Microsoft has not invested a lot of time and effort in developing or promoting MS Query over the years. Indeed, most people using MS Query would agree that the interface is a bit dated and the documentation is modest at best. Alas, with new and exciting XML capabilities at Excel's doorstep, MS Query is not likely to get very much attention any time soon. Nevertheless, MS Query still has its role to play in helping Excel link to external data sources.

Throughout this chapter, you will learn basic techniques that explain the process of using external data as it pertains to pivot tables. Keep in mind that although these techniques are based in an Excel environment, using Excel wizards, the engine behind this functionality is MS Query.

9

> **TIP**
>
> In order to keep this book focused on pivot tables, you will just skim the surface of using external data with Excel. If you are interested in a more detailed lesson on data management using Excel and MS Query, you may want to look into a book titled *Managing Data with Excel (Business Solutions)*, (ISBN 0789731002) by Conrad Carlberg. This book, recently updated and re-released by Que, is an excellent guide to the brilliant things you can do with Excel as it pertains to data management.

CASE STUDY

Analyze a Dataset with More Than 83,000 Records with a Pivot Table

Say that you have an Access database called MyExternalData.mdb on your system. You want to analyze the data in the database with an Excel pivot table, but there are more than 83,000 rows of data in the table. Although you cannot import this data into Excel as local data, you can build a pivot table using external data.

> **TIP**
>
> The MyExternalData.mdb Access file can be found at http://www.MrExcel.com/pivotbookdata.html. Simply download the file anywhere on your system, making sure you note its path and location for use in this walkthrough.

To start building a pivot table from an external data source, simply go to the application toolbar, select Data, and then select PivotTable and PivotChart Report. After you have activated the PivotTable and PivotChart Wizard, select External Data Source, as shown in Figure 9.1, and click the Next button.

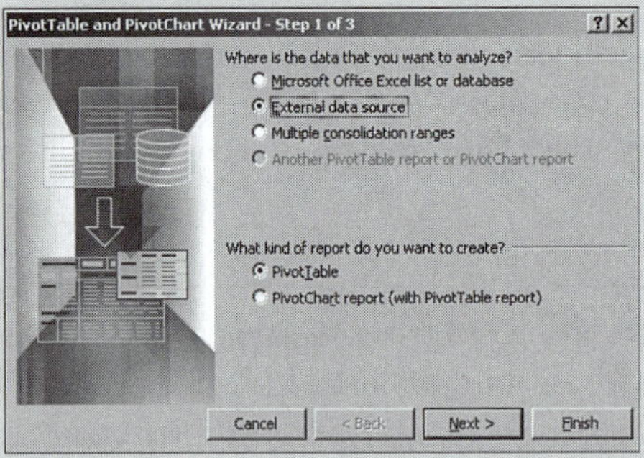

Figure 9.1
Select Data and then PivotTable and PivotChart Report. Next, select External Data Source and click Next.

The next dialog box, shown in Figure 9.2, is PivotTable and PivotChart Wizard – Step 2 of 3. Select Get Data to initiate MS Query and to start defining your data source.

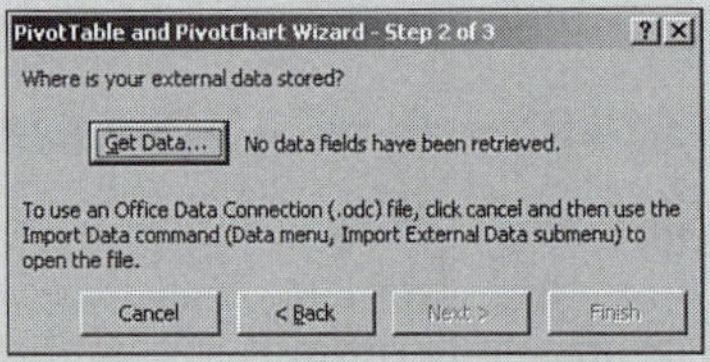

Figure 9.2
Selecting Get Data will initiate MS Query.

Looking at Figure 9.3, you will notice that your dialog box no longer refers to creating a pivot table. This is because, at this point, you are no longer working with an Excel wizard. You are now working with a MS Query wizard aimed at collecting all the definitions needed to establish your external data source.

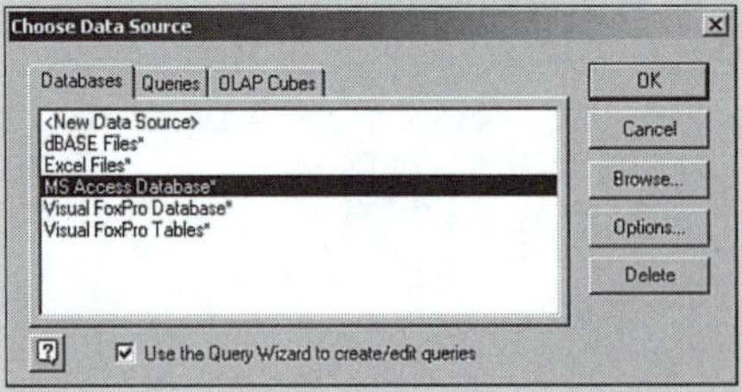

Figure 9.3
Select the MS Access Database entry and place a check in the Use the Query Wizard to Create/Edit Queries check box. Click OK to continue.

The first step in defining an external data source for your pivot table is to choose a data source. In this case, your data source is in an Access file, so you would select MS Access Database. In order to continue using the wizard, you will need to check the Use the Query Wizard to Create/Edit Queries check box. Click OK to continue.

Now that MS Query knows that you are working with an Access database, you will have to identify which Access database you want to work with. To do this, simply use the browser to find your database then click OK.

The dialog box that comes up next is a field selector. Use the tree view on the left to expand the tables in your database and view the fields. Then move the fields you will need in your pivot table to the list on the right using the buttons in the middle, as shown in Figure 9.4.

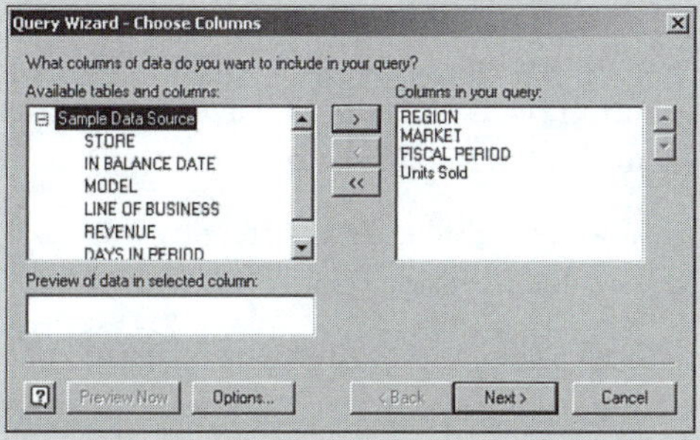

Figure 9.4
Move the desired fields using the ">" button.

The two dialog boxes you skipped over in this walkthrough provide for some basic filtering and sorting options that are, for the most part, self-explanatory. In this walkthrough, you will not make use of these features.

After you are satisfied that you have all the fields you will need, click the Next button three times until you come to the dialog box titled Query Wizard Finish.

You will finally have to tell MS Query what you want to do with your resulting query. You have the option of returning the data to Microsoft Excel, opening MS Query to view and edit your query, or creating an OLAP cube from your resulting data. In this scenario, you want to select the option Return Data to Microsoft Office Excel, as shown in Figure 9.5.

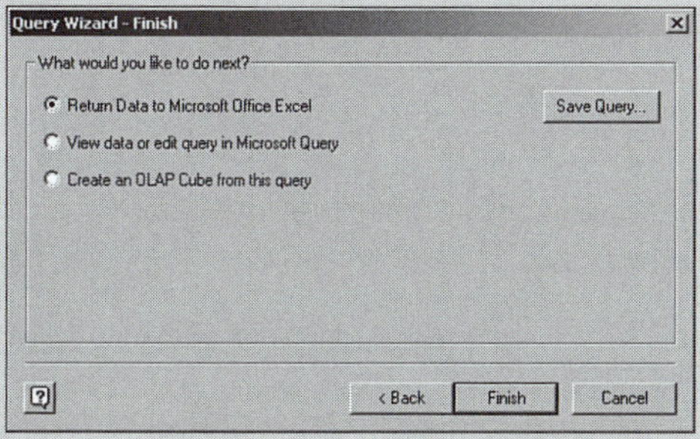

Figure 9.5
Select the Return Data to Microsoft Office Excel option and then click Finish.

9

When you are creating a pivot table with external data, the option Return Data to Microsoft Excel does not place the resulting data directly into your spreadsheet, as this option would suggest. Instead, the resulting data goes directly into your pivot table's pivot cache. The benefit of this behavior is that you can create pivot tables using datasets that exceed the 65,536-row limit of Excel.

You will be taken back to the PivotTable and PivotChart Wizard – Step 2 of 3 dialog box, as shown previously in Figure 9.2. You are once again working with the Excel wizard. Notice the text next to the Get Data button reads "Data fields have been retrieved." This is the sign that all has gone well and you are ready to go to the next step.

Step 3 of the PivotTable Wizard will seem like familiar territory again. In this step, you select where you want your pivot table to reside.

The resulting pivot table is shown in Figure 9.6. After your data has been brought into Excel, you can create, refresh, and manage your pivot table, just as you would any other.

Figure 9.6
After your data has been brought into Excel, you can create, refresh, and manage your pivot table, just as you would any other pivot table.

	A	B	C	D	E	F
1						
2						
3	Sum of Units Sold		FISCAL ▼			
4	REGION ▼	MARKET ▼	200205	200206	200207	200208
5	North	Great Lakes	1354	1310	1288	1446
6		New England	1312	1272	1432	1346
7		New York North	1312	1378	1320	1290
8		New York South	1068	1072	1082	978
9		Ohio	1472	1380	1544	1658
10		Shenandoah Valley	2060	1956	2352	1840
11		South Carolina	1078	1200	1140	1144
12	North Total		9656	9568	10158	9702
13	South	Florida	1660	1586	1738	1630
14		Gulf Coast	1586	1632	1584	1586
15		Illinois	1514	1682	1392	1478
16		Indiana	1476	1544	1468	1468
17		Kentucky	1174	1224	1170	1214
18		North Carolina	1000	1226	1326	1084
19		Tennessee	920	1018	1030	992
20		Texas	1422	1472	1314	1460
21	South Total		10752	11384	11022	10912

To add and edit fields used in your pivot cache, simply right-click anywhere inside your pivot table, select PivotTable Wizard, click the Back button, and then select Get Data. You will be taken to the dialog box previously shown in Figure 9.4.

CAUTION

If you move or rename your Access database after you have created your pivot table, you will not be able to refresh your pivot table.

If you do get an error when trying to refresh, simply click OK to close the error message box, select Database in the subsequent dialog box, and then use the browser to locate your file again. Click OK twice to get back to your pivot table, which is now pointed to the correct file.

Importing and Using External Data Without the PivotTable Wizard

You have just successfully built a pivot table that analyzes more than 80,000 rows of data. This would be impossible (or at least difficult) to do with local data. The reason you were able to do this is that you brought external data directly into your pivot cache using the PivotTable Wizard. By bringing external data directly into a pivot cache, you avoid the physical limitations of a spreadsheet.

The drawback to using the PivotTable Wizard to bring in external data is that you won't have immediate access to detailed records. That is, your raw dataset is not hard-coded onto a spreadsheet where you can AutoFilter it, see items not in your pivot table, or perform any number of other actions against it. Luckily, as with most actions in Excel, there is more than one way to bring in and use external data.

You have the option of importing and writing your external data directly onto your spreadsheet. You can do this by going up to the application menu and selecting Data, Import External Data, New Database Query. This will initiate the same MS Query wizards you went through in the first case study of this chapter.

> NOTE
>
> If you are using Excel 2000, you will not find Import External Data under the Data menu. Instead, this selection is called Get External Data.

After your external dataset has been imported, you can create a pivot table from it just as you would do with a local data source. The benefit of using this method is that you can create a pivot table summary of the data on one sheet and a formatted view of the details on another sheet. This method is ideal if you are distributing a report to users who need to have both summary and details in one workbook. Keep in mind though, that because you are writing data directly into a spreadsheet, you are limited to the spreadsheet's physical limitations (that is, 256 columns, 65,536 rows).

Creating Dynamic Pivot Table Reporting Systems

One of the more useful ways to utilize imported external data is in the creation of a dynamic reporting system. What does that mean?

Imagine for a moment that you have distributed, to 10 users, an Excel workbook that consists of one pivot table report. This report provides data on weekly sales. If your pivot table uses a data source within the Excel workbook, you have essentially given your users a static report. Although it is true that the pivot table is dynamic in and of itself, it will never show new data because the source data used to feed the pivot table is hard-coded locally. The bottom line is that every week, you will have to distribute a new weekly sales report to the same 10 users with the latest data.

Now imagine that the same pivot table report uses an imported external data source. With this new arrangement, you can dynamically link back to your source data and refresh the data that feeds your pivot table. Better yet, any of the users consuming data from your report can refresh the data source when needed at the touch of a button. Because they will always have access to the latest data, the need to redistribute subsequent reports is eliminated.

CASE STUDY

Create a Standalone Dynamic Pivot Table Reporting System

> **NOTE**
>
> There is no sample file for this case study. In this example, the data source being used is a SQL server. The reason for this is that using a data source that can be updated and maintained on a server is more conducive to the kind of report building being demonstrated here. Unfortunately, it is difficult to provide a sample file for this case study because the essence of this demonstration is the interaction between Excel and a SQL server data source, and we cannot pass you a SQL Server environment.

In order to report the latest customer retention numbers, you have been distributing the same pivot table report repeatedly to the same managers every month. In the meantime, much of your data has been moved to a new SQL server.

You decide to take advantage of the new data situation and create a dynamic pivot table report that uses the SQL server as an external data source. This will give your managers the ability to refresh their customer retention report at the touch of a button, not to mention save you the time and effort it took to create and send new reports every month.

This task can be broken out into five steps:

1. Create your external data source.
2. Define your query.
3. Import your results.
4. Create and format your pivot table report.
5. Create a macro that refreshes the report with the latest data.

Create Your External Data Source

The first thing you will need to do is create the external data source. In a new workbook, go to the application menu and select Data, Import External Data, New Database Query.

This will initiate the MS Query Wizard. As shown in Figure 9.7, the first dialog box will ask you to identify the data source you would like to use. In this case, you want to use a SQL Server database. Because your desired data source is not shown here, you will have to select <New Data Source> and then click OK.

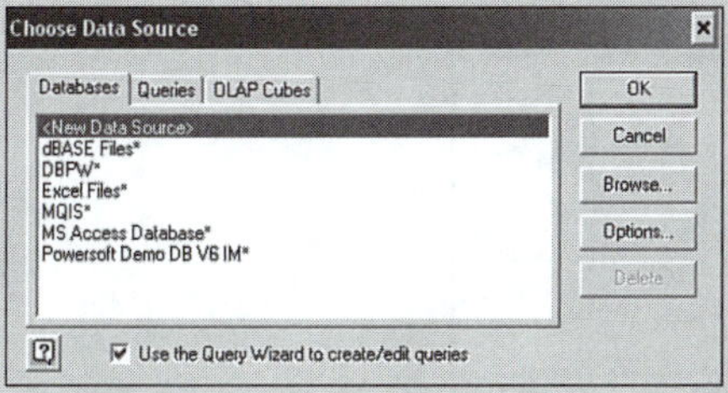

Figure 9.7
Because your SQL Server database is not shown here, select <New Data Source> then click OK.

In the next dialog box, enter the name you would like to give to your data source and identify which database driver should be used to connect to the data source.

A database driver is the translator between an application and the database. You cannot connect to any external data source without its appropriate driver. In Figure 9.8, you are using the SQL Server driver because your data source will be a SQL Server database. After you have named your data source and selected the appropriate driver, click the Connect button to continue.

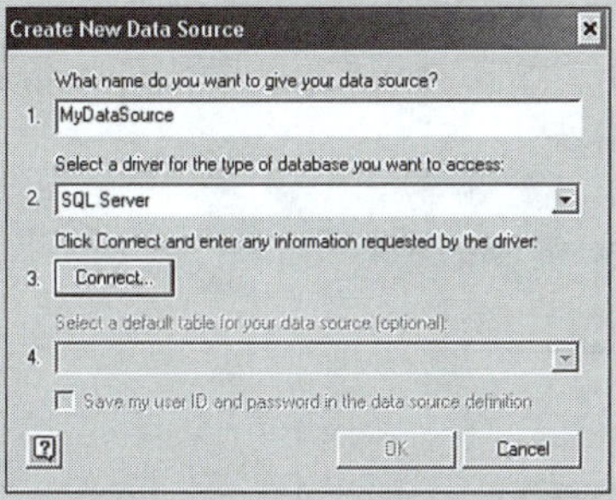

Figure 9.8
Enter a name for your data source and then select the appropriate driver. Click the Connect button to continue.

> **NOTE**
> Microsoft Office comes with default database drivers for the following data sources: SQL Server, Access, dBASE, FoxPro, Excel, Oracle, Paradox, various text files, and a select few third-party drivers. If you do not see a selection for your database driver, you will need to install it before any connection can be made.

Next, you will have to enter three pieces of information: server, login ID, and password.

To identify the server you are connecting to, you can use either an IP address or a DNS (Domain Name System), as shown in Figure 9.9. For the purposes of this case study, your server has been assigned a DNS of SOPS, so you do not have to use the actual IP address. It is always best to use a DNS if you have the option for a number of security and functional reasons.

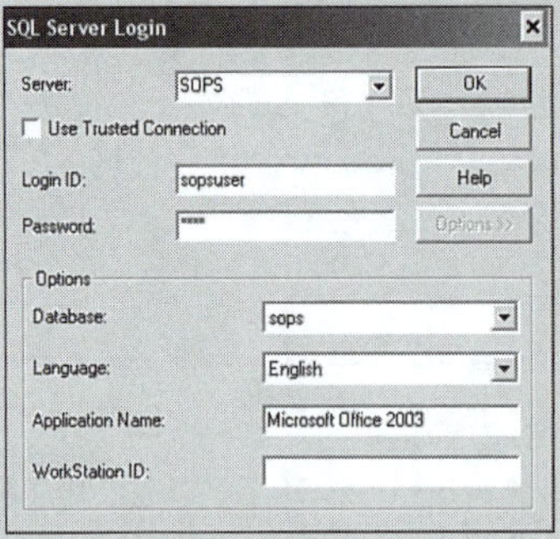

Figure 9.9
In the Server input, enter the server's IP address or, preferably, the server's DNS (Domain Name System).

Next enter your login ID and password (normally provided by your Database Administrator). Click OK twice to complete the creation of your data source.

Define Your Query

At this point, you will see your new data source as a selection in your list of data sources. In this case, your new data source is called MyDataSource, as shown in Figure 9.10. Select your new data source, check the Use the Query Wizard to Create/Edit Queries check box, and then click OK to continue.

Figure 9.10
Select your new data source, place a check in the Use the Query Wizard to Create/Edit Queries check box, and then click OK to continue.

As shown in Figure 9.11, the dialog box that comes up next is a field selector. Use the tree view on the left to expand the tables in your database and view the fields. Then move the fields you will need to the list on the right using the buttons in the middle. When you are satisfied that you have all the fields you will need, click the Next button three times until you come to the dialog box titled Import Data.

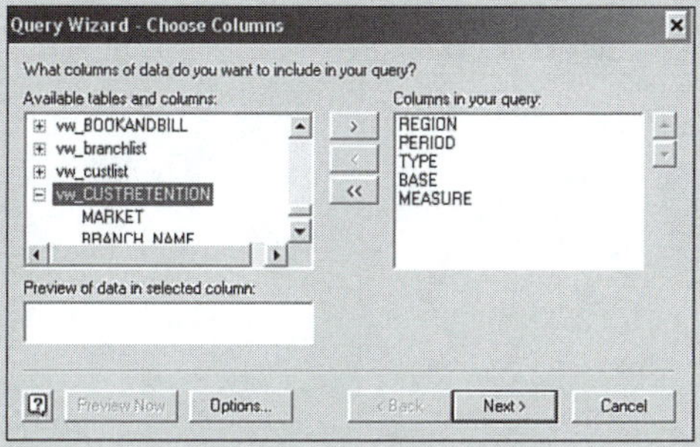

Figure 9.11
Simply move the fields you will need from the list on the left to the list on the right using the buttons in the middle.

Import Your Results

As shown in Figure 9.12, select where you would like to place the resulting dataset. Keep in mind that if your resulting dataset has more than 65,536 rows, Excel will cut your data short.

Figure 9.12
Choose where you would like to place your resulting dataset and then click OK.

After your new dataset has been imported, right-click anywhere inside the dataset and then select External Data Range Properties. This will activate the External Data Range Properties dialog box, as shown in Figure 9.13. Place a check inside the Save Password check box. This setting will embed the password for the data source in the workbook, allowing your users to refresh data without requiring a password.

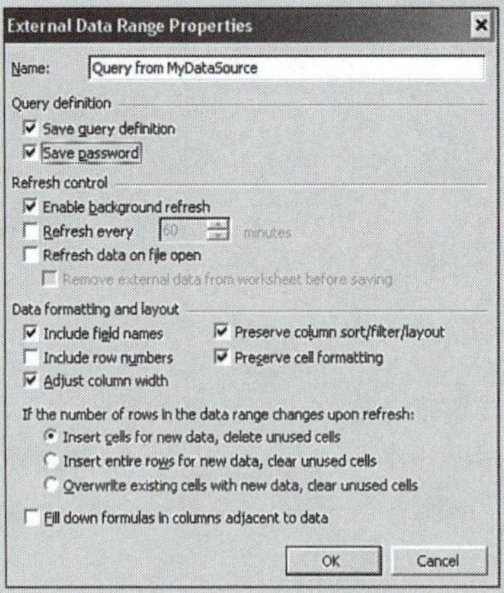

Figure 9.13
Use this dialog to save the password for the query.

Use Caution When Saving Passwords

When you enable the Save Password setting, as shown in Figure 9.13, you are essentially embedding the password into your Excel workbook. This means that anyone who is interested enough could open your Excel workbook with a text editor, such as WordPad, and extract the embedded password. Figure 9.14 shows an example of this.

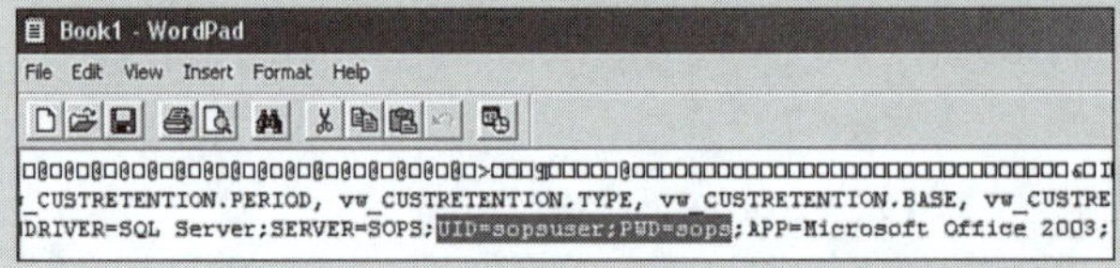

Figure 9.14
Anyone determined enough can examine your Excel file with a text editor to find the password.

Here are a few actions you can take to help minimize the potential impact of this security flaw:

- Employ the use of views where possible.
- Use "read-only" tables that are isolated and dedicated to your dynamic reports.
- Use a dedicated user ID and password used only for your dynamic reports.
- Avoid using IP addresses in your data sources.

Create and Format Your Pivot Table Report

Create a pivot table using the external data you imported into your workbook. After your pivot table is built, you can link a chart to it and format your report to suit your needs, as shown in Figure 9.15.

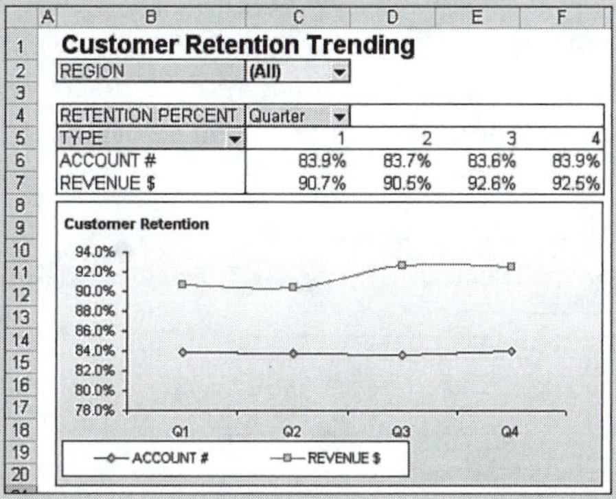

Figure 9.15
Create your base pivot table and then add a chart and some formatting.

	A	B	C	D	E	F
1		**Customer Retention Trending**				
2		REGION	(All)			
3						
4		RETENTION PERCENT	Quarter			
5		TYPE		1	2	3	4
6		ACCOUNT #		83.9%	83.7%	83.6%	83.9%
7		REVENUE $		90.7%	90.5%	92.6%	92.5%
8						
9		Customer Retention				
10		94.0%				
11		92.0%				
12		90.0%				
13		88.0%				
14		86.0%				
15		84.0%				
16		82.0%				
17		80.0%				
18		78.0%	Q1	Q2	Q3	Q4
19		◆ ACCOUNT #	☐ REVENUE $			
20						

Create a Macro That Refreshes the Report with the Latest Data

After your users have this report in their hands, they can technically refresh their report to get the latest data any time they want by performing the following actions: right-click anywhere inside the source data, select Refresh Data, go to the pivot table, right-click anywhere inside the pivot table, and select Refresh Data.

Although this series of actions seems simple, some of your users will not have the Excel savvy or the inclination to begin to refresh their report. The good news is that you can create a macro that will perform these actions for the user anytime they fire it.

First, go up to the application menu and select Tools, Macro and then select Record New Macro. When the dialog box shown in Figure 9.16 activates, name your macro "Refresh Data." In the Shortcut Key Input field, type in the letter *R*. This will allow your users to fire the macro with the keyboard. In this case, the combination of keys that will fire this macro is the Control key, the Shift Key, and the R key. Click OK to start recording your actions.

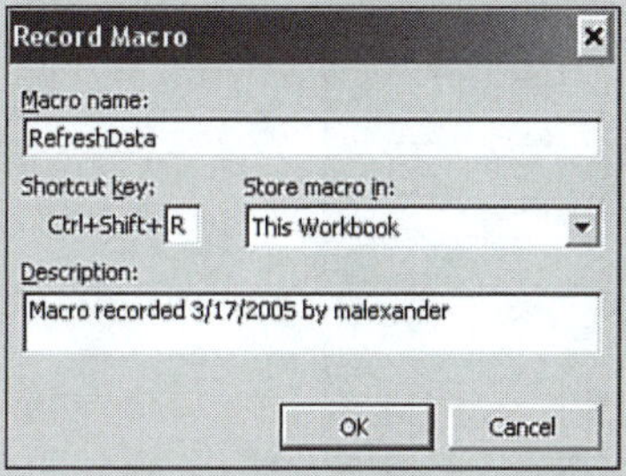

Figure 9.16
Give the macro a name and a shortcut key.

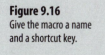

Record Macro

Macro name:
RefreshData

Shortcut key: Ctrl+Shift+ R

Store macro in: This Workbook

Description:
Macro recorded 3/17/2005 by malexander

OK   Cancel

1. Go to your source data.

2. Right-click and select Refresh Data.

3. Right-click on your pivot table and select Refresh Data.

When you are done, go up to the application menu and select Tools, Macro and then select Stop Recording. Now your users do not have to know every action it takes to refresh their data. They simply press the shortcut keys you defined, and the macro does all the work! To make the shortcut key easy to remember, add a note to your worksheet, as shown in Figure 9.17.

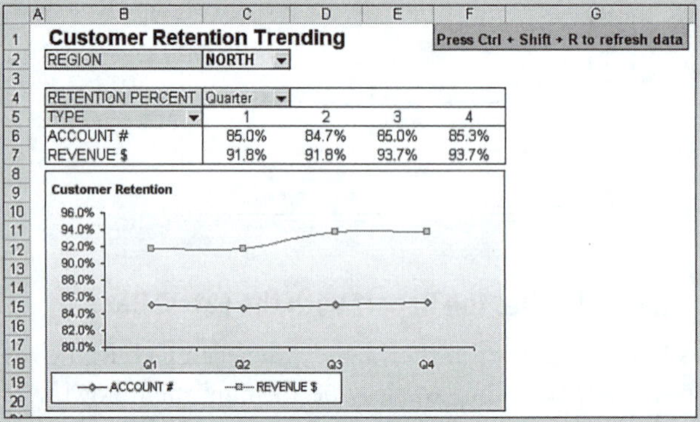

Figure 9.17
With a little additional formatting, you have created a dynamic reporting tool that you can now distribute to your users as a standalone Excel file.

Pivot Table Data Options

Some pivot table options deal specifically with how a pivot table interacts with external data. Although you've seen the PivotTable Options dialog box before, several options in the lower third of the dialog are specific to external data queries. To display the dialog box shown in Figure 9.18, right-click inside the pivot table and choose Table Options. The options specific to external data are listed here:

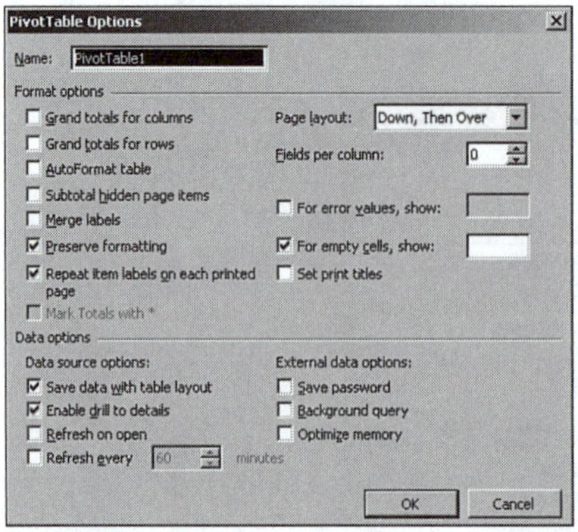

Figure 9.18
The options in the lower third of this dialog box are all specific to external data queries.

- **Save data with table layout**—This option means that Excel will save your external data in the workbook so that the data is immediately available upon opening the file. Keep in mind that this behavior adds to your file size. By default, the setting for this state is "enabled."

- **Enable drill to details**—When you double-click a data item in a pivot table, the default behavior for Excel is to drill into the details beneath that data item. Clearing the check box for this setting prevents this behavior. This option is not available for reports based on OLAP databases without special add-ins.

- **Refresh on open**—Enabling this setting will ensure that the pivot table is automatically refreshed with the source data whenever the workbook is opened.

- **Refresh every**—Select this check box to automatically refresh the PivotTable at an interval you specify.

- **Save password**—Select this option to store the external data source password as part of the workbook. This will ensure that you will not be required to reenter your password when you refresh your data.

- **Background query**—If you have a large external dataset that takes an extraordinarily long time to refresh, you can enable this setting so that you can continue your work while your data is updating. This option is not available for reports based on OLAP databases.

- **Optimize memory**—When this option is enabled, Excel evaluates the results of the external query before it populates the pivot cache to determine whether storage of each row or column array in the results can be optimized for performance. Unfortunately, documentation on this option is thin, and it is unclear how this is actually done or how this option affects performance.

Next Steps

Chapter 10, "Leveraging the Power of OLAP Cubes," will introduce you to the world of OLAP reporting, where OLAP cubes enhance your interaction with pivot tables. You will learn how OLAP functionality can give your pivot tables access to millions of records in databases far larger than the ones you can create with Microsoft Access.

Leveraging the Power of OLAP Cubes

10

Defining OLAP?

OLAP is short for *Online Analytical Processing*. It is a category of tools that allow data analysts to analyze multidimensional data.

An OLAP server is a tool that sits between the data warehouse and your computer. The OLAP server understands how data is organized in the database and has special functions for aggregating and presenting that data.

Common OLAP servers include products such as Essbase from Hyperion and SQL Server with Analysis Tools from Microsoft.

An OLAP server will take a few hundred million records from a data warehouse and create a multi-dimensional data structure. This structure, known as an OLAP cube, will make querying faster.

Benefits of OLAP Cubes

In Chapter 9, "Using External Data Sources for Your Pivot Table," you learned how to use external data sources to handle datasets larger than 65,536 records. An Access database or SQL server might be able to deliver a few hundred thousand records to an Excel pivot table. What happens if you have a lot more data? Millions, or even billions of records?

Here are two contrasting examples. In a very small bank with just a few branches, you might have only a few thousand customers. You can easily create a dataset that would fit in Excel about those customers' balances and loans. You could then use pivot tables to generate all sorts of interesting aggregations.

However, if you're working for a medium-sized chain of convenience stores and are tracking all the daily sales, that's a set of data that is several orders of magnitudes larger. Imagine that the chain has 250 stores, and each store is averaging 1,000 sales per day. Over the course of a year, you'll see more than 91 million sales occur, each one involving an average of 2.3 products.

You will want to know which items sell fast and which aren't worth the shelf space. You will want to compare this year to prior years, and you will have more than 200 million records per year (one record for each item sold). Can Excel, by itself, handle all this data? No. Isn't there some other way? Yes, if you have an OLAP server.

When your database involves millions of records, most likely you're already using a full-blown relational database management system (RDBMS) such as Microsoft SQL Server 2000 or later. SQL Server brings with it several other excellent tools to build solutions for making sense from all that raw data. Some other RDBMS products also have associated tools for building business intelligence solutions. Your database administrator (DBA) or data warehouse architect can use these tools to build a data warehouse and OLAP cubes and keep them up to date with new data as it comes in.

The biggest conceptual change in using OLAP cubes is that the data is already prepared for you. When you've got hundreds of millions of records, it's too much to query them all on the front end. More than likely you have a full-time DBA tending to them on the back end. The DBA will be experienced in the arcana of data warehousing and will create and maintain the OLAP cube(s), which you will access using pivot tables.

Introduction to Data Warehouses and OLAP Cubes

You will want to be familiar with what OLAP cubes are so that you can make full use of them. You can trace how operational data becomes an OLAP cube in this section.

Operational Data

A traditional Online Transaction Processing (OLTP) database such as Access or SQL Server will store data across several related tables. In the convenience store chain, the cash registers might store data in tables called Customers, Orders, Order Details, and Products. Figure 10.1 shows the table structure for the cash register.

Figure 10.1
Sales at the convenience store are likely stored across several tables in a relational database.

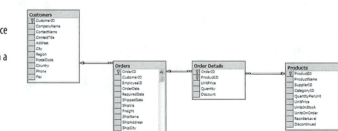

The cash register database is recording all sales, so you can keep a record of what you're selling, know when to replenish your store's inventory, and calculate the profit margin on all your items and the day's total sales. Of course, that database is going to keep on growing with each day's new sales.

Rather than leaving the data to grow on the cash registers, where it won't be of much use to the executives back at the home office, it is sent upstream (daily, hourly, or perhaps even as each sale happens) to the companywide sales database.

After just a few months of receiving data from your 250 stores, you've got a whole lot of data in that database in the home office. No single record makes much difference to you, really, because one record or sale by itself doesn't tell you where your business has been or where it is headed. You need summaries and other aggregations of all kinds if you want to pull meaningful information out of the raw data. However, you don't want to send in long-running queries to this database, because it's very busy receiving so much operational information from the stores. Trying to generate reports on all that data, or even a subset of it, would slow things down on the operations side.

The answer is to move the data from that companywide sales database into another database that is structured for easier and faster querying. This is known as a *data warehouse*.

Warehousing Your Data

The format of the data warehouse, although still a relational database, looks very different from the transaction database. As shown in Figure 10.2, sales are stored in a central fact table, with lookups out to other tables in order to provide product hierarchies, store hierarchies, and time hierarchies as shown in Figure 10.2.

Figure 10.2
The central fact table will contain hundreds of millions of records per year.

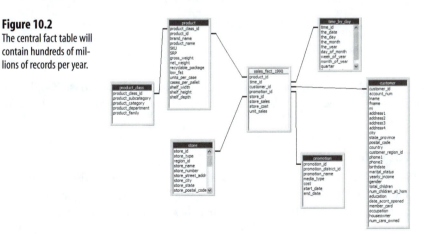

Each record in the fact table will have two categories of information. The first category is dimensional information, such as what time the sale was made, in what store, and what item was sold. The second category is measure information, examples of which include the price of the item, the cost of the item, and how many of that item were sold in that particular transaction.

Measure information is typically numeric. This is the data you can total and otherwise aggregate.

Dimension information provides meaning to the totals. You can slice your total sales along the time dimension and the product dimension to find out that between 3:00 a.m. and 5:00 a.m., stores in the Central Time Zone sell more laundry detergent than any other region does at that time of night.

Enter the Cube

A *summary table* is a prebuilt file that contains every possible aggregation of every measure, by each dimension. One way to prebuild all the possible summary tables is to create a multidimensional data structure (commonly called a *cube*). This is different from the usual relational database data structure, wherein each cell (the intersection of a field and record) holds one and only one piece of data. Any "cell" in a cube can have multiple pieces of data, or even none; further, each cell's data is aggregated on one or more dimensions. The OLAP server will handle converting the fact table in Figure 10.2 to the virtual cube shown in Figure 10.3.

Figure 10.3
An OLAP cube summarizes measures along various dimensions.

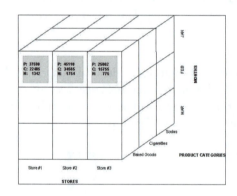

If this structure is called a *cube*, does that mean it is limited to three dimensions? People call it a cube to enable you to visualize the data in your mind. However, it is possible to have far more than three dimensions.

Cubes Offer Prebuilt Data Views

The bottom line is that when you have data in Excel, you might have to go through the work described in Chapter 2, "Creating a Basic Pivot Table," to groom and organize your data. However, when you have an OLAP cube, the data has already been groomed and organized for you.

An OLAP cube is essentially a data structure that already contains all the possible aggregations by all the available dimensions. Now all you have to do is point Excel's pivot table at that OLAP cube, and then you can use just about any neat pivot table trick discussed in this book to generate various reports and charts.

Connecting to an OLAP Cube

Now that your DBA has the company data flowing into an OLAP cube, you want to view that information. To work through the examples in this book, you can download a local version of an OLAP cube from http://www.mrexcel.com/pivotbookdata.html. Or, if your company has SQL Server 2000 and a DBA, you can ask your DBA to set up the Sales cube for the Foodmart database using MS Analysis Services. Analysis Services can be installed from the SQL Server 2000 CD. Analysis Manager contains an excellent tutorial for setting up this demo cube.

Make the Connection to a Local Cube

Select PivotTable and PivotChart Report from the Data menu. In step 1 of 3 of the wizard, select External Data Source as you did in Chapter 9 (see Figure 10.4).

Figure 10.4
In step 1 of the wizard, select External Data Source.

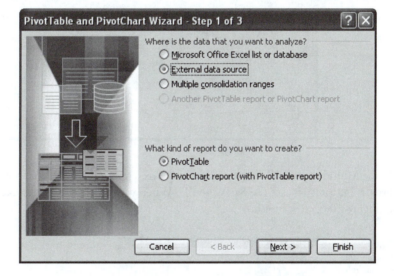

In step 2 of the wizard, click the Get Data button.

In the Choose Data Source dialog box, select the OLAP Cubes tab. If this is your first time using the local Cube file, select New Data Source and click OK.

As shown in Figure 10.5, the Create New Data Source dialog box will be displayed. Give your cube a name, such as Sales. In the OLAP Provider field, choose the Microsoft OLE DB provider. In step 3, click the Connect button.

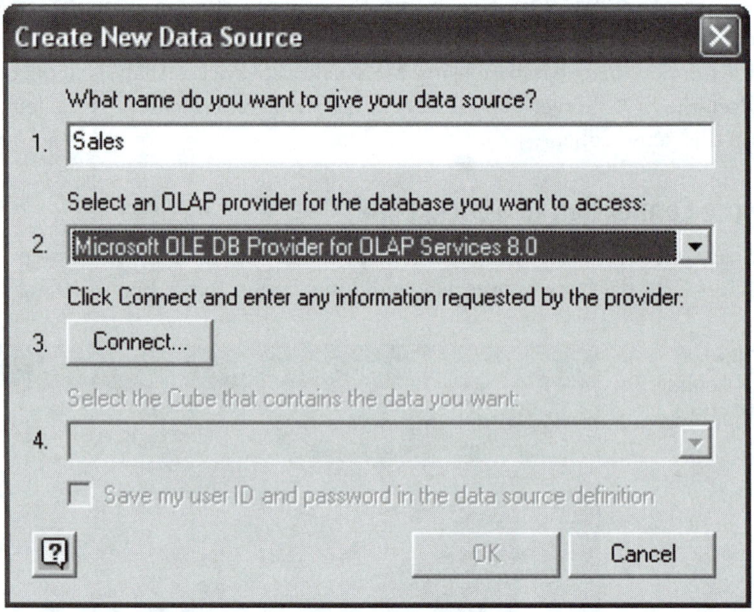

Figure 10.5
Even though the cube exists, you must give the connection to the cube a name.

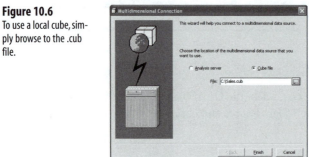

Create New Data Source

What name do you want to give your data source?

1. Sales

Select an OLAP provider for the database you want to access:

2. Microsoft OLE DB Provider for OLAP Services 8.0

Click Connect and enter any information requested by the provider:

3. Connect...

Select the Cube that contains the data you want:

4.

☐ Save my user ID and password in the data source definition

OK   Cancel

In the Multidimensional Connection dialog box, choose the Cube File option. Use the browse button to locate the Sales.cub file. When your dialog box looks like the one shown in Figure 10.6, click Finish.

Figure 10.6
To use a local cube, simply browse to the .cub file.

Multidimensional Connection

This wizard will help you connect to a multidimensional data source.

Choose the location of the multidimensional data source that you want to use.

○ Analysis server   ● Cube file

File: C:\Sales.cub

< Back   Finish   Cancel

Click OK to close the Create Data Source and Choose Data Source dialog boxes. You will be taken back to step 2 of the PivotTable Wizard. Click Next.

You will then be at step 3 of the wizard, as shown in Figure 10.7. Because you don't have an existing worksheet with transactional data, the default is to place the pivot table on the blank existing worksheet. Click Finish.

Figure 10.7
In step 3 of the wizard, create the pivot table on the existing blank worksheet.

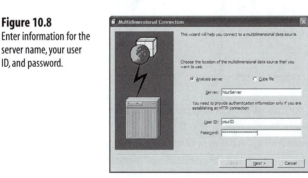

Make the Connection to a Server Cube

If you have a real OLAP server, you will want to connect to the server instead of a local cube file. In Figure 10.6 (shown earlier), you would instead select the Analysis Server option. You then have to supply a server name, user ID, and password. Your DBA should be able to provide this information, as shown in Figure 10.8.

Figure 10.8
Enter information for the server name, your user ID, and password.

When connecting to a server-based cube, you will have an extra step of specifying the database. In the Foodmart example, the only option is the Foodmart database, as shown in Figure 10.9. Click the Finish button.

Figure 10.9
Choose the database. In this example, there is only one choice.

Continue with the steps to return to the PivotTable Wizard and then click Finish in step 3 of the wizard.

Working with an OLAP Pivot Table

You now have a blank pivot table, just as if your data was on another worksheet in Excel. As soon as you start dragging and dropping dimensions and measures, you'll have an eyeful of meaningful data. Let's start slicing the cube.

Arranging the Data

As with regular Excel pivot tables, there is a PivotTable toolbar and a PivotTable Field List. You will notice in Figure 10.10 that each field in the field list has an icon next to it. The fields Store Cost, Store Sales, and Unit Sales have an icon with two rows of ones and zeroes. This icon denotes that these fields are numeric measures. The other fields have an icon with a blue and grey hierarchy. These fields are the dimension fields. If your DBA correctly followed the Analysis Services tutorial, you'll see five dimensions: Customer, Product, Promotion, Store, and Time.

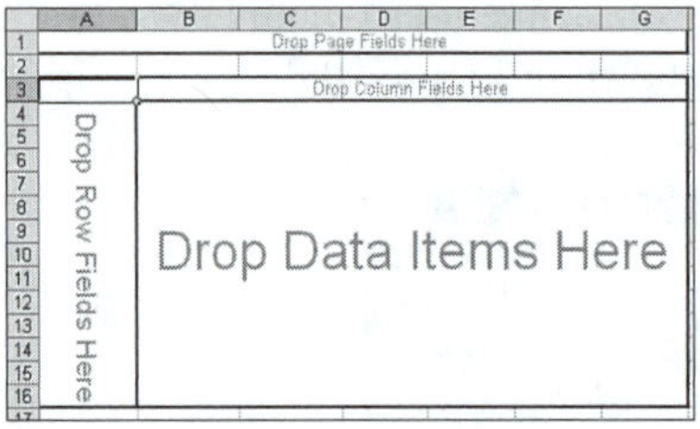

Figure 10.10
Icons in the field list indicate whether a field is a measure or a dimension.

On the worksheet, you can see an outline of the pivot table layout. There are four areas: page, row, column, and data. The data area is where you'll be dragging measures. You remember measures; those are the pieces of data you want to see summarized or otherwise aggregated. The page, row, and column areas are for dimensions, which are the attributes by which you want to do the aggregating.

Click and hold on Store Sales and then drag it over to the data area. When you drop it, it shows you the total dollars of revenue for all your stores. Of course, that's not very interesting. Drag the Store Sales measure out of the upper-left corner of the layout to any area away from the layout, until you see it accompanied by a red X; letting it go now removes that field from the layout. Now you are back to your beginning layout.

Drag and drop the Customer dimension into the Drop Row Fields Here area. Drag and drop the Time dimension into the Drop Column Fields Here area. Drag and drop the Store Sales into the Data area.

Immediately and without any other effort, a summary of 200+ million records shows the 1998 sales figures for the three countries in which Foodmart operates, as shown in Figure 10.11.

Figure 10.11
This OLAP pivot table appears similar to a regular pivot table, except it is summarizing 200+ million records.

	A	B	C
1	Drop Page Fields Here		
2			
3	Store Sales	Year ▼	
4	Country ▼	1998	Grand Total
5	Canada	98045.46	98045.46
6	Mexico	430293.59	430293.59
7	USA	550808.42	550808.42
8	Grand Total	1079147.47	1079147.47

Drilling Into the Cube

Examine Figure 10.11. Although you had dropped a field called Customer to the row area of the pivot table, the actual pivot table shows a field called Country. This is because the Customer dimension is a hierarchy of data. Choose the plus sign next to Customer in the PivotTable Field List. You will see that customers are stored by Lname but are grouped by city, state, and country, as shown in Figure 10.12.

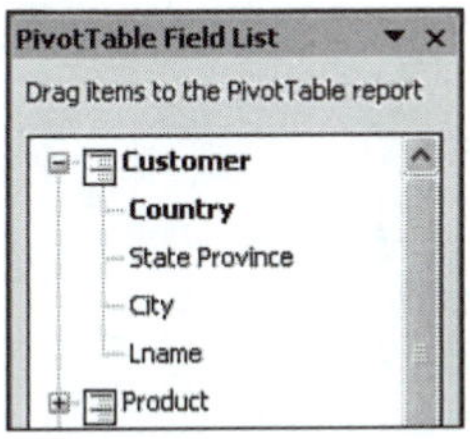

Figure 10.12
Dimension fields in the PivotTable Field List can be expanded to show all the aggregations available.

PivotTable Field List ▼ ✕

Drag items to the PivotTable report

- **Customer**
  - **Country**
  - State Province
  - City
  - Lname
- Product

By default, when you drag Customer to the pivot table, you will see the most summarized view of the data. The default pivot table shown in Figure 10.11 included data by country and year.

It is very easy to start drilling down into the data. Double-click on Mexico, and you will see the layout automatically expands to show eight Mexican states, as shown in Figure 10.13.

Figure 10.13
OLAP cubes have groups already built-in. Simply double-click to drill into the data.

	A	B	C	D
1	Drop Page Fields Here			
2				
3	Store Sales		Year ▼	
4	Country ▼	State Province	1998	Grand Total
5	Canada		98045.46	98045.46
6	Mexico	DF	75131	75131
7		Guerrero	30838.58	30838.58
8		Jalisco	4328.87	4328.87
9		Mexico	20395.4	20395.4
10		Sinaloa	18251.45	18251.45
11		Veracruz	52142.07	52142.07
12		Yucatan	79063.13	79063.13
13		Zacatecas	150143.09	150143.09
14	Mexico Total		430293.59	430293.59
15	USA		550808.42	550808.42
16	Grand Total		1079147.47	1079147.47

10

Double-click on Zacatecas, and the layout will expand to show the two cities within Zacatecas.

Go up to the cell named 1998 and double-click on it. The layout expands to show the four quarters of 1998. Double-click on each quarter to see each month, as shown in Figure 10.14.

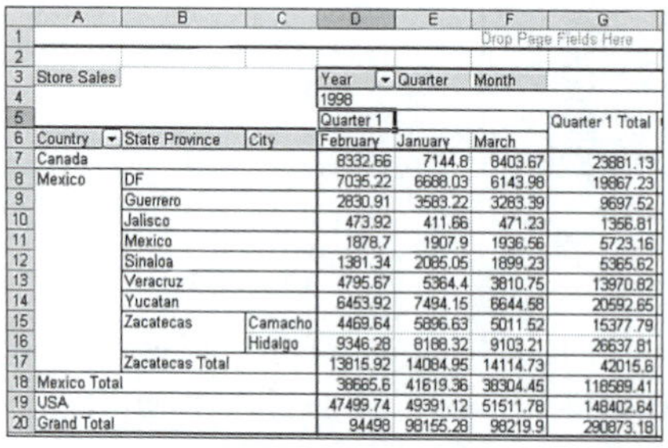

Figure 10.14
Only a few clicks are required to drill down to this data.

To go back to a previous rollup of the data, you have to hide the detail for a measure. In Figure 10.15, select Zacatecas in cell B15 and click the Hide Detail button in the PivotTable toolbar.

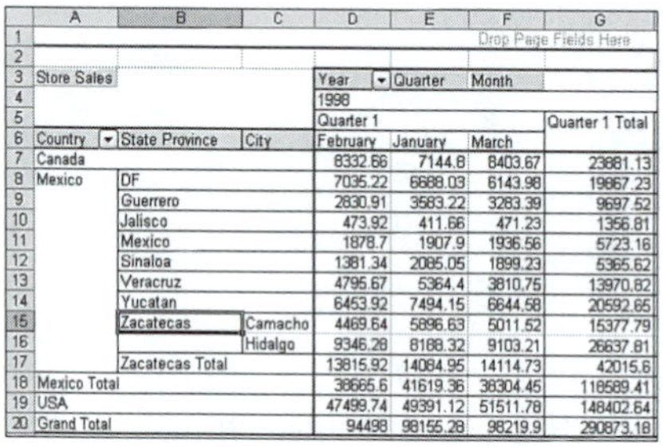

Figure 10.15
Use the icon with the red minus sign to hide detail for Zacatecas.

Using Page Fields

Now try dragging and dropping some other dimension, such as Product, up to the Drop Page Fields Here area. The page area acts as a filter. By default, it shows All Product. Select the drop-down to see a list of categories. Click the plus sign next to Baking Goods, as shown in Figure 10.16, to reveal product subcategories. Choose Cooking Oil.

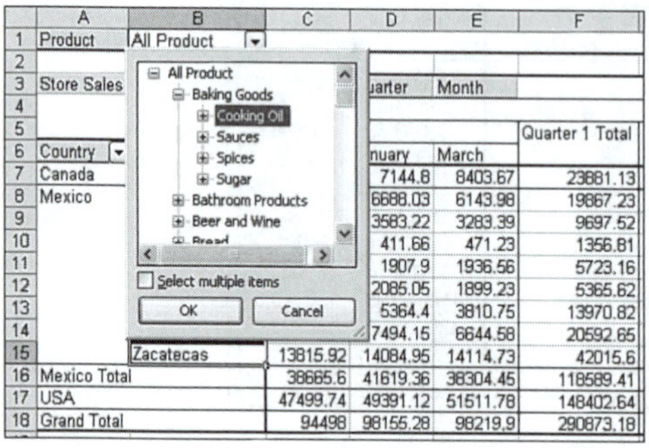

Figure 10.16
The Product page field offers a number of hierarchical choices as well. Click any plus sign to expand it.

Click the Cooking Oil drop-down. Expand the Cooking Oil subcategory to choose the BBB brands. You may notice at this point that not every state carries this brand; those that don't will show an empty cell, as shown in Figure 10.17.

Figure 10.17
If you drill down far enough, you may begin to encounter sparse data. The state of Jalisco did not purchase any of this brand in Q1.

	A	B	C	D	E	F
1	Product	BBB Best ▼				
2						
3	Store Sales		Year ▼	Quarter	Month	
4			1998			
5			Quarter 1			Quarter 1 Total
6	Country ▼	State Province	February	January	March	
7	Canada		21.26	38.16	42.16	101.58
8	Mexico	DF	16.96	4.62	5.52	27.1
9		Guerrero	3.68	22.73	3.68	30.09
10		Jalisco				
11		Mexico	7.36			7.36
12		Sinaloa	11.98			11.98
13		Veracruz	4.62	10.06		14.68
14		Yucatan	24.3	7.36	12.15	43.81
15		Zacatecas	33.3	25.65	38.31	97.26
16	Mexico Total		102.2	70.42	59.66	232.28
17	USA		144.48	61.87	122.62	328.97
18	Grand Total		267.94	170.45	224.44	662.83

What you're doing is drilling down through levels of detail, and at each level you can see the aggregations of the measures are immediately presented to you. There's no pausing for any calculating, because all those summarized totals are already (either in actuality or virtually) prepared and stored in the OLAP cube. Feel free to experiment, combining multiple dimensions in the rows, in the columns, and in the page filter.

Comparing OLAP Cubes' Pivot Tables to Excel Data

You've seen the basic idea of what an OLAP cube is. You've also seen that connecting to a cube is fairly simple, and that using one is very much like using pivot tables to work with raw data in an Excel worksheet. So what are the differences between using pivot tables on Excel-stored data and using pivot tables on OLAP data?

OLAP Handles More Data, Faster

The biggest difference is in the amount of data an OLAP cube can handle. As mentioned earlier, in a typical data warehouse there will be millions and more likely billions of records. Organizing aggregations of all that data into a usable structure is beyond even the amazing capabilities of Excel.

Now, not only can you access mountains of data, you can also sift through that data in the blink of an eye. There is no processing time to generate any of the aggregations because they have all been preprocessed for you. As you slice the cube from any point of view of interest to you, the preaggregated results appear nearly instantaneously.

Dimensions or Measures

In an OLAP cube, each field is either marked as a "measure" or a "dimension." Measures are generally the numeric fields such as Revenue, Cost, and Quantity. Unlike using Excel data, you can only drop measures in the data area. You cannot drop a measure in the row, column, or page area.

Similarly, the remaining dimension fields cannot be dropped in the data area. This is different from using regular Excel data, where it would be possible to drop the Region field in the data area (for example, to get a count of records).

OLAP Measures Are Already Grouped

It is likely that your DBA has defined groups in the data cube. For example, a year dimension may already contain quarters, months, and days. Simply double-click on the year to expand the group to show quarters.

This is a great benefit of OLAP data. It is possible to set up similar groups in regular Excel data, but this requires a fair amount of steps, as described in the section "Grouping Pivot Fields" in Chapter 5, "Controlling the Way You View Your Pivot Data."

If your DBA did not set up groups, it is possible to add groups to OLAP pivot tables using the techniques described in Chapter 5.

Drill-Through of OLAP Data

With regular Excel data, you can double-click any number in the pivot table to see all the records used to calculate that number.

The double-click method does not natively work with OLAP datasets. For Excel 2002 or newer, you can drill through by using an Excel add-in provided by Microsoft. It's called the Excel 2002/2003 add-in for SQL Server Analysis Services and is located here:

http://www.microsoft.com/downloads/details.aspx?FamilyId=DAE82128-9F21-475D-88A4-4B6E6C069FF0&displaylang=en

Other Excel-oriented OLAP tools offer add-ins of their own.

> **CAUTION**
>
> You cannot drill through a local cube. With OLAP, the drill-through capability requires a server to query the original transactional data. A local cube is the resultant data file, without the server capable of conducting the back-end query.

Calculated Fields with OLAP

As you've seen in previous chapters, you can have calculated cells and members. You can do this locally, or you can ask your DBA to make those kinds of changes in the cube as needed. Calculations do not work in local cubes.

Other Pivot Table Features Operate the Same

Any pivot table feature not described thus far will work with OLAP cubes just like it would work with local data. Specifically, you can easily format a table using the AutoFormat feature described in Chapter 4, "Formatting Your Pivot Table Report." You can create pivot charts as described in Chapter 7, "Creating and Using Pivot Charts." You can use AutoSort to sequence the pivot table as described in Chapter 5. And, you can display the top or bottom records using the Top 10 AutoShow feature, also described in Chapter 5.

Other Considerations When Using OLAP Cubes

You have a few items to consider when using OLAP cubes. Note that OLAP is a rich and broad topic. These are just a few of the features.

Viewing an OLAP Cube Online

One of the tools provided in Excel allows you to display a spreadsheet or pivot table as a web page, and you can even make it interactive for the user. The same is true for working with an OLAP cube. Likewise, you can control whether opening the web page will force a refresh of the data, and you'll have the same formatting issues with numerical data and with charts. It's possible to create VBA code to handle the formatting for you. You can also export from the web page back down to a new Excel file for further analysis if so desired.

Writing Back to a Cube

If the cube has been write-enabled, and if that cube's aggregations are all of the sum variety, then the user can paste data back to the cube, directly altering the values in cube cells. This allows the analyst to engage in "what-if" scenarios. For example, if the cube has a measure for the state tax rate on liquor sales, you can write-back to that measure postulating that the rate for a given state is raised by two percentage points and see immediately the impact this will have on your bottom line. That kind of information can help you decide whether you will want to stop selling alcohol in that state, raise your retail prices, or fight the proposed tax hike.

Setting Actions in a Cube

Perhaps while you are browsing a cube that has been set up for inventory data, you notice that a regional Foodmart warehouse is running low on some item. If the DBA has made use of the Actions feature, you can select a restocking action directly from the cube, which then starts the ordering process or sends a notification to the appropriate manager.

Combining Cubes

If you have several cubes you would like to look at as if they were one cube, you can ask your DBA to create a virtual cube. This is much like the use of database views to combine various fields from multiple tables. To you, the virtual cube won't appear any different.

Building a Local Cube

Building a local cube requires connecting to an OLAP cube on an Analysis Server. On the PivotTable window, open the PivotTable drop-down. Choose Client-Server Settings, and on that dialog box click the button labeled Create Local Data File. Click Next, choose which dimensions you want to include, click Next, choose which measures you want to include, click Next, choose the name for and where to store the local cube file, and then click Finish.

Next Steps

In Chapter 11, "Enhancing Your Pivot Table Reports with Macros," you will learn how macros can help you enhance your pivot table reports and empower your clients to do their own data analysis.

Enhancing Your Pivot Table Reports with Macros

11

Why Use Macros with Your Pivot Table Reports?

Imagine that you could be in multiple locations at one time, with multiple clients at one time, helping them with their pivot table reports. Suppose you could help multiple clients refresh their data, extract the top 20 records, group by months, or sort by revenue—even all at the same time. The fact is that you can do just that by using Excel macros.

A *macro* is a series of keystrokes that have been recorded and saved. Once saved, the macro can be played back on command. In other words, you can record your actions in a macro, save the macro, and then allow your clients to play back your actions with a touch of a button. It would be as though you were there with them! This functionality is especially useful when distributing pivot table reports.

For example, suppose that you want to give your clients the option of grouping their pivot table report by month, by quarter, or by year. Although the process of grouping can be technically performed by anyone, some of your clients may not have a clue how to do it. In this case, you could record a macro to group by month, a macro to group by quarter, and a macro to group by year. Then you could create three buttons, one for each macro. In the end, your clients, having little experience with pivot tables, will need only to click a button to group their pivot table report.

A major benefit of using macros with your pivot table reports is the power you can give your clients to easily perform pivot table actions that they would not normally be able to perform on their own, thus empowering them to more effectively analyze the data you provide.

Recording Your First Macro

Take a look at the pivot table shown in Figure 11.1. You know that you can refresh this pivot table by right-clicking inside the pivot table and selecting Refresh Data. Now if you were to record your actions with a macro while you refreshed your pivot table, you, or anyone else, could replicate your actions and refresh this pivot table by running the macro.

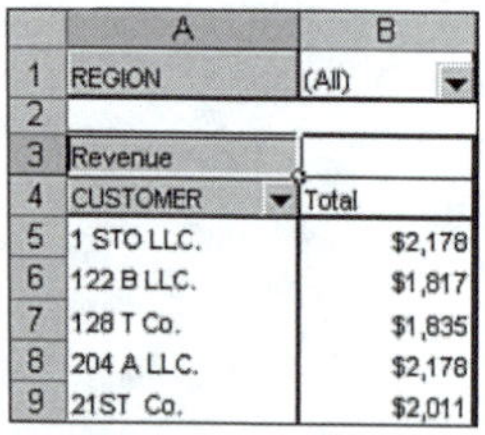

Figure 11.1

Recording your actions while refreshing this pivot table will allow you to simply run a macro the next time you have to refresh.

	A	B
1	REGION	(All) ▼
2		
3	Revenue	
4	CUSTOMER ▼	Total
5	1 STO LLC.	$2,178
6	122 B LLC.	$1,817
7	128 T Co.	$1,835
8	204 A LLC.	$2,178
9	21ST Co.	$2,011

> **NOTE** If you are using Excel 2000 or a later version, your macro security settings may be set to High, effectively disabling all macros. In order to utilize macros, you will have to set your security settings to Medium or Low. Go up to the application menu and select Tools, Macro, Security. It's generally a good rule to set the macro security level to Medium. This will allow macros to run, only after you explicitly enable them when you open Excel.

The first step in recording a macro is to initiate the Record Macro dialog box. Go up to the application menu and select Tools, Macro, Record New Macro.

When the Record Macro dialog box activates, you will fill in a few key pieces of information about the macro:

- **Macro name**—Enter a name for your macro. You should generally enter a name that describes the action being performed.

- **Shortcut key**—You can enter any letter into this input box. That letter becomes part of a set of keys on your keyboard that can be pressed to play back the macro. This is optional.

- **Store macro in**—Specify where you want the macro to be stored. If you are distributing your pivot table report, you will want to select the option This Workbook in order for the macro to be available to your clients.

- **Description**—You can enter a few words that give more detail about the macro.

Because this macro will refresh your pivot table when it is played, you will name your macro RefreshData. You will also assign a shortcut key of R. You will notice that the dialog box, shown in Figure 11.2, gives you a shortcut key of Ctrl+Shift+R. Keep in mind that you will use the shortcut key to play your macro once it is created. Be sure to store the macro in This Workbook. Click OK to continue.

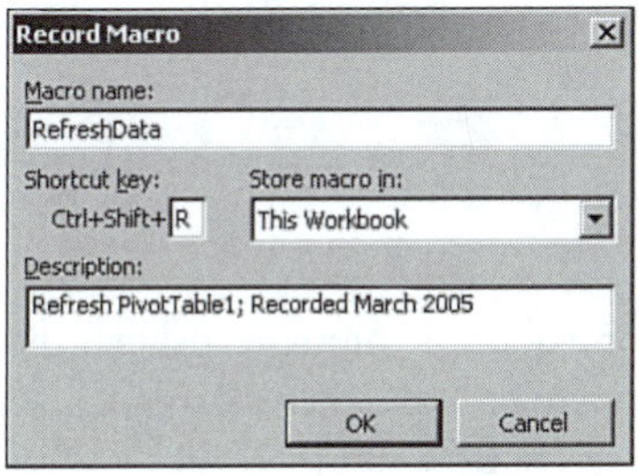

Figure 11.2
Fill in the Record Macro dialog box as shown here.

When you click OK from the Record Macro dialog box, you initiate the recording process. At this point, any action you perform is recorded by Excel. That being the case, you want to record the process of refreshing your pivot table.

Right-click anywhere inside the pivot table and select Refresh Data. After you have refreshed your pivot table, you can stop the recording process by going up to the application menu and selecting Tools, Macro, Stop Recording.

Congratulations! You have just recorded your first macro. You can now play your macro by pressing Ctrl, Shift, and R on your keyboard at the same time.

Creating a User Interface with Form Controls

Making your clients run your macro with shortcut keys, such as Ctrl+Shift+R, can be a satisfactory solution if you have only one macro in your pivot table report. However, suppose you want to allow your clients to perform several macro actions. You will want to give your clients a clear and easy way to run each macro without having to remember a gaggle of shortcut keys. A basic user interface provides the perfect solution. You can think of a user interface as a set of controls such as buttons, scrollbars, and other devices that allow a user to run macros with a simple click of the mouse.

It just so happens that Excel offers a set of controls designed specifically for creating user interfaces directly on a spreadsheet. These controls are called *form controls*. The general idea behind form controls is that you can place one on a spreadsheet and then assign a macro it—meaning a macro you have already recorded. After a macro is assigned to the control, that macro is executed, or played, when the control is clicked. Form controls can be found on the Forms toolbar. To get to the Forms toolbar, go up to the application menu and select View, Toolbars, Forms.

In the example shown in Figure 11.3, you want to allow your clients to refresh the pivot table with a click of a button. In this case, you can assign the RefreshData macro you recorded earlier to a command button from the Forms toolbar.

Figure 11.3

Open the Forms toolbar and select the command button control. Move your cursor onto the spreadsheet and left-click.

After you drop the command button control onto your spreadsheet, the Assign Macro dialog box, shown in Figure 11.4, will open and ask you to assign a macro to this button. Select the macro you want to assign to the button and then click OK.

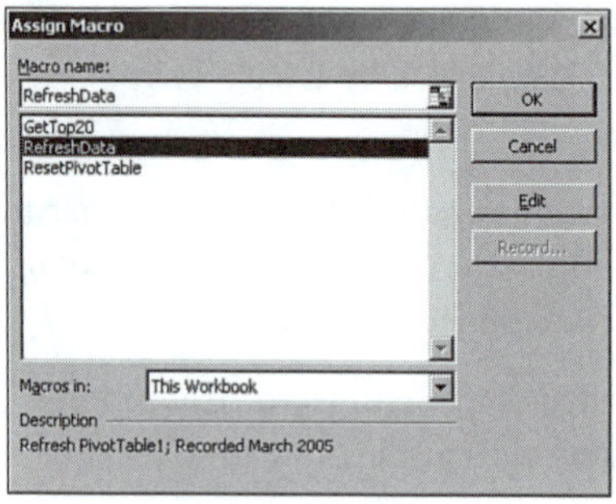

Figure 11.4

Select the macro you want to assign to the button and then click OK. In this case, you want to select RefreshData.

Figure 11.5 shows your Refresh Pivot Table button ready to go. You will also see a couple other buttons to demonstrate that if you have multiple macros in a workbook, you can assign each macro to a different control. Keep in mind that all the controls in the Forms toolbar work in the same way as the command button, in that you assign a macro to run when the control is selected.

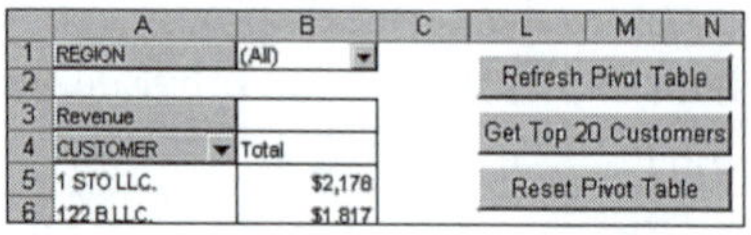

Figure 11.5

If you have multiple macros, you can assign each one to a different form control and then name the controls to distinguish between them.

When you have all the controls you need for your pivot table report, you can format the controls and surrounding spreadsheet to create a basic interface. Figure 11.6 shows your pivot table report after it has been formatted to give your users the feeling of a graphical interface.

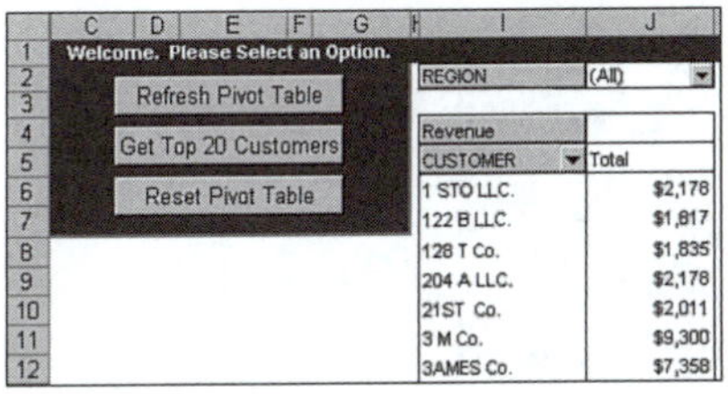

Figure 11.6
You can easily create the feeling of an interface with a handful of macros, a few form controls, and a little formatting.

Recording Macros in Excel 2002 and Later Versions

Be aware that if you distribute a pivot table report with macros that were recorded in Excel 2002 or later, your interface may not work properly for someone using Excel 2000. This is because, after 2000, Microsoft introduced new objects and parameters to Excel VBA that are not recognized by Excel 2000.

For example, if you record a macro to refresh a pivot table in Excel 2003, Excel will generate the following code:

```
ActiveSheet.PivotTables("PivotTable1").PivotCache.Refresh
```

The same macro recorded in Excel 2000, will generate this code:

```
ActiveSheet.PivotTables("PivotTable1").RefreshTable
```

Because the Object and Method combination of `PivotCache.Refresh` does not exist in Excel 2000, the macro generated with Excel 2003 will fail.

There are only three ways around this problem:

- Create your macros using Excel 2000. (Excel 2000 code will run fine in later versions of Excel.)
- Make Excel 2002, or above, a requirement for using your pivot table reports.
- Edit your macros manually to make them compatible with Excel 2000.

Altering a Recorded Macro to Add Functionality

When you record a macro, Excel creates a module that stores the recorded steps of your actions. These recorded steps are actually lines of VBA code that make up your macro. You can add some interesting functionality to your pivot table reports by tweaking your macro's VBA code in order to achieve various effects.

To get a better understanding of how this works, start by creating a new macro that will extract the top five records by customer. Go up to the application menu and select Tools, Macro, Record New Macro. The dialog box shown in Figure 11.7 will be activated.

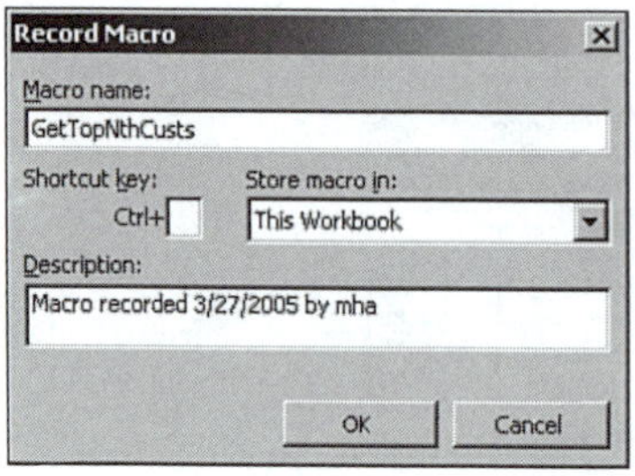

Figure 11.7
Name your new macro "GetTopNthCusts" and specify that you want to store the macro in This Workbook. Click OK to start recording.

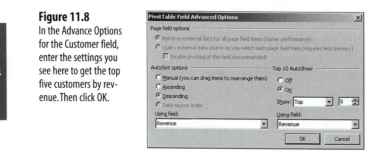

After you have started recording, right-click on the Customer field and select Field Settings. Click the Advanced button and enter the settings you see in Figure 11.8. These settings will give you the top five customers by revenue.

Figure 11.8
In the Advance Options for the Customer field, enter the settings you see here to get the top five customers by revenue. Then click OK.

After successfully recording the steps to extract out the top five customers by revenue, go up to the application menu and select Tools, Macro, Stop Recording.

You now have a macro that, when played, will filter your pivot table to the top five customers by revenue. The plan is to tweak this macro to respond to a scrollbar. That is, you will force the macro to base the number used to filter the pivot table on the number represented by a scrollbar in your user interface. In other words, a user will be able to get the top five, top eight, or top 32, simply by moving a scrollbar up and down.

To get a scrollbar onto your spreadsheet, activate the Forms toolbar, select a scrollbar, and place it onto your spreadsheet. Unlike a command button, the scrollbar control requires some initial setup before you can use it. Right-click on the scrollbar and select Format Control. You will see the Format Object dialog box shown in Figure 11.9.

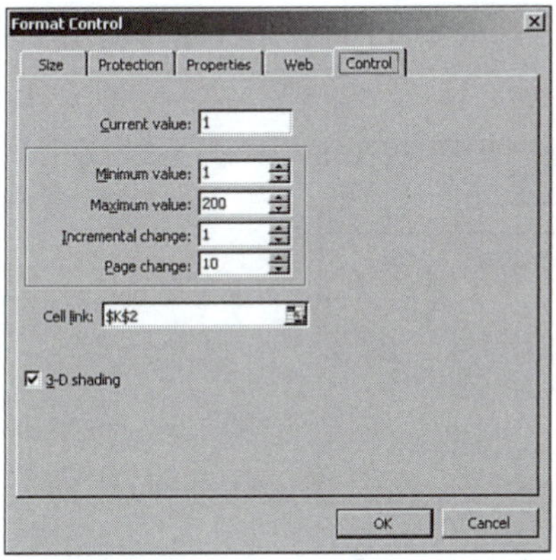

Figure 11.9
After you have placed a scrollbar on your spreadsheet, right-click on the scrollbar and select Format Control.

While you're in the Format Control dialog box, make the following setting changes: Set Minimum Level to 1 so the scrollbar cannot go below 1, set Maximum Level to 200 so the scrollbar cannot go above 200, and set the Cell Link to K2 so that the number represented by the scrollbar will output to cell K2. Click the OK button to apply to your changes.

Next, right-click on your newly formatted scrollbar and select Assign Macro to activate the dialog box shown in Figure 11.10. Assign the GetTopNthCusts macro you just recorded to your scrollbar. This will ensure that this macro will play each time the scrollbar is clicked.

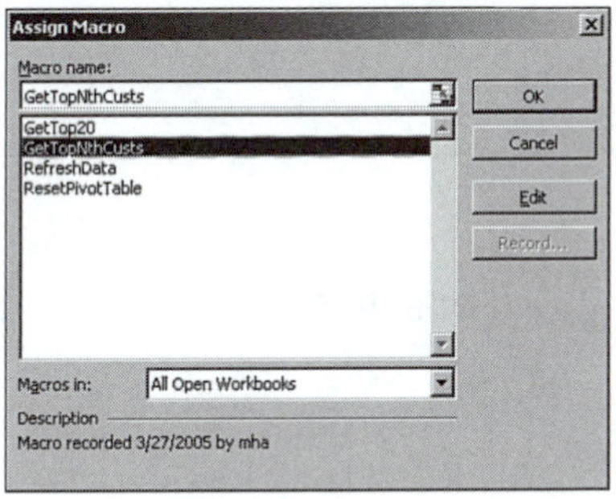

Figure 11.10
Right-click on the scrollbar and select Assign Macro. Select the GetTopNthCusts macro from the list and then click OK.

At this point, test your scrollbar by clicking on it. When you click on your scrollbar, two things should happen: The GetTopNthCusts macro should play, and the number in cell K2 should change to reflect your scrollbar's position. The number in K2 is important because that is the number you are going to use to tie your macro to your scrollbar.

The only thing left to do now is to tweak your macro to respond to the number in cell K2, effectively tying it to your scrollbar. In order to do this, you will have to get to the VBA code that makes up the macro. There are several ways to get you there, but for the purposes of this example, select Tools, Macro, Macros. This will open up the Macro dialog box shown in Figure 11.11, exposing several options. From here, you can run, delete, step into, or edit a selected macro. To get to the VBA code that makes up your macro, select the macro and then click Edit.

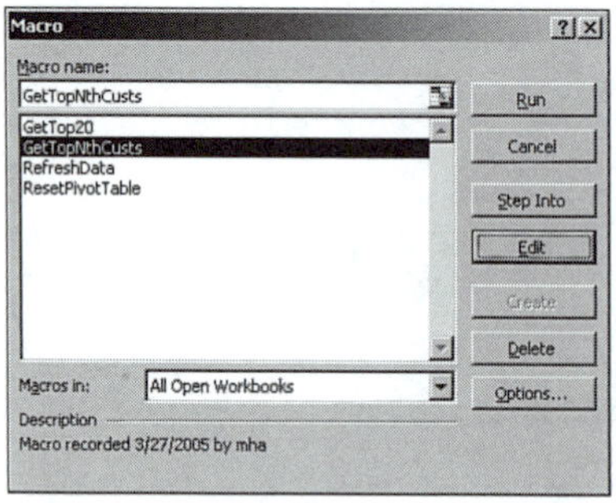

Figure 11.11
To get to the VBA code that makes up the GetTopNthCusts macro, select the macro and then click Edit.

As you can see in Figure 11.12, the Visual Basic Editor will open up with a detailed view of all the VBA code that makes up this macro. Your goal here is to replace the hard-coded number 5, as specified when you originally recorded your macro, with the value in cell K2, which is tied to your scrollbar.

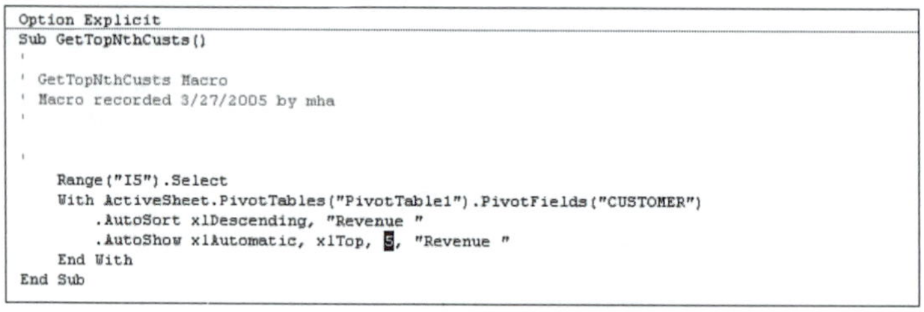

Figure 11.12
You will notice that the number 5 is hard-coded as part of your macro. This is because you originally recorded your macro to filter the top five customers by revenue.

```
Option Explicit
Sub GetTopNthCusts()
'
' GetTopNthCusts Macro
' Macro recorded 3/27/2005 by mha
'

    Range("I5").Select
    With ActiveSheet.PivotTables("PivotTable1").PivotFields("CUSTOMER")
        .AutoSort xlDescending, "Revenue"
        .AutoShow xlAutomatic, xlTop, 5, "Revenue "
    End With
End Sub
```

You will delete the number 5 and replace it with the following:

```
ActiveSheet.Range("K2").Value
```

Your macro's code should look similar to the code shown in Figure 11.13.

Figure 11.13
Simply delete the hard-coded number 5 and replace it with this reference to cell K2:
`ActiveSheet.`
`Range("K2").`
`Value.`

```
Option Explicit
Sub GetTopNthCusts()
'
' GetTopNthCusts Macro
' Macro recorded 3/27/2005 by mha
'

'
    Range("I5").Select
    With ActiveSheet.PivotTables("PivotTable1").PivotFields("CUSTOMER")
        .AutoSort xlDescending, "Revenue "
        .AutoShow xlAutomatic, xlTop, ActiveSheet.Range("K2").Value, "Revenue "
    End With
End Sub
```

Close the Visual Basic Editor to get back to your pivot table report. Test your scrollbar by setting it to 11. Your macro should play and filter out the top 11 customers by revenue, as shown here in Figure 11.14.

Figure 11.14
After a little formatting, you have a clear and easy way for your clients to get the top customers by revenue.

	A	B	C	D	E	F	G	H	I	J	K
1	Welcome. Please Select an Option.										Get Top
2		Refresh Pivot Table				REGION	(All)	▼		▲	11
3											
4		Get Top 20 Customers				Revenue					
5						CUSTOMER	▼ Total				
6		Reset Pivot Table				PENSK Co.	$1,045,375				
7						AUTO Co.	$178,070			▼	
8						MIDAS Co.	$173,920				
9						GOODY Co.	$141,103				
10						DQ CO Co.	$130,202				
11						ANNIS Co.	$119,918				
12						UPS 0 Co.	$116,645				
13						ROADW Co.	$93,510				
14						CITY Co.	$88,761				
15						SOUTH Co.	$85,566				
16						GRA G Co.	$84,338				

11

CASE STUDY

Synchronize Two Pivot Tables with One Combo Box

The pivot table report in Figure 11.15 contains two pivot tables. Each pivot table has a page field for allowing you to select a market. The problem is that every time you select a market from the page field in one pivot table, you have to select the same market from the page field in the other pivot table to ensure you are analyzing the correct Units Sold versus Revenue.

Figure 11.15
With two pivot tables containing page fields that filter out a market, you will have to ensure that you synchronize both pivot tables when analyzing data for a particular market.

	A	B	C	D	E
1					
2	**Revenues**				
3	MARKET	(All) ▼			
4					
5	Revenue	Quarters ▼			
6	LINE OF BUSINESS ▼	Qtr1	Qtr2	Qtr3	Qtr4
7	Copier Sale	19,847,240	21,827,116	22,391,657	22,515,676
8	Parts	20,923,077	20,773,707	20,667,813	21,573,896
9	Printer Sale	16,368,698	16,975,476	17,609,516	17,415,088
10	Service Plan	147,352,010	144,861,312	138,576,497	143,716,260
11					
12	**Equipment Sales**				
13	MARKET	(All) ▼			
14					
15	Units Sold	Quarters ▼			
16	LINE OF BUSINESS ▼	Qtr1	Qtr2	Qtr3	Qtr4
17	Copier Sale	6630	7361	7485	7535
18	Printer Sale	3464	3542	3655	3683

Not only is it a bit of a hassle to have to synchronize both pivot tables every time you want to analyze a new market's data, but there is a chance you, or your clients, may forget to do so.

One way to synchronize these pivot tables is to use a combo box. The idea is to record a macro that selects a market from the Market field of both tables. Then create a combo box and fill it with the market names that exist in your two pivot tables. Finally, alter your macro to filter both pivot tables, using the value from your combo box.

Here are the steps in performing this task:

1. Create a new macro and call it SynchMarkets. When recording starts, select the California market from the Market field in both pivot tables and then stop recording.

2. Activate the Forms toolbar and place a combo box onto your spreadsheet.

3. Create a hard-coded list of all the markets that exist in your pivot table. Note that the first entry in your list is (All). You must include this entry if you want to be able to select all markets with your combo box.

   At this point, your pivot table report should look similar to the one shown in Figure 11.16.

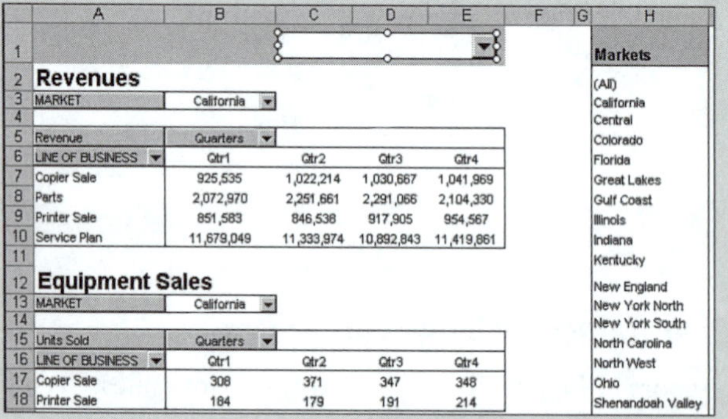

Figure 11.16
You now have all the tools you need—a macro that changes the Market field of both pivot tables, a combo box on your spreadsheet, and a list of all the markets that exist in your pivot table.

4. Right-click on your combo box and select Format Control to perform the initial setup.

First, specify an input range for the list you are using to fill your combo box, as shown in Figure 11.17. In this case, this means the market list you created in step 3. Next, specify a cell link. That is, the cell that will show the index number of the item you select (cell I1 is the cell link in this example). Finally, click OK.

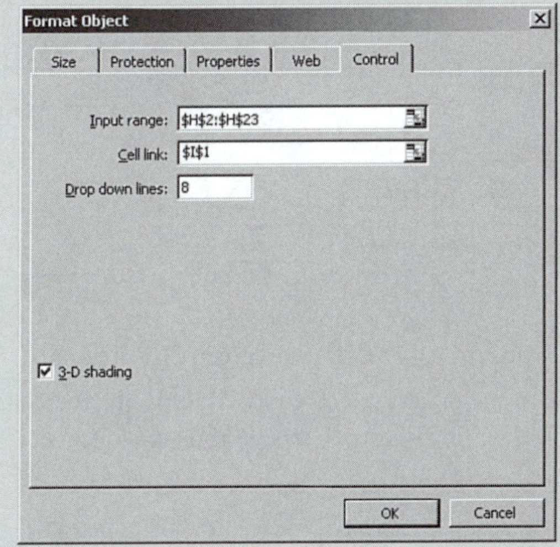

Figure 11.17

The settings for your combo box should reference your market list as the input range and specify a cell link close to your market list. In this case, the cell link is cell I1.

As you can see in Figure 11.18, you should now be able to select a market from your combo box and see the associated index number in cell I1.

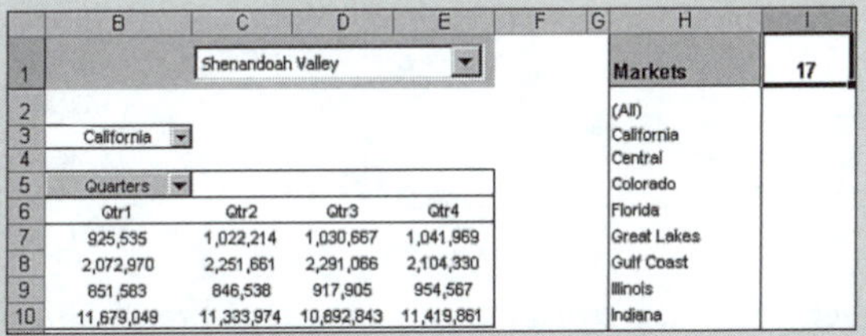

Figure 11.18

Your combo box, now filled with market names, will output an index number in cell I1 when a market is selected.

NOTE The only output of a combo box form control is an index number. In Figure 11.18, the selection of Shenandoah Valley from the combo box resulted in the number 17 in cell I1. This means that Shenandoah Valley was the 17th item in the combo box. In order to make use of this index number, you will have to pass it through the INDEX function. The INDEX function converts an index number to a value that can be recognized.

5. Enter an INDEX function that converts the index number in cell I1 to a value.

An INDEX function requires two arguments in order to work properly. The first argument is the range of the list you are working with. In most cases, you will use the same range that is feeding your combo box. The second argument is the index number. If the index number is in a cell (for example, cell I1 in Figure 11.19), you can simply reference the cell.

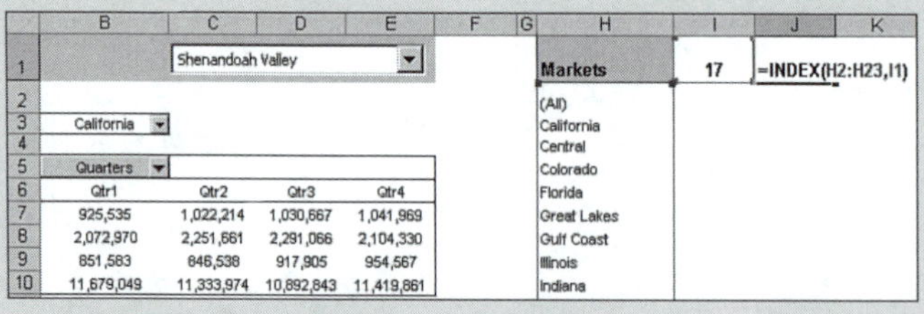

Figure 11.19
The INDEX function in cell J1 will convert the index number in cell I1 to a value. You will eventually use the value in cell J1 to alter your macro.

6. Edit the SynchMarkets macro using the value in cell J1 instead of a hard-coded value.

7. Go up to the application menu and select Tools, Macro, Macros. Select the SynchMarkets macro shown in Figure 11.20 and then click Edit.

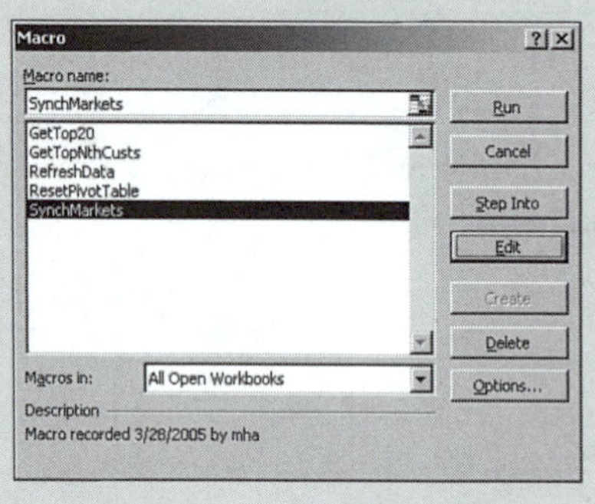

Figure 11.20
To get to the VBA code that makes up your macro, select the SynchMarkets macro and then click Edit.

When you recorded your macro originally, you selected the California market from the Market field in both pivot tables. As you can see in Figure 11.21, the subsequent result is that California is hard-coded in your macro's VBA code.

Figure 11.21
The California market is hard-coded in your macro's VBA code.

```
Sub SynchMarkets()
'
' SynchMarkets Macro
' Macro recorded 3/28/2005 by mha
'

'
ActiveSheet.PivotTables("PivotTable2").PivotFields("MARKET").CurrentPage = _
        "California"

ActiveSheet.PivotTables("PivotTable3").PivotFields("MARKET").CurrentPage = _
        "California"

End Sub
```

8. Replace "California" with ActiveSheet.Range("J1").Value, which references the value in cell J1. At this point, your macro code should look similar to that shown in Figure 11.22. After you have edited the macro, close the Visual Basic Editor to get back to the spreadsheet.

Figure 11.22
Replace "California" with ActiveSheet. Range("J1"). Value and then close the Visual Basic Editor.

```
Sub SynchMarkets()
'
'  SynchMarkets Macro
'  Macro recorded 3/28/2005 by mha
'
'
ActiveSheet.PivotTables("PivotTable2").PivotFields("MARKET").CurrentPage = _
        ActiveSheet.Range("J1").Value

ActiveSheet.PivotTables("PivotTable3").PivotFields("MARKET").CurrentPage = _
        ActiveSheet.Range("J1").Value

End Sub
```

9. All that is left to do is to ensure that the macro will play when you select a market from the combo box. Right-click on the combo box and select Assign Macro. Select the SynchMarkets macro and then click OK.

10. Hide the rows and columns that hold the page fields in your pivot tables, hide the market list you created, and, finally, hide the index formulas.

Figure 11.23 shows your final result. You now have a user-friendly interface that allows your clients to select a market in both pivot tables simply by selecting the market in one combo box.

Figure 11.23
Your pivot table report is ready to use!

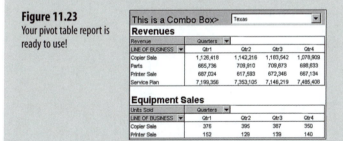

This is a Combo Box>	Texas			▼

Revenues

Revenue	Quarters ▼			
LINE OF BUSINESS ▼	Qtr1	Qtr2	Qtr3	Qtr4
Copier Sale	1,126,418	1,142,216	1,183,542	1,078,909
Parts	665,736	709,910	709,873	698,633
Printer Sale	687,024	617,593	672,346	667,134
Service Plan	7,199,356	7,353,105	7,146,219	7,485,408

Equipment Sales

Units Sold	Quarters ▼			
LINE OF BUSINESS ▼	Qtr1	Qtr2	Qtr3	Qtr4
Copier Sale	376	395	387	350
Printer Sale	152	129	139	140

Next Steps

In Chapter 12, "Using VBA to Create Pivot Tables," you will go beyond recording macros. You will learn how to utilize Visual Basic for Applications to create powerful, behind-the-scenes, processes and calculations using pivot tables.

Using VBA to Create Pivot Tables

Introduction to VBA

Version 5 of Excel introduced a powerful new macro language called Visual Basic for Application (VBA). Every copy of Excel shipped since 1993 has had a copy of the powerful VBA language hiding behind the worksheets.

Enable VBA in Your Copy of Excel

If you are using Excel 2000 or newer, VBA may be disabled. Before you can start using VBA, you need to enable macros on the Security dialog box. From the application menu, choose Tools, Macro, Security. Set the macro security level to medium. This will allow VBA macros to run, but you will have to explicitly enable them when you open Excel.

Visual Basic Editor

From Excel, type Alt+F11 or from the application menu, select Tools, Macro, Visual Basic Editor to open the Visual Basic Editor, as shown in Figure 12.1. The three main sections of the VBA Editor are described here. If this is your first time using VBA, some of these items may be disabled. Follow the instructions given in the following list to make sure that each is enabled:

- **Project Explorer**—This pane displays a hierarchical tree of all open workbooks. Expand the tree to see the worksheets and code modules present in the workbook. If the Project Explorer is not visible, enable it with Ctrl+R.

- **Properties window**—The Properties window is important when you begin to program user forms. It has some use when writing normal code, so enable it with F4.

■ **Code window**—This is the area where you will write your code. Code is stored in one or more code modules attached to your workbook. To add a code module to a workbook, select Insert, Code Module from the application menu.

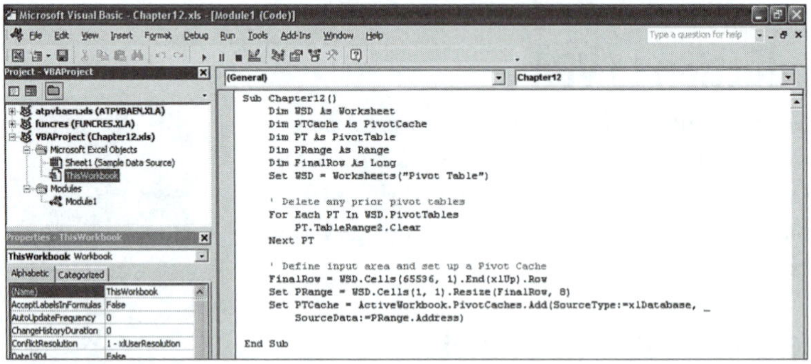

Figure 12.1
The Visual Basic Editor window is lurking behind every copy of Excel shipped since 1993.

Visual Basic Tools

Visual Basic is a powerful development environment. Although this chapter cannot offer a complete course on VBA, if you are new to VBA, you will want to take advantage of these important tools in VBA:

■ As you begin to type code, Excel may offer a drop-down with valid choices. This feature, known as AutoComplete, allows you to type code faster and eliminate typing mistakes.

■ For assistance on any keyword, put the cursor in the keyword and press the F1 key. You might need your installation CDs because the VBA help file is not in the default install.

■ Excel checks each line of code as you finish it. Lines in error will appear in red. Comments will appear in green. You can add a comment by typing a single apostrophe. Use lots of comments so you can remember what each section of code is doing.

■ Despite the aforementioned error checking, Excel may still encounter an error at runtime. If this happens, click the Debug button. The line that caused the error will be highlighted in yellow. Hover your cursor over any variable to see the current value of the variable.

■ When you are in Debug mode, use the Debug menu to step line by line through code. You can toggle back and forth between Excel and VBA to see the effect of running a line of code on the worksheet.

■ Other great debugging tools are breakpoints, the Watch window, the Object Browser, and the Immediate window. Read about these in the Excel help menu.

The Macro Recorder

Excel offers a macro recorder that is about 90% perfect. Unfortunately, the last 10% is frustrating. Code that you record to work with one dataset will be hard-coded to work only with that dataset. This might work fine if your transactional database occupies cells A1:K41550 every single day, but if you are pulling in a new invoice register every day, it is unlikely that you will have the same number of rows each day. Given that you might need to work with other data, it would be a lot better if Excel could record selecting cells using the End key. This is one of the shortcomings of the macro recorder.

In reality, Excel pros will use the macro recorder to record code, but then expect to have to clean up the recorded code.

Understanding Object-Oriented Code

If you took a class in BASIC a long time ago, the recorded code in VBA is going to appear rather foreign to you. Whereas BASIC is a procedural language, VBA is an object-oriented language. Most lines of VBA code follow the Noun.Verb syntax. Except, in VBA, it is called Object.Method. Objects can be workbooks, worksheets, cells, or ranges of cells. Methods can be typical Excel actions, such as `.Copy`, `.Paste`, `.PasteSpecial`. Many methods allow adverbs—parameters you use to specify how to perform the method. If you see a construct with a colon/equal sign, you know that the macro recorder is describing how the method should work. The final type of code that you might see is where you assign a value to the adjectives of an object. In VBA, adjectives are called *properties*. If you set `ActiveCell.Font.ColorIndex = 3`, you are setting the font color of the active cell to red. Note that when you are dealing with properties, there is only an equal sign, not a colon/equal sign.

Tricks of the Trade

You need to master a few simple techniques in order to write efficient VBA code. These techniques will help you make the jump to writing effective code.

Write Code to Handle Any Size Data Range

The macro recorder will hard-code that your data is in a range, such as A1:K41550. Although this will work for today's dataset, it may not work as you get new datasets. Write code that can deal with different size datasets.

The macro recorder will use syntax such as `Range("H12")` to refer to a cell. However, it is more flexible to use `Cells(12, 8)` to refer to the cell in row 12, column 8. Similarly, the macro recorder will refer to a rectangular range as `Range("A1:K41550")`. However, it is more flexible to use the `Cells` syntax to refer to the upper-left corner of the range and then use the `Resize()` syntax to refer to the number of rows and columns in the range. The equivalent way to describe the preceding range is `Cells(1, 1).Resize(41550,11)`.

This is more flexible because you can replace any of the numbers with a variable.

In the Excel user interface, you can use the End key on the keyboard to jump to the end of a range of data. If you move the cellpointer to the final row on the worksheet and press the End key followed by the up-arrow key, the cell pointer will jump to the last row with data. The equivalent of doing this in VBA is to use the following code:

```
Range("A65536").End(xlUp).Select
```

You don't need to select this cell—you just need to find the row number that contains the last row. The following code will locate this row and save the row number to a variable named FinalRow:

```
FinalRow = Range("A65536").End(xlUp).Row
```

There is nothing magic about the variable name FinalRow. You could call this variable something such as x or y, or even your dog's name. However, because VBA allows you to use meaningful variable names, you should use something such as FinalRow to describe the final row.

> **NOTE**
>
> Excel has offered 65,536 rows for eight years and 256 columns for 20 years. Some predict that Microsoft will finally offer more rows and columns in Excel 2006. To make your code flexible enough to handle newer versions of Excel, you can use Application.Rows.Count to learn the total number of rows in this version of Excel. The preceding code could then be generalized like so:
>
> ```
> FinalRow = Cells(Application.Rows.Count, 1).End(xlUp).Row
> ```

It is also possible to find the final column in a dataset. If you are relatively sure that the dataset will begin in row 1, you can use the End key in combination with the left-arrow key to jump from IV1 to the last column with data. To generalize for the possibility that Excel 2006 includes more columns, you can use the following code:

```
FinalCol = Cells(1, Application.Columns.Count).End(xlToLeft).Column
```

End+Down Versus End+Up

You might be tempted to find the final row by starting in cell A1 and using the End key in conjunction with the down-arrow key. Avoid this. Data coming from another system is imperfect. If your program will import 50,000 rows from a legacy computer system every day for the next five years, a day will come when someone manages to key a null value into the dataset. This will cause a blank cell or even a blank row to appear in the middle of your dataset. Using Range("A1").End(xlDown) will stop prematurely at the blank cell instead of including all your data. This blank cell will cause that day's report to miss thousands of rows of data, a potential disaster that will call into question the credibility of your report. Take the extra step of starting at the last row in the worksheet in order to greatly reduce the risk of problems.

Use Super-Variables—Object Variables

In typical programming languages, a variable holds a single value. You might use x = 4 to assign a value of 4 to the variable x.

Think about a single cell in Excel. There are many properties that describe a cell. A cell might contain a value such as 4, but the cell also has a font size, font color, a row, a column, possibly a formula, possibly a comment, a list of precedents, and more. It is possible in VBA to create a super-variable that contains all the information about a cell or about any object. A statement to create a typical variable such as x = Range("A1") will assign the current value of A1 to the variable x. However, use the Set keyword to create an object variable:

```
Set x = Range("A1")
```

You've now created a super-variable that contains all the properties of the cell. Instead of having a variable with only one value, you have a variable where you can access the value of many properties associated with the variable. You can reference x.Formula to learn the formula in A1, or x.Font.ColorIndex to learn the color of the cell.

Versions

Pivot tables have been evolving. They were introduced in Excel 5 and perfected in Excel 97. In Excel 2000, pivot table creation in VBA was dramatically altered. Some new parameters were added in Excel 2002. Therefore, you need to be extremely careful when writing code in Excel 2003 that might be run in Excel 2000 or Excel 97.

Just a few simple tweaks make 2003 code run in 2000, but a major overhaul is required to make 2003 code run in Excel 97. Because it has been eight years since the release of Excel 97 (and because Microsoft has not supported that product for 3+ years), this chapter will focus on using only the pivot cache method introduced in Excel 2000. At the end of the chapter, you will briefly learn the PivotTable Wizard method, which is your only option if you need code to run in Excel 97.

Build a Pivot Table in Excel VBA

Keep in mind that this chapter is not meant to imply that you use VBA to build pivot tables to give to your users! Rather, its purpose is to remind you that pivot tables can be used as a means to an end; you can use a pivot table to extract a summary of data and then use that summary elsewhere.

> **TIP**
> The code listings from this chapter are available for download at http://www.MrExcel.com/pivotbookdata.html.

In Excel 2000 and newer, you first build a pivot cache object to describe the input area of the data:

```
Dim WSD As Worksheet
Dim PTCache As PivotCache
Dim PT As PivotTable
Dim PRange As Range
Dim FinalRow As Long
Dim FinalCol As Long
Set WSD = Worksheets("PivotTable")

' Delete any prior pivot tables
For Each PT In WSD.PivotTables
    PT.TableRange2.Clear
Next PT

' Define input area and set up a Pivot Cache
FinalRow = WSD.Cells(Application.Rows.Count, 1).End(xlUp).Row
FinalCol = WSD.Cells(1, Application.Columns.Count).End(xlToLeft).Column
Set PRange = WSD.Cells(1, 1).Resize(FinalRow, FinalCol)
Set PTCache = ActiveWorkbook.PivotCaches.Add(SourceType:=xlDatabase, _
    SourceData:=PRange)
```

After the pivot cache is defined, use the `CreatePivotTable` method to create a blank pivot table based on the defined pivot cache:

```
Set PT = PTCache.CreatePivotTable(TableDestination:=WSD.Cells(2, FinalCol + 2), _
    TableName:="PivotTable1")
```

In the `CreatePivotTable` method, you specify the output location and optionally give the table a name. After running this line of code, you have a strange-looking blank pivot table, like the one shown in Figure 12.2.

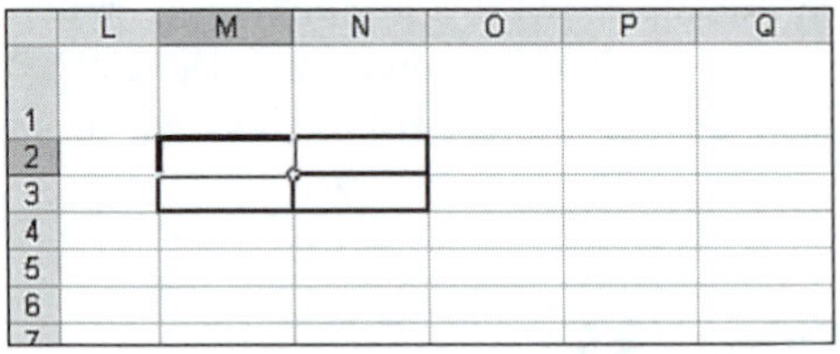

Figure 12.2
Immediately after you use the `CreatePivotTable` method, Excel gives you a four-cell blank pivot table that is not very useful. You now have to use code to drop fields onto the table.

If you are using the Layout dialog box in the user interface to build the pivot table, Excel does not recalculate the pivot table after you drop each field onto the table. By default in VBA, Excel calculates the pivot table as you execute each step of building the table. This could require the pivot table to be executed a half-dozen times before you get to the final result. To speed up your code execution, you can temporarily turn off calculation of the pivot table by using the `ManualUpdate` property:

```
PT.ManualUpdate = True
```

You can now run through the steps needed to lay out the pivot table. In the `.AddFields` method, you can specify one or more fields that should be in the row, column, or page area of the pivot table:

```
' Set up the row & column fields
PT.AddFields RowFields:=Array("Line of Business", "Model"), _
    ColumnFields:="Region"
```

To add a field such as Revenue to the data area of the table, you change the `Orientation` property of the field to be `xlDataField`.

Getting a Sum Instead of a Count

Excel is smart. When you build a report with revenue, it assumes you want to sum the revenue. But, there is a problem. Say that one of the revenue cells is accidentally blank. When you build the pivot table, even though 99.9% of fields are numeric, Excel assumes you have alphanumeric data and offers to count this field. This is annoying. It seems to be an anomaly that on one hand, you are expected to make sure that 100% of your cells have numeric data, but on the other hand, the results of the pivot table are often filled with non-numeric blank cells.

When you build the pivot table in the Excel interface, you should take care in the Layout dialog box to notice that the field reads Count of Revenue instead of Sum of Revenue. At that point, the right thing is to go back and fix the data, but what people usually do is double-click the Count of Revenue button and change it to Sum of Revenue.

In VBA, you should always explicitly define that you are creating a sum of revenue by explicitly setting the `Function` property to `xlSum`:

```
' Set up the data fields
With PT.PivotFields("Revenue")
    .Orientation = xlDataField
    .Function = xlSum
    .Position = 1
End With
```

At this point, you've given VBA all the settings required to correctly generate the pivot table. If you set `ManualUpdate` to `False`, Excel calculates and draws the pivot table. You can immediately thereafter set this back to `True`:

```
' Calc the pivot table
PT.ManualUpdate = False
PT.ManualUpdate = True
```

12

At this point, you will have a complete pivot table like the one shown in Figure 12.3.

Figure 12.3

Less than 50 lines of code create this pivot table in under a second.

	M	N	O	P	Q	R
2	Sum of REVENUE		REGION			
3	LINE OF BUSINESS	MODEL	West	North	South	Grand Total
4	Copier Sale	2500C	23976601	25893618	36711470	86581689
5	Copier Sale Total		23976601	25893618	36711470	86581689
6	Parts	3002C	5674090	4155214	5334767	15164071
7		3002P	9826610	15525824	14960290	40312724
8		4055T	3841454	4157167	4778067	12776688
9		5001C	2996689	3772983	4477480	11247152
10		5001P	1331210	1451983	1654665	4437858
11	Parts Total		23670053	29063171	31205269	83938493
12	Printer Sale	2500P	19594197	20621317	28153264	68368778
13	Printer Sale Total		19594197	20621317	28153264	68368778
14	Service Plan	3002C	16855085	22435572	27317650	66608307
15		3002P	55532410	90867809	98282491	244682710
16		4500C	46967756	64532173	76674818	188174747
17		4500P	1249362	8707258	7562089	17518709
18		5001C	4623183	2670363	2538423	9831969
19		5001P	24113465	12201336	11374836	47689637
20	Service Plan Total		149341261	201414511	223750307	574506079
21	Grand Total		216582112	276992617	319820310	813395039

Here is the complete code used to generate the pivot table:

```
Sub CreatePivot()
    Dim WSD As Worksheet
    Dim PTCache As PivotCache
    Dim PT As PivotTable
    Dim PRange As Range
    Dim FinalRow As Long
    Dim FinalCol As Long
    Set WSD = Worksheets("PivotTable")

    ' Delete any prior pivot tables
    For Each PT In WSD.PivotTables
        PT.TableRange2.Clear
    Next PT

    ' Define input area and set up a Pivot Cache
    FinalRow = WSD.Cells(Application.Rows.Count, 1).End(xlUp).Row
    FinalCol = WSD.Cells(1, Application.Columns.Count). _
        End(xlToLeft).Column
    Set PRange = WSD.Cells(1, 1).Resize(FinalRow, FinalCol)
    Set PTCache = ActiveWorkbook.PivotCaches.Add(SourceType:= _
        xlDatabase, SourceData:=PRange)

    ' Create the Pivot Table from the Pivot Cache
    Set PT = PTCache.CreatePivotTable(TableDestination:=WSD. _
        Cells(2, FinalCol + 2), TableName:="PivotTable1")

    ' Turn off updating while building the table
    PT.ManualUpdate = True

    ' Set up the row & column fields
    PT.AddFields RowFields:=Array("Line of Business", "Model"), _
        ColumnFields:="Region"

    ' Set up the data fields
    With PT.PivotFields("Revenue")
        .Orientation = xlDataField
```

```
        .Function = xlSum
        .Position = 1
    End With

    ' Calc the pivot table
    PT.ManualUpdate = False
    PT.ManualUpdate = True

End Sub
```

Cannot Move or Change Part of a Pivot Report

Although pivot tables are incredible, they have annoying limitations. You cannot move or change just a part of a pivot table. For example, try to run a macro that would delete column R, which contains the Grand Total column of the pivot table. The macro comes to a screeching halt with an error 1004, as shown in Figure 12.4.

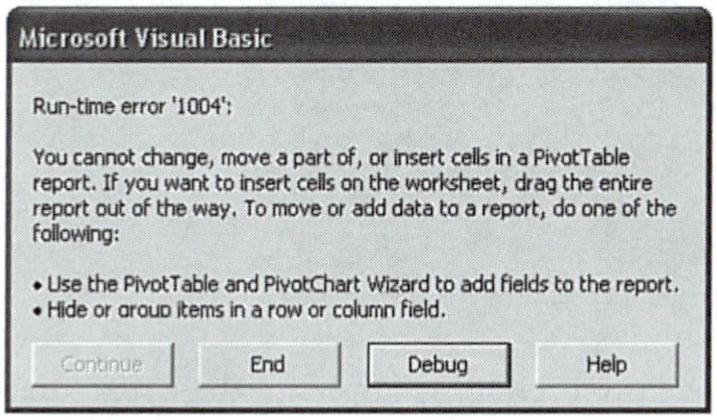

Figure 12.4
You cannot delete just a part of a pivot table. To get around this limitation, you can change the summary from a pivot table to just values.

Size of a Finished Pivot Table

It is difficult to know the size of a pivot table in advance. If you run a report of transactional data on one day, you may or may not have sales from the West region, for example. This could cause your table to be either five or six columns wide. Therefore, you should use the special property TableRange2 to refer to the entire resultant pivot table.

Because of the limitations of pivot tables, you should generally copy the results of a pivot table to a new location on the worksheet and then delete the original pivot table. The code in CreateSummaryReportUsingPivot() creates a small pivot table. Note that you can set the ColumnGrand and RowGrand properties of the table to False to prevent the totals from being added to the table.

PT.TableRange2 includes the entire pivot table. In this case, this includes the extra row at the top with the button Sum of Revenue. To eliminate that row, the code copies PT.TableRange2, but offsets this selection by one row by using .Offset(1, 0). Depending on the nature of your pivot table, you might need to use an offset of two or more rows to get rid of extraneous information at the top of the pivot table.

12

The code copies `PT.TableRange2` and does a `PasteSpecial` to a cell three rows below the current pivot table. At that point in the code, your worksheet appears as shown in Figure 12.5. The table in M2 is a live pivot table, and the table in M16 is just the copied results.

Figure 12.5
An intermediate result of the macro. Only the summary in M16:P25 will remain after the macro finishes.

	M	N	O	P
2	Sum of REVENUE	REGION		
3	MODEL	West	North	South
4	2500C	23976601	25893618	36711470
5	2500P	19594197	20621317	28153264
6	3002C	22529175	26590786	32652417
7	3002P	65359020	106393633	113242781
8	4055T	3841454	4157167	4778067
9	4500C	46967756	64532173	76674818
10	4500P	1249362	8707258	7562089
11	5001C	7619872	6443346	7015903
12	5001P	25444675	13653319	13029501
13				
14				
15				
16	MODEL	West	North	South
17	2500C	23976601	25893618	36711470
18	2500P	19594197	20621317	28153264
19	3002C	22529175	26590786	32652417
20	3002P	65359020	106393633	113242781
21	4055T	3841454	4157167	4778067
22	4500C	46967756	64532173	76674818
23	4500P	1249362	8707258	7562089
24	5001C	7619872	6443346	7015903
25	5001P	25444675	13653319	13029501
26				

You can then totally eliminate the pivot table by applying the `Clear` method to the entire table. If your code is then going on to do additional formatting, you should remove the pivot cache from memory by setting `PTCache` equal to `Nothing`:

```
Sub CreateSummaryReportUsingPivot()
    ' Use a Pivot Table to create a static summary report
    ' with model going down the rows and regions across
    Dim WSD As Worksheet
    Dim PTCache As PivotCache
    Dim PT As PivotTable
    Dim PRange As Range
    Dim FinalRow As Long
    Dim FinalCol As Long
    Set WSD = Worksheets("PivotTable")

    ' Delete any prior pivot tables
    For Each PT In WSD.PivotTables
        PT.TableRange2.Clear
    Next PT

    ' Define input area and set up a Pivot Cache
    FinalRow = WSD.Cells(Application.Rows.Count, 1).End(xlUp).Row
    FinalCol = WSD.Cells(1, Application.Columns.Count). _
        End(xlToLeft).Column
```

```vba
    Set PRange = WSD.Cells(1, 1).Resize(FinalRow, FinalCol)
    Set PTCache = ActiveWorkbook.PivotCaches.Add(SourceType:= _
        xlDatabase, SourceData:=PRange)

    ' Create the Pivot Table from the Pivot Cache
    Set PT = PTCache.CreatePivotTable(TableDestination:=WSD. _
        Cells(2, FinalCol + 2), TableName:="PivotTable1")

    ' Turn off updating while building the table
    PT.ManualUpdate = True

    ' Set up the row fields
    PT.AddFields RowFields:="Model", ColumnFields:="Region"

    ' Set up the data fields
    With PT.PivotFields("Revenue")
        .Orientation = xlDataField
        .Function = xlSum
        .Position = 1
    End With

    With PT
        .ColumnGrand = False
        .RowGrand = False
        .NullString = "0"
    End With

    ' Calc the pivot table
    PT.ManualUpdate = False
    PT.ManualUpdate = True

    ' PT.TableRange2 contains the results. Move these to J10
    ' as just values and not a real pivot table.
    PT.TableRange2.Offset(1, 0).Copy
    WSD.Cells(5 + PT.TableRange2.Rows.Count, FinalCol + 2). _
        PasteSpecial xlPasteValues

    ' At this point, the worksheet looks like Figure 12.5

    ' Delete the original Pivot Table & the Pivot Cache
    PT.TableRange2.Clear
    Set PTCache = Nothing
End Sub
```

The preceding code will create the pivot table. It then copies the results as values and pastes them as values in M16:P25. Figure 12.5 shows an intermediate result just before the original pivot table is cleared.

So far, you've walked through building the simplest of pivot table reports. Pivot tables offer far more flexibility. Read on for more complex reporting examples.

Revenue by Model for a Product Line Manager

A typical report might provide a list of models with revenue by year. This report could be given to product line managers to show them which models are selling well. In this example, you want to show the models in descending order by revenue with years going across the columns. A sample report is shown in Figure 12.6.

Figure 12.6

A typical request is to take transactional data and produce a summary by model for product line managers. You can use a pivot table to get 90% of this report, and then a little formatting to finish it.

	A	B	C	D	E
1	Revenue by Market and Year				
2					
3	LINE OF BUSINESS	MARKET	2006	2007	Grand Total
4	Copier Sale	California	1,946K	2,075K	4,020K
5	Copier Sale	Central US	1,766K	1,741K	3,507K
6	Copier Sale	Colorado	1,274K	1,840K	3,114K
7	Copier Sale	Florida	1,727K	2,057K	3,784K
8	Copier Sale	Great Lakes	886K	1,043K	1,930K
9	Copier Sale	Gulf Coast	2,921K	2,910K	5,831K
10	Copier Sale	Illinois	1,503K	1,486K	2,990K
11	Copier Sale	Indiana	1,748K	1,869K	3,617K
12	Copier Sale	Kentucky	2,564K	3,308K	5,872K
13	Copier Sale	New England		3,176K	3,176K
14	Copier Sale	New York North	1,761K	2,172K	3,933K
15	Copier Sale	New York South	743K	899K	1,642K
16	Copier Sale	North Carolina	1,514K	2,249K	3,763K
17	Copier Sale	North West	1,444K	1,735K	3,179K
18	Copier Sale	Ohio	3,892K	1,326K	5,217K
19	Copier Sale	Shenandoah Valley	1,994K	2,251K	4,245K
20	Copier Sale	South Carolina	2,657K	3,095K	5,751K
21	Copier Sale	Southwest	2,175K	2,357K	4,532K
22	Copier Sale	Tennessee	2,968K	3,356K	6,324K
23	Copier Sale	Texas	2,193K	2,338K	4,531K
24	Copier Sale	Topeka	2,657K	2,968K	5,625K
25	Copier Sale Total		40,332K	46,250K	86,582K

The key to producing this data quickly is to use a pivot table. Although pivot tables are incredible for summarizing data, they are quirky and their presentation is downright ugly. The final result is rarely formatted in a manner that is acceptable to line managers. There is not a good way to insert page breaks between each product in the pivot table.

To create this report, start with a pivot table that has Line of Business and Market as row fields, In Balance Date grouped by year as a column field, and Sum of Revenue as the data field. Figure 12.7 shows the default pivot table created with these settings.

Here are just a few of the annoyances that most pivot tables present in their default state:

■ The Outline view is horrible. In Figure 12.7, the value "Copier Sale" appears in the product column only once and is followed by 20 blank cells. This is the worst feature of pivot tables, and there is absolutely no way to correct it. Although humans can understand that this entire section is for product copier sales, it is radically confusing if your Copier section spills to a second or third page. Page 2 starts without any indication that the report is for copier sales. If you intend to repurpose the data, you need the Copier Sales value to be on every row.

Figure 12.7
Use the power of the pivot table to get the summarized data, but then use your own common sense in formatting the report.

	M	N	O	P	Q
2	Sum of REVENUE		IN BALANCE DATE ▼		
3	LINE OF BUSINESS ▼	MARKET ▼	2006	2007	Grand Total
4	Copier Sale	California	1945645	2074740	4020385
5		Central US	1765979	1740738	3506717
6		Colorado	1273808	1839783	3113591
7		Florida	1726585	2057032	3783617
8		Great Lakes	886356	1043161	1929517
9		Gulf Coast	2920984	2909904	5830888
10		Illinois	1503380	1486388	2989768
11		Indiana	1747801	1868886	3616687
12		Kentucky	2564272	3308158	5872430
13		New England		3175850	3175850
14		New York North	1760975	2171906	3932881
15		New York South	742995	898975	1641970
16		North Carolina	1513984	2249174	3763158
17		North West	1443962	1735179	3179141
18		Ohio	3891500	1325633	5217133
19		Shenandoah Valley	1994123	2250647	4244770
20		South Carolina	2656626	3094871	5751497
21		Southwest	2174879	2357268	4532147
22		Tennessee	2968320	3355517	6323837
23		Texas	2192673	2338412	4531085
24		Topeka	2657004	2967616	5624620
25	Copier Sale Total		40331851	46249838	86581689
26	Parts	California	4535393	4184634	8720027

■ The report contains blank cells instead of zeroes. In Figure 12.7, customer New England had no copier sales in 2006. Excel produces a pivot table where cell O13 is blank instead of zero. This is simply bad form. Excel experts rely on being able to "ride the range," using the End and arrow keys. Blank cells ruin this ability.

■ The title is boring. Most people would agree that "Sum of Revenue" is an annoying title.

■ Some captions are extraneous. The words "In Balance Date" floating in cell O2 of Figure 12.7 really does not belong in a report.

■ The default alphabetical sort order is rarely useful. Product line managers are going to want the top markets at the top of the list. It would be helpful to have the report sorted in descending order by revenue.

■ The borders are ugly. Excel draws in a myriad of borders that really make the report look awful.

■ The default number format is General. It would be better to set this up as data with commas to serve as thousands of separators, or perhaps even data in thousands or millions.

12

- Pivot tables offer no intelligent page break logic. If you want to be able to produce one report for each line of business manager, there is no fast method for indicating that each product should be on a new page.

- Because of the page break problem, you may find it is easier to do away with the pivot table's subtotal rows and have the Subtotal method add subtotal rows with page breaks. You need a way to turn off the pivot table subtotal rows offered for Line of Business in Figure 12.7. These show up automatically whenever you have two or more row fields. If you would happen to have four row fields, you would want to turn off the automatic subtotals for the three outermost row fields.

Even with all these problems in default pivot tables, they are still the way to go. Each complaint can be overcome, either by using special settings within the pivot table or by entering a few lines of code after the pivot table is created and then copied to a regular dataset.

Eliminate Blank Cells in the Data Area

People started complaining about the blank cells immediately when pivot tables were first introduced. Anyone using Excel 97 or later can easily replace blank cells with zeroes. In the user interface, the setting can be found in the PivotTable Options dialog box. Choose the For Empty Cells, Show option and type **0** in the box.

The equivalent operation in VBA is to set the NullString property for the pivot table to "0".

> **NOTE**
> Although the proper code is to set this value to a text zero, Excel actually puts a real zero in the empty cells.

Control the Sort Order with AutoSort

The Excel user interface offers an AutoSort option that enables you to show markets in descending order based on revenue. The equivalent code in VBA to sort the customer field by descending revenue uses the AutoSort method:

```
PT.PivotFields("Line of Business").AutoSort Order:=xlDescending, _
    Field:="Sum of Revenue"
```

Default Number Format

To change the number format in the user interface, double-click the Sum of Revenue title, click the Number button, and set an appropriate number format.

When you have large numbers, it helps to have the thousands separator displayed. To set this up in VBA code, use the following:

```
PT.PivotFields("Sum of Revenue").NumberFormat = "#,##0"
```

Some companies often have customers who typically buy thousands or millions of dollars of goods. You can display numbers in thousands by using a single comma after the number format. Of course, you will want to include a "K" abbreviation to indicate that the numbers are in thousands:

```
PT.PivotFields("Sum of Revenue").NumberFormat = "#,##0,K"
```

Of course, local custom dictates the thousands abbreviation. If you are working for a relatively young computer company where everyone uses "K" for the thousands separator, you're in luck because Microsoft makes it easy to use the K abbreviation. However, if you work at a 100+ year-old soap company where you use "M" for thousands and "MM" for millions, you have a few more hurdles to jump. You are required to prefix the M character with a backslash to have it work:

```
PT.PivotFields("Sum of Revenue").NumberFormat = "#,##0,\M"
```

Alternatively, you can surround the M character with a double quote. To put a double quote inside a quoted string in VBA, you must put two sequential quotes. To set up a format in tenths of millions that uses the `#,##0.0,,"MM"` format, you would use this line of code:

```
PT.PivotFields("Sum of Revenue").NumberFormat = "#,##0.0,,""M"""
```

In case it is hard to read, the format is quote, pound, comma, pound, pound, zero, period, zero, comma, comma, quote, quote, M, quote, quote, quote. The three quotes at the end are correct. Use two quotes to simulate typing one quote in the custom number format box and a final quote to close the string in VBA.

Suppress Subtotals for Multiple Row Fields

As soon as you have more than one row field, Excel automatically adds subtotals for all but the innermost row field. However, you may want to suppress subtotals for any number of reasons. Although this may be a relatively simple task to accomplish manually, the VBA code to suppress subtotals is surprisingly complex.

You must set the `Subtotals` property equal to an array of 12 `False` values. Read the VBA help for all the gory details, but it goes something like this: The first `False` turns off automatic subtotals, the second `False` turns off the Sum subtotal, the third `False` turns off the Count subtotal, and so on. It is interesting that you have to turn off all 12 possible subtotals, even though Excel displays only one subtotal. This line of code suppresses the Product subtotal:

```
PT.PivotFields("Line of Business").Subtotals = Array(False, False, False, False, _
    False, False, False, False, False, False, False, False)
```

A different technique is to turn on the first subtotal. This will automatically turn off the other 11 subtotals. You can then turn off the first subtotal to make sure that all subtotals are suppressed:

```
PT.PivotFields("Line of Business").Subtotals(1) = True
PT.PivotFields("Line of Business").Subtotals(1) = False
```

12

Suppress Grand Total for Rows

Because you are going to be using VBA code to add automatic subtotals, you can get rid of the Grand Total row. If you turn off Grand Total for Rows, you delete the column called Grand Total. Thus, to get rid of the Grand Total row, you must uncheck Grand Total for Columns. This is handled in the code with the following line:

```
PT.ColumnGrand = False
```

Handle Additional Annoyances

You've reached the end of the adjustments that you can make to the pivot table. To achieve the final report, you have to make the remaining adjustments after converting the pivot table to regular data.

Figure 12.8 shows the pivot table with all the adjustments described in the previous sections made and with `PT.TableRange2` selected.

Figure 12.8

It took less than one second and 30 lines of code to get 90% of the way to the final report. To solve the last five annoying problems, you have to change this data from a pivot table to regular data.

	M	N	O	P	Q
2	Sum of REVENUE		IN BALANCE DATE ▾		
3	LINE OF BUSINESS ▾	MARKET ▾	2006	2007	Grand Total
4	Copier Sale	California	1,946K	2,075K	4,020K
5		Central US	1,766K	1,741K	3,507K
6		Colorado	1,274K	1,840K	3,114K
7		Florida	1,727K	2,057K	3,784K
8		Great Lakes	886K	1,043K	1,930K
9		Gulf Coast	2,921K	2,910K	5,831K
10		Illinois	1,503K	1,486K	2,990K
11		Indiana	1,748K	1,869K	3,617K
12		Kentucky	2,564K	3,308K	5,872K
13		New England		3,176K	3,176K
14		New York North	1,761K	2,172K	3,933K
15		New York South	743K	899K	1,642K
16		North Carolina	1,514K	2,249K	3,763K
17		North West	1,444K	1,735K	3,179K
18		Ohio	3,892K	1,326K	5,217K
19		Shenandoah Valley	1,994K	2,251K	4,245K
20		South Carolina	2,657K	3,095K	5,751K
21		Southwest	2,175K	2,357K	4,532K
22		Tennessee	2,968K	3,356K	6,324K
23		Texas	2,193K	2,338K	4,531K
24		Topeka	2,657K	2,968K	5,625K
25	Parts	California	4,535K	4,185K	8,720K
26		Central US	1,332K	1,155K	2,487K

New Workbook to Hold the Report

Say that you want to build the report in a new workbook so that it can be easily mailed to the product managers. This is fairly easy to do. To make the code more portable, assign object variables to the original workbook, the new workbook, and the first worksheet in the new workbook. At the top of the procedure, add these statements:

```
Dim WSR As Worksheet
Dim WBO As Workbook
Dim WBN As Workbook
Set WBO = ActiveWorkbook
Set WSD = Worksheets("Pivot Table")
```

After the pivot table has been successfully created, build a blank Report workbook with this code:

```
' Create a New Blank Workbook with one Worksheet
Set WBN = Workbooks.Add(xlWorksheet)
Set WSR = WBN.Worksheets(1)
WSR.Name = "Report"
' Set up Title for Report
With WSR.Range("A1")
    .Value = "Revenue by Market and Year"
    .Font.Size = 14
End With
```

Summary on a Blank Report Worksheet

Imagine that you have submitted the pivot table in Figure 12.8, and your manager hates the borders, hates the title, and hates the words "Line of Business" in cell O2. You can solve all three of these problems by excluding the first row(s) of PT.TableRange2 from the .Copy method and then using PasteSpecial(xlPasteValuesAndNumberFormats) to copy the data to the report sheet.

> **CAUTION**
>
> In Excel 2000 and earlier, xlPasteValuesAndNumberFormats was not available. You would have to Paste Special twice: once as xlPasteValues and once as xlPasteFormats.

In the current example, the .TableRange2 property includes only one row to eliminate, row 2, as shown in Figure 12.8. If you had a more complex pivot table with several column fields and/or one or more page fields, you would have to eliminate more than just the first row of the report. It helps to run your macro to this point, look at the result, and figure out how many rows you need to delete. You can effectively not copy these rows to the report by using the Offset property. Copy the TableRange2 property, offset by one row. Purists will note that this code does copy one extra blank row from below the pivot table, but this really does not matter, because the row is blank. After doing the copy, you can erase the original pivot table and destroy the pivot cache:

```
' Copy the Pivot Table data to row 3 of the Report sheet
' Use Offset to eliminate the title row of the pivot table
PT.TableRange2.Offset(1, 0).Copy
WSR. Range("A3").PasteSpecial Paste:=xlPasteValuesAndNumberFormats
PT.TableRange2.Clear
Set PTCache = Nothing
```

Note that you used the Paste Special option to paste just values and number formats. This gets rid of both borders and the pivot nature of the table. You might be tempted to use the All Except Borders option under Paste, but this keeps the data in a pivot table, and you won't be able to insert new rows in the middle of the data.

Fill Outline View

The report is almost complete. You are nearly a Data, Subtotals command away from having everything you need. Before you can use the Subtotals command, however, you need to fill in all the blank cells in the outline view of column A.

Fixing the Outline view requires just a few obscure steps. Here are the steps in the user interface:

1. Select all the cells in column A that make up the report.
2. Select Edit, GoTo to bring up the GoTo dialog box. Click the Special button to bring up the GoTo Special dialog box. Select Blanks to select only the blank cells.
3. Enter an R1C1-style formula to fill the blank with the cell above it. This formula is =R[1]C. In the user interface you would type an equals sign, press the up-arrow key, and then press Ctrl+Enter.
4. Reselect all the cells in column A that make up the report. This is necessary because the Paste Special step cannot work with noncontiguous selections.
5. Copy the formulas in column A and convert them to values by using the Values option in the Paste Special dialog box.

Fixing the Outline view in VBA requires fewer steps. The equivalent VBA logic is shown here:

1. Find the last row of the report.
2. Enter the formula =R[-1]C in the blank cells in A.
3. Change those formulas to values.

The code to do this follows:

```
Dim FinalReportRow as Long
    ' Fill in the Outline view in column A
    ' Look for last row in column B since many rows
    ' in column A are blank
FinalReportRow = WSR.Range("B65536").End(xlUp).Row
With Range("A3").Resize(FinalReportRow - 2, 1)
    With .SpecialCells(xlCellTypeBlanks)
        .FormulaR1C1 = "=R[-1]C"
    End With
    .Value = .Value
End With
```

Final Formatting

The last steps for the report involve some basic formatting tasks and then adding the subtotals. You can bold and right-justify the headings in row 3. Set rows 1–3 up so that the top three rows print on each page:

```
' Do some basic formatting
' Autofit columns, bold the headings, right-align
```

```
Selection.Columns.AutoFit
Range("A3").EntireRow.Font.Bold = True
Range("A3").EntireRow.HorizontalAlignment = xlRight
Range("A3:B3").HorizontalAlignment = xlLeft

' Repeat rows 1-3 at the top of each page
WSR.PageSetup.PrintTitleRows = "$1:$3"
```

Add Subtotals

Automatic subtotals are a powerful feature found on the Data menu. Figure 12.9 shows the Subtotal dialog box. Note the option Page Break Between Groups.

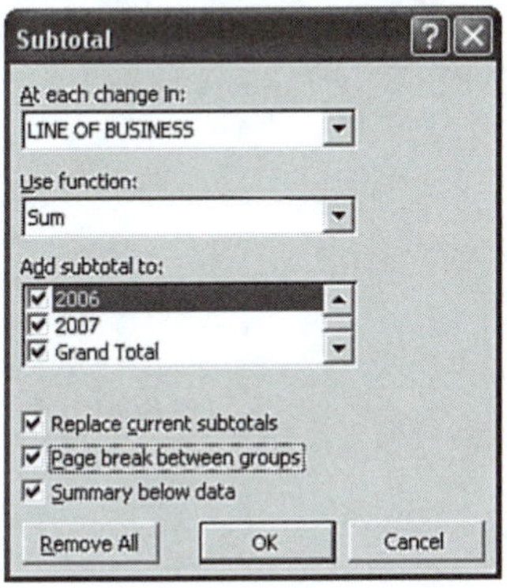

Figure 12.9

Use automatic subtotals because doing so enables you to add a page break after each product. This ensures that each product manager has a clean report with only his or her product on it.

If you were sure that you would always have two years and a total, the code to add subtotals for each Line of Business group would be the following:

```
' Add Subtotals by Product.
' Be sure to add a page break at each change in product
Selection.Subtotal GroupBy:=1, Function:=xlSum, TotalList:=Array(3, 4, 5), _
    PageBreaks:=True
```

However, this code fails if you have more or less than one year. The solution is to use this convoluted code to dynamically build a list of the columns to total, based on the number of columns in the report:

```
Dim TotColumns()
Dim I as Integer
FinalCol = Cells(3, 255).End(xlToLeft).Column
ReDim Preserve TotColumns(1 To FinalCol - 2)
For i = 3 To FinalCol
    TotColumns(i - 2) = i
Next i
Selection.Subtotal GroupBy:=1, Function:=xlSum, TotalList:=TotColumns,_
    Replace:=True, PageBreaks:=True, SummaryBelowData:=True
```

Finally, with the new totals added to the report, you need to AutoFit the numeric columns again with this code:

```
Dim GrandRow as Long
' Make sure the columns are wide enough for totals
```

```
GrandRow = Range("A65536").End(xlUp).Row
Cells(3, 3).Resize(GrandRow - 2, FinalCol - 2).Columns.AutoFit
Cells(GrandRow, 3).Resize(1, FinalCol - 2).NumberFormat = "#,##0,K"
' Add a page break before the Grand Total row, otherwise
' the product manager for the final Line will have two totals
WSR.HPageBreaks.Add Before:=Cells(GrandRow, 1)
```

Put It All Together

Listing 12.1 produces the product line manager reports in a few seconds.

Listing 12.1   Code That Produces the Product Line Report in Figure 12.10

```vba
Sub ProductLineReport()
    ' Line of Business and Market as Row
    ' Years as Column
    Dim WSD As Worksheet
    Dim PTCache As PivotCache
    Dim PT As PivotTable
    Dim PRange As Range
    Dim FinalRow As Long
    Dim GrandRow As Long
    Dim FinalReportRow as Long
    Dim i as Integer
    Dim TotColumns()

    Set WSD = Worksheets("PivotTable")
    Dim WSR As Worksheet
    Dim WBO As Workbook
    Dim WBN As Workbook
    Set WBO = ActiveWorkbook

    ' Delete any prior pivot tables
    For Each PT In WSD.PivotTables
        PT.TableRange2.Clear
    Next PT

    ' Define input area and set up a Pivot Cache
    FinalRow = WSD.Cells(Application.Rows.Count, 1).End(xlUp).Row
    FinalCol = WSD.Cells(1, Application.Columns.Count). _
        End(xlToLeft).Column
    Set PRange = WSD.Cells(1, 1).Resize(FinalRow, FinalCol)
    Set PTCache = ActiveWorkbook.PivotCaches.Add(SourceType:= _
        xlDatabase, SourceData:=PRange.Address)

    ' Create the Pivot Table from the Pivot Cache
    Set PT = PTCache.CreatePivotTable(TableDestination:=WSD. _
        Cells(2, FinalCol + 2), TableName:="PivotTable1")

    ' Turn off updating while building the table
    PT.ManualUpdate = True

    ' Set up the row fields
    PT.AddFields RowFields:=Array("Line of Business", _
        "In Balance Date"), ColumnFields:="Market"

    ' Set up the data fields
    With PT.PivotFields("Revenue")
```

```vba
            .Orientation = xlDataField
            .Function = xlSum
            .Position = 1
    End With

    ' Calc the pivot table
    PT.ManualUpdate = False
    PT.ManualUpdate = True

    ' Group by Year
    Cells(3, FinalCol + 3).Group Start:=True, End:=True, _
        Periods:=Array(False, False, False, False, False, False, True)

    ' Move In Balance Date to columns
    PT.PivotFields("In Balance Date").Orientation = xlColumnField
    PT.PivotFields("Market").Orientation = xlRowField

    PT.PivotFields("Sum of Revenue").NumberFormat = "#,##0,K"
    PT.PivotFields("Line of Business").Subtotals(1) = True
    PT.PivotFields("Line of Business").Subtotals(1) = False
    PT.ColumnGrand = False

    ' Calc the pivot table
    PT.ManualUpdate = False
    PT.ManualUpdate = True

    ' PT.TableRange2.Select

    ' Create a New Blank Workbook with one Worksheet
    Set WBN = Workbooks.Add(xlWBATWorksheet)
    Set WSR = WBN.Worksheets(1)
    WSR.Name = "Report"
    ' Set up Title for Report
    With WSR.[A1]
        .Value = "Revenue by Market and Year"
        .Font.Size = 14
    End With

    ' Copy the Pivot Table data to row 3 of the Report sheet
    ' Use Offset to eliminate the title row of the pivot table
    PT.TableRange2.Offset(1, 0).Copy
    WSR.[A3].PasteSpecial Paste:=xlPasteValuesAndNumberFormats
    PT.TableRange2.Clear
    Set PTCache = Nothing

    ' Fill in the Outline view in column A
    ' Look for last row in column B since many rows
    ' in column A are blank
    FinalReportRow = WSR.Range("B65536").End(xlUp).Row
    With Range("A3").Resize(FinalReportRow - 2, 1)
        With .SpecialCells(xlCellTypeBlanks)
            .FormulaR1C1 = "=R[-1]C"
        End With
        .Value = .Value
    End With

    ' Do some basic formatting
```

```
' Autofit columns, bold the headings, right-align
Selection.Columns.AutoFit
Range("A3").EntireRow.Font.Bold = True
Range("A3").EntireRow.HorizontalAlignment = xlRight
Range("A3:B3").HorizontalAlignment = xlLeft

' Repeat rows 1-3 at the top of each page
WSR.PageSetup.PrintTitleRows = "$1:$3"

' Add subtotals
FinalCol = Cells(3, 255).End(xlToLeft).Column
ReDim Preserve TotColumns(1 To FinalCol - 2)
For i = 3 To FinalCol
    TotColumns(i - 2) = i
Next i
Selection.Subtotal GroupBy:=1, Function:=xlSum, _
    TotalList:=TotColumns, Replace:=True, _
    PageBreaks:=True, SummaryBelowData:=True

' Make sure the columns are wide enough for totals
GrandRow = Range("A65536").End(xlUp).Row
Cells(3, 3).Resize(GrandRow - 2, FinalCol - 2).Columns.AutoFit
Cells(GrandRow, 3).Resize(1, FinalCol - 2).NumberFormat = "#,##0,K"
' Add a page break before the Grand Total row, otherwise
' the product manager for the final Line will have two totals
WSR.HPageBreaks.Add Before:=Cells(GrandRow, 1)

End Sub
```

Figure 12.10 shows the report produced by this code.

Figure 12.10
It takes less than two seconds to convert 50,000 rows of transactional data to this useful report if you use the code that produced this example. Without pivot tables, the code would be far more complex.

	A	B	C	D	E
1	Revenue by Market and Year				
2					
3	LINE OF BUSINESS	MARKET	2006	2007	Grand Total
4	Copier Sale	California	1,946K	2,075K	4,020K
5	Copier Sale	Central US	1,766K	1,741K	3,507K
6	Copier Sale	Colorado	1,274K	1,840K	3,114K
7	Copier Sale	Florida	1,727K	2,057K	3,784K
8	Copier Sale	Great Lakes	886K	1,043K	1,930K
9	Copier Sale	Gulf Coast	2,921K	2,910K	5,831K
10	Copier Sale	Illinois	1,503K	1,486K	2,990K
11	Copier Sale	Indiana	1,748K	1,869K	3,617K
12	Copier Sale	Kentucky	2,564K	3,308K	5,872K
13	Copier Sale	New England		3,176K	3,176K
14	Copier Sale	New York North	1,761K	2,172K	3,933K
15	Copier Sale	New York South	743K	899K	1,642K
16	Copier Sale	North Carolina	1,514K	2,249K	3,763K
17	Copier Sale	North West	1,444K	1,735K	3,179K
18	Copier Sale	Ohio	3,892K	1,326K	5,217K
19	Copier Sale	Shenandoah Valley	1,994K	2,251K	4,245K
20	Copier Sale	South Carolina	2,657K	3,095K	5,751K
21	Copier Sale	Southwest	2,175K	2,357K	4,532K
22	Copier Sale	Tennessee	2,968K	3,356K	6,324K
23	Copier Sale	Texas	2,193K	2,338K	4,531K
24	Copier Sale	Topeka	2,657K	2,968K	5,625K
25	**Copier Sale Total**		40,332K	46,250K	86,582K

Issues with Two or More Data Fields

So far, you have built some powerful summary reports, but you've touched only a portion of the powerful features available in pivot tables. The prior example produced a report but had only one data field.

It is possible to have multiple fields in a pivot report.

The data in this example includes not just revenue, but also units. The CFO will probably appreciate a report by product that shows quantity sold, revenue, and average price.

When you have two or more data fields, you have a choice of placing the data fields in one of four locations. By default, Excel builds the pivot report with the data field as the inner-most row field. It is often preferable to have the data field as the outermost row field or as a column field.

When a pivot table is going to have more that one data field, you have a virtual field named Data. Where you place the Data field in the .AddFields method determines which view of the data you get.

The default setup, with the data fields arranged as the innermost row field, as shown in Figure 12.11, would have this AddFields line:

Figure 12.11
The default pivot table report has the multiple data fields as the inner-most row field.

	A	B	C	D	E	F
1			Drop Page Fields Here			
2						
3			REGION ▾			
4	Data ▾	LINE OF BUSINESS ▾	West	North	South	Grand Total
5	Sum of REVE	Copier Sale	23976601	25893618	36711470	86581689
6		Parts	23670053	29063171	31205269	83938493
7		Printer Sale	19594197	20621317	28153264	68368778
8		Service Plan	149341261	201414511	223750307	574506079
9	Sum of UNITS	Copier Sale	8081	8706	12224	29011
10		Parts	0	0	0	0
11		Printer Sale	4135	4313	5876	14324
12		Service Plan	0	0	0	0
13	Total Sum of REVENUE		216582112	276992617	319820310	813395039
14	Total Sum of UNITS SOLD		12216	13019	18100	43335

```
PT.AddFields RowFields:=Array("Line of Business", "Data")
```

The view shown in Figure 12.12 would use this code:

```
PT.AddFields RowFields:=Array("Data", "Line of Business")
```

Figure 12.12
By moving the Data field to the first row field, you can obtain this view of the multiple data fields.

	A	B	C
1		Drop Page Fields Here	
2			
3		Data ▾	
4	MODEL ▾	Sum of REVENUE	Sum of UNITS SOLD
5	2500C	86581689	29011
6	2500P	68368778	14324
7	3002C	81772378	0
8	3002P	284995434	0
9	4055T	12776688	0
10	4500C	188174747	0
11	4500P	17518709	0
12	5001C	21079121	0
13	5001P	52127495	0
14	Grand Total	813395039	43335

The view that you need for this report would have Data as a column field:

```
PT.AddFields RowFields:="Model", ColumnFields:="Data"
```

After adding a column field called Data, you would then go on to define two data fields:

```
' Set up the data fields
With PT.PivotFields("Revenue")
    .Orientation = xlDataField
    .Function = xlSum
    .Position = 1
    .NumberFormat = "#,##0"
End With

With PT.PivotFields("Units Sold")
    .Orientation = xlDataField
    .Function = xlSum
    .Position = 2
    .NumberFormat = "#,##0"
End With
```

Calculated Data Fields

Pivot tables offer two types of formulas. The most useful type defines a formula for a calculated field. This adds a new field to the pivot table. Calculations for calculated fields are always done at the summary level. If you define a calculated field for average price as Revenue divided by Units Sold, Excel first adds up the total revenue and the total quantity, and then it does the division of these totals to get the result. In many cases, this is exactly what you need. If your calculation does not follow the associative law of mathematics, it might not work as you expect.

To set up a calculated field, use the Add method with the CalculatedFields object. You have to specify a field name and a formula. Note that if you create a field called Average Price, the default pivot table produces a field called Sum of Average Price. This is misleading and downright silly. What you have is actually the average of the sums of prices. The solution is to use the Name property when defining the data field to replace Sum of Average Price with something such as Avg Price. Note that this name must be different from the name for the calculated field.

Listing 12.2 produces the report shown in Figure 12.13.

Figure 12.13

The virtual "Data" dimension contains two fields from your dataset plus a calculation. It is shown along the column area of the report.

	M	N	O	P
2		Data		
3	MARKET	Sum of REVENUE	Sum of UNITS SOLD	Avg Price
4	California	61,636,732	2,142	28,775.32
5	Central US	30,503,842	1,913	15,945.55
6	Colorado	26,217,201	1,723	15,216.02
7	Florida	47,362,461	2,203	21,499.07
8	Great Lakes	36,992,638	1,314	28,152.69
9	Gulf Coast	45,159,185	2,518	17,934.55
10	Illinois	42,101,421	1,761	23,907.68
11	Indiana	41,043,454	2,227	18,429.93
12	Kentucky	37,363,632	2,753	13,571.97
13	New England	34,505,390	1,795	19,223.06
14	New York North	41,493,673	2,396	17,317.89
15	New York South	29,482,893	796	37,038.81
16	North Carolina	34,082,354	1,738	19,610.10
17	North West	28,923,143	1,669	17,329.62
18	Ohio	45,539,552	2,581	17,644.15
19	Shenandoah Valley	56,233,581	1,962	28,661.36
20	South Carolina	32,744,890	2,175	15,055.12
21	Southwest	29,325,287	2,209	13,275.37
22	Tennessee	33,564,381	2,832	11,851.83
23	Texas	39,143,422	2,068	18,928.15
24	Topeka	39,975,907	2,560	15,615.59
25	Grand Total	813,395,039	43,335	18,769.93

Listing 12.2   Code That Calculates an Average Price Field as a Second Data Field

```vba
Sub TwoDataFields()
    Dim WSD As Worksheet
    Dim PTCache As PivotCache
    Dim PT As PivotTable
    Dim PRange As Range
    Dim FinalRow As Long

    Set WSD = Worksheets("PivotTable")
    Dim WSR As Worksheet
    Dim WBO As Workbook
    Dim WBN As Workbook
    Set WBO = ActiveWorkbook

    ' Delete any prior pivot tables
    For Each PT In WSD.PivotTables
        PT.TableRange2.Clear
    Next PT

    ' Define input area and set up a Pivot Cache
    FinalRow = WSD.Cells(Application.Rows.Count, 1).End(xlUp).Row
    FinalCol = WSD.Cells(1, Application.Columns.Count). _
        End(xlToLeft).Column
    Set PRange = WSD.Cells(1, 1).Resize(FinalRow, FinalCol)
    Set PTCache = ActiveWorkbook.PivotCaches.Add(SourceType:= _
        xlDatabase, SourceData:=PRange.Address)

    ' Create the Pivot Table from the Pivot Cache
    Set PT = PTCache.CreatePivotTable(TableDestination:=WSD. _
        Cells(2, FinalCol + 2), TableName:="PivotTable1")

    ' Turn off updating while building the table
    PT.ManualUpdate = True

    ' Set up the row fields
    PT.AddFields RowFields:="Market", ColumnFields:="Data"

    ' Define Calculated Fields
    PT.CalculatedFields.Add Name:="AveragePrice", Formula:="=Revenue/Units Sold"

    ' Set up the data fields
    With PT.PivotFields("Revenue")
        .Orientation = xlDataField
        .Function = xlSum
        .Position = 1
        .NumberFormat = "#,##0"
    End With

    With PT.PivotFields("Units Sold")
        .Orientation = xlDataField
        .Function = xlSum
        .Position = 2
        .NumberFormat = "#,##0"
    End With

    With PT.PivotFields("AveragePrice")
```

12

```
            .Orientation = xlDataField
            .Function = xlSum
            .Position = 3
            .NumberFormat = "#,##0.00"
            .Name = "Avg Price"
        End With

        ' Ensure that you get zeroes instead of blanks in the data area
        PT.NullString = "0"

        ' Calc the pivot table
        PT.ManualUpdate = False
        PT.ManualUpdate = True

    End Sub
```

Calculated Items

Say that in your company the vice president of sales is responsible for copier sales and printer sales. The idea behind a calculated item is that you can define a new item along the Line of Business field to calculate the total of copier sales and printer sales. Listing 12.3 produces the report shown in Figure 12.14.

Figure 12.14

Unless you love restating numbers to the SEC, avoid using calculated items.

	M	N
2	Sum of REVENUE	
3	LINE OF BUSINESS ▼	Total
4	Copier Sale	86,581,689
5	Printer Sale	68,368,778
6	PrinterCopier	154,950,467
7	Parts	83,938,493
8	Service Plan	574,506,079
9	Grand Total	968,345,506

Listing 12.3   Code That Adds a New Item Along the Line of Business Dimension

```
Sub CalcItemsProblem()
    Dim WSD As Worksheet
    Dim PTCache As PivotCache
    Dim PT As PivotTable
    Dim PRange As Range
    Dim FinalRow As Long

    Set WSD = Worksheets("PivotTable")
    Dim WSR As Worksheet

    ' Delete any prior pivot tables
    For Each PT In WSD.PivotTables
        PT.TableRange2.Clear
    Next PT

    ' Define input area and set up a Pivot Cache
```

```vb
    FinalRow = WSD.Cells(Application.Rows.Count, 1).End(xlUp).Row
    FinalCol = WSD.Cells(1, Application.Columns.Count). _
        End(xlToLeft).Column
    Set PRange = WSD.Cells(1, 1).Resize(FinalRow, FinalCol)
    Set PTCache = ActiveWorkbook.PivotCaches.Add(SourceType:= _
        xlDatabase, SourceData:=PRange.Address)

    ' Create the Pivot Table from the Pivot Cache
    Set PT = PTCache.CreatePivotTable(TableDestination:=WSD. _
        Cells(2, FinalCol + 2), TableName:="PivotTable1")

    ' Turn off updating while building the table
    PT.ManualUpdate = True

    ' Set up the row fields
    PT.AddFields RowFields:="Line of Business"

    ' Define calculated item along the product dimension
    PT.PivotFields("Line of Business").CalculatedItems _
        .Add "PrinterCopier", "='Copier Sale'+'Printer Sale'"
    ' Resequence so that the report has printers and copiers first
    PT.PivotFields("Line of Business"). _
        PivotItems("Copier Sale").Position = 1
    PT.PivotFields("Line of Business"). _
        PivotItems("Printer Sale").Position = 2
    PT.PivotFields("Line of Business"). _
        PivotItems("PrinterCopier").Position = 3

    ' Set up the data fields
    With PT.PivotFields("Revenue")
        .Orientation = xlDataField
        .Function = xlSum
        .Position = 1
        .NumberFormat = "#,##0"
    End With

    ' Ensure that you get zeroes instead of blanks in the data area
    PT.NullString = "0"

    ' Calc the pivot table
    PT.ManualUpdate = False
    PT.ManualUpdate = True

End Sub
```

12

Look closely at the results shown in Figure 12.14. The calculation for PrinterCopier is correct. PrinterCopier is a total of Printers + Copiers. Some quick math confirms that 86 million + 68 million is about 154 million. However, the grand total should be 154 million + 83 million + 574 million, or about 811 million. Instead, Excel gives you a grand total of $968 million. The total revenue for the company just increased by $150 million. Excel gives the wrong grand total when a field contains both regular and calculated items. The only plausible method for dealing with this is to attempt to hide the products that make up PrinterCopier. The results are shown in Figure 12.15:

```
With PT.PivotFields("Line of Business")
    .PivotItems("Copier Sale").Visible = False
    .PivotItems("Printer Sale").Visible = False
End With
```

Figure 12.15

After the components that make up the calculated PrinterCopier item are hidden, the total revenue for the company is again correct. However, it would be easier to add a new field to the original data with a Responsibility field.

	M	N
2	Sum of REVENUE	
3	LINE OF BUSINESS ▼	Total
4	PrinterCopier	154,950,467
5	Parts	83,938,493
6	Service Plan	574,506,079
7	Grand Total	813,395,039

Summarize Date Fields with Grouping

With transactional data, you will often find your date-based summaries having one row per day. Although daily data might be useful to a plant manager, many people in the company want to see totals by month or quarter and year.

The great news is that Excel handles the summarization of dates in a pivot table with ease. For anyone who has ever had to use the arcane formula =A2+1-Day(A2) to change daily dates into monthly dates, you will appreciate the ease with which you can group transactional data into months or quarters.

Creating a group with VBA is a bit quirky. The .Group method can be applied to only a single cell in the pivot table, and that cell must contain a date or the Date field label. This is the first example in this chapter where you must allow VBA to calculate an intermediate pivot table result.

You must define a pivot table with In Balance Date in the row field. Turn off `ManualCalculation` to allow the Date field to be drawn. You can then use the `LabelRange` property to locate the date label and group from there. Figure 12.16 shows the result of Listing 12.4.

Figure 12.16

The In Balance Date field is now composed of three fields in the pivot table, representing year, quarter, and month.

	M	N	O	P	Q	R	S
2	Sum of REVENUE			REGION ▼			
3	Years ▼	Quarters ▼	IN BALANCE DATE ▼	West	North	South	Grand Total
4	2006	Qtr1	Jan	8,720,476	11,236,439	12,727,533	32,684,448
5			Feb	9,225,674	11,185,957	13,679,193	34,090,824
6			Mar	9,225,618	11,953,742	13,469,631	34,648,991
7		Qtr2	Apr	9,041,189	11,549,559	13,368,172	33,958,920
8			May	9,516,441	11,765,501	13,830,922	35,112,864
9			Jun	9,119,339	11,054,716	13,530,350	33,704,405
10		Qtr3	Jul	9,158,797	10,880,363	13,094,448	33,133,608
11			Aug	8,938,174	10,928,843	13,124,048	32,991,065
12			Sep	8,765,593	10,602,069	12,937,835	32,305,497
13		Qtr4	Oct	9,366,436	11,724,578	13,354,434	34,445,448
14			Nov	8,808,645	11,616,640	13,319,244	33,744,529
15			Dec	8,623,556	11,300,522	13,127,058	33,051,136
16	2007	Qtr1	Jan	9,016,346	11,353,880	13,372,402	33,742,628
17			Feb	8,817,997	11,322,225	13,343,066	33,483,288
18			Mar	9,499,545	12,458,951	13,882,350	35,840,846
19		Qtr2	Apr	8,961,701	11,567,922	13,180,773	33,710,396
20			May	9,217,324	11,741,321	13,500,566	34,459,211
21			Jun	8,818,100	11,557,867	13,115,848	33,491,815
22		Qtr3	Jul	9,009,295	11,559,512	13,182,356	33,751,163
23			Aug	8,974,245	11,786,294	13,468,008	34,228,547
24			Sep	8,649,972	11,393,225	12,792,406	32,835,603
25		Qtr4	Oct	9,185,147	12,424,305	13,609,530	35,218,982
26			Nov	9,165,534	12,527,651	14,011,254	35,704,439
27			Dec	8,756,968	11,500,535	12,798,883	33,056,386
28	Grand Total			216,582,112	276,992,617	319,820,310	813,395,039

Listing 12.4   Code That Uses the Group Feature to Roll Daily Dates Up to Monthly Dates

```
Sub ReportByMonth()
    Dim WSD As Worksheet
    Dim PTCache As PivotCache
    Dim PT As PivotTable
    Dim PRange As Range
    Dim FinalRow As Long

    Set WSD = Worksheets("PivotTable")
    Dim WSR As Worksheet

    ' Delete any prior pivot tables
    For Each PT In WSD.PivotTables
        PT.TableRange2.Clear
    Next PT

    ' Define input area and set up a Pivot Cache
    FinalRow = WSD.Cells(Application.Rows.Count, 1).End(xlUp).Row
    FinalCol = WSD.Cells(1, Application.Columns.Count). _
        End(xlToLeft).Column
    Set PRange = WSD.Cells(1, 1).Resize(FinalRow, FinalCol)
    Set PTCache = ActiveWorkbook.PivotCaches.Add(SourceType:= _
        xlDatabase, SourceData:=PRange.Address)

    ' Create the Pivot Table from the Pivot Cache
    Set PT = PTCache.CreatePivotTable(TableDestination:=WSD. _
        Cells(2, FinalCol + 2), TableName:="PivotTable1")

    ' Turn off updating while building the table
```

12

```
    PT.ManualUpdate = True

    ' Set up the row fields
    PT.AddFields RowFields:="In Balance Date", ColumnFields:="Region"

    ' Set up the data fields
    With PT.PivotFields("Revenue")
        .Orientation = xlDataField
        .Function = xlSum
        .Position = 1
        .NumberFormat = "#,##0"
    End With

    ' Ensure that you get zeroes instead of blanks in the data area
    PT.NullString = "0"

    ' Calc the pivot table to allow the date label to be drawn
    PT.ManualUpdate = False
    PT.ManualUpdate = True

    ' Group ShipDate by Month, Quarter, Year
    PT.PivotFields("In Balance Date").LabelRange.Group Start:=True, _
        End:=True, Periods:= _
        Array(False, False, False, False, True, True, True)

    ' Calc the pivot table
    PT.ManualUpdate = False
    PT.ManualUpdate = True

End Sub
```

Group by Week

You probably noticed that Excel allows you to group by day, month, quarter, and year. There is no standard grouping for week. You can, however, define a group that bunches up groups of seven days.

By default Excel starts the week based on the first date found in the data. This means that the default week would run from Tuesday January 1, 2006 through Monday December 31, 2007. You can override this by changing the Start parameter from True to an actual date. Use the WeekDay function to determine how many days to adjust the start date.

There is one limitation to grouping by week. When you group by week, you cannot also group by any other measure. It is not valid to group by week and quarter.

Listing 12.5 creates the report shown in Figure 12.17.

Figure 12.17
Use the Number of Days setting to group by week.

	M	N	O	P	Q
2	Sum of REVENUE	REGION			
3	IN BALANCE DATE	West	North	South	Grand Total
4	1/2/2006 - 1/8/2006	1,907,865	2,674,724	3,694,750	8,277,339
5	1/9/2006 - 1/15/2006	2,384,129	1,869,308	3,017,787	7,271,224
6	1/16/2006 - 1/22/2006	2,117,490	3,071,926	2,114,682	7,304,098
7	1/23/2006 - 1/29/2006	1,909,951	2,789,489	3,135,694	7,835,134
8	1/30/2006 - 2/5/2006	2,168,063	2,756,914	2,526,931	7,451,908
9	2/6/2006 - 2/12/2006	1,755,401	2,385,247	3,681,971	7,822,619
10	2/13/2006 - 2/19/2006	2,332,649	2,386,434	2,315,164	7,034,247
11	2/20/2006 - 2/26/2006	1,943,883	2,628,402	3,769,099	8,341,384
12	2/27/2006 - 3/5/2006	3,451,687	4,292,381	4,134,886	11,878,954
13	3/6/2006 - 3/12/2006	1,757,286	2,535,487	3,711,548	8,004,321
14	3/13/2006 - 3/19/2006	2,223,687	2,224,709	3,116,171	7,564,567
15	3/20/2006 - 3/26/2006	2,153,934	3,038,399	3,089,593	8,281,926

Listing 12.5   The Code Used to Group by Week Must Figure Out the Monday Nearest the Start of Your Data

```
Sub ReportByWeek()
    Dim WSD As Worksheet
    Dim PTCache As PivotCache
    Dim PT As PivotTable
    Dim PRange As Range
    Dim FinalRow As Long

    Set WSD = Worksheets("PivotTable")
    Dim WSR As Worksheet

    ' Delete any prior pivot tables
    For Each PT In WSD.PivotTables
        PT.TableRange2.Clear
    Next PT

    ' Define input area and set up a Pivot Cache
    FinalRow = WSD.Cells(Application.Rows.Count, 1).End(xlUp).Row
    FinalCol = WSD.Cells(1, Application.Columns.Count). _
        End(xlToLeft).Column
    Set PRange = WSD.Cells(1, 1).Resize(FinalRow, FinalCol)
    Set PTCache = ActiveWorkbook.PivotCaches.Add(SourceType:= _
        xlDatabase, SourceData:=PRange.Address)

    ' Create the Pivot Table from the Pivot Cache
    Set PT = PTCache.CreatePivotTable(TableDestination:=WSD. _
        Cells(2, FinalCol + 2), TableName:="PivotTable1")

    ' Turn off updating while building the table
    PT.ManualUpdate = True

    ' Set up the row fields
    PT.AddFields RowFields:="In Balance Date", ColumnFields:="Region"

    ' Set up the data fields
    With PT.PivotFields("Revenue")
        .Orientation = xlDataField
        .Function = xlSum
        .Position = 1
        .NumberFormat = "#,##0"
```

12

```
    End With

    ' Ensure that you get zeroes instead of blanks in the data area
    PT.NullString = "0"

    ' Calc the pivot table to allow the date label to be drawn
    PT.ManualUpdate = False
    PT.ManualUpdate = True

    ' Group Date by Week.
    'Figure out the first Monday before the minimum date
    FirstDate = PT.PivotFields("In Balance Date").LabelRange. _
        Offset(1, 0).Value
    WhichDay = Weekday(FirstDate, 3)
    StartDate = FirstDate - WhichDay
    PT.PivotFields("In Balance Date").LabelRange.Group _
        Start:=StartDate, End:=True, By:=7, _
        Periods:=Array(False, False, False, True, False, False, False)

    ' Calc the pivot table
    PT.ManualUpdate = False
    PT.ManualUpdate = True

End Sub
```

Advanced Pivot Table Techniques

You may be a pivot table pro and never have run into some of the really advanced techniques available with pivot tables. The next four sections discuss such techniques.

AutoShow Feature to Produce Executive Overviews

If you are designing an executive dashboard utility, you might want to spotlight the top five markets.

As with the AutoSort option, you could be a pivot table pro and never have stumbled across the AutoShow feature in Excel. This setting lets you select either the top or bottom n records based on any data field in the report.

The code to use AutoShow in VBA uses the .AutoShow method.

```
' Show only the top 5 Markets
PT.PivotFields("Market").AutoShow Top:=xlAutomatic, Range:=xlTop, _
    Count:=5, Field:="Sum of Revenue"
```

When you create a report using the AutoShow method, it is often helpful to copy the data and then go back to the original pivot report to get the totals for all markets. In the following code, this is achieved by removing the Market field from the pivot table and copying the grand total to the report. Listing 12.6 produces the report shown in Figure 12.18.

Figure 12.18
The Top 5 Markets report contains two pivot tables.

	A	B	C	D	E	F
1	Top 5 Markets					
2						
3	MARKET	Copier Sale	Parts	Printer Sale	Service Plan	Grand Total
4	California	4,020,385	8,720,027	3,570,593	45,325,727	61,636,732
5	Shenandoah Valley	4,244,770	6,967,670	2,329,461	42,691,680	56,233,581
6	Florida	3,783,617	5,037,083	4,823,314	33,718,447	47,362,461
7	Ohio	5,217,133	4,692,767	3,960,185	31,669,467	45,539,552
8	Gulf Coast	5,830,888	4,889,568	2,685,703	31,753,026	45,159,185
9	Top 5 Total	23,096,793	30,307,115	17,369,256	185,158,347	255,931,511
10						
11	Total Company	86,581,689	83,938,493	68,368,778	574,506,079	813,395,039

Listing 12.6   Code Used to Create the Top 5 Markets Report

```
Sub Top5Markets()
    ' Produce a report of the top 5 markets
    Dim WSD As Worksheet
    Dim WSR As Worksheet
    Dim WBN As Workbook
    Dim PTCache As PivotCache
    Dim PT As PivotTable
    Dim PRange As Range
    Dim FinalRow As Long
    Set WSD = Worksheets("PivotTable")

    ' Delete any prior pivot tables
    For Each PT In WSD.PivotTables
        PT.TableRange2.Clear
    Next PT

    ' Define input area and set up a Pivot Cache
    FinalRow = WSD.Cells(Application.Rows.Count, 1).End(xlUp).Row
    FinalCol = WSD.Cells(1, Application.Columns.Count). _
        End(xlToLeft).Column
    Set PRange = WSD.Cells(1, 1).Resize(FinalRow, FinalCol)
    Set PTCache = ActiveWorkbook.PivotCaches.Add(SourceType:= _
        xlDatabase, SourceData:=PRange.Address)

    ' Create the Pivot Table from the Pivot Cache
    Set PT = PTCache.CreatePivotTable(TableDestination:=WSD. _
        Cells(2, FinalCol + 2), TableName:="PivotTable1")

    ' Turn off updating while building the table
    PT.ManualUpdate = True

    ' Set up the row fields
    PT.AddFields RowFields:="Market", ColumnFields:="Line of Business"

    ' Set up the data fields
    With PT.PivotFields("Revenue")
```

```
        .Orientation = xlDataField
        .Function = xlSum
        .Position = 1
        .NumberFormat = "#,##0"
        .Name = "Total Revenue"
End With

' Ensure that you get zeroes instead of blanks in the data area
PT.NullString = "0"

' Sort markets descending by sum of revenue
PT.PivotFields("Market").AutoSort Order:=xlDescending, _
    Field:="Total Revenue"

' Show only the top 5 markets
PT.PivotFields("Market").AutoShow Type:=xlAutomatic, Range:=xlTop, _
    Count:=5, Field:="Total Revenue"

' Calc the pivot table to allow the date label to be drawn
PT.ManualUpdate = False
PT.ManualUpdate = True

' Create a new blank workbook with one worksheet
Set WBN = Workbooks.Add(xlWBATWorksheet)
Set WSR = WBN.Worksheets(1)
WSR.Name = "Report"
' Set up ritle for report
With WSR.[A1]
    .Value = "Top 5 Markets"
    .Font.Size = 14
End With

' Copy the pivot table data to row 3 of the report sheet
' Use offset to eliminate the title row of the pivot table
PT.TableRange2.Offset(1, 0).Copy
WSR.[A3].PasteSpecial Paste:=xlPasteValuesAndNumberFormats
LastRow = WSR.Cells(65536, 1).End(xlUp).Row
WSR.Cells(LastRow, 1).Value = "Top 5 Total"

' Go back to the pivot table to get totals without the AutoShow
PT.PivotFields("Market").Orientation = xlHidden
PT.ManualUpdate = False
PT.ManualUpdate = True
PT.TableRange2.Offset(2, 0).Copy
WSR.Cells(LastRow + 2, 1).PasteSpecial Paste:=xlPasteValuesAndNumberFormats
WSR.Cells(LastRow + 2, 1).Value = "Total Company"

' Clear the pivot table
PT.TableRange2.Clear
Set PTCache = Nothing

' Do some basic formatting
' Autofit columns, bold the headings, right-align
WSR.Range(WSR.Range("A3"), WSR.Cells(LastRow + 2, 6)).Columns.AutoFit
Range("A3").EntireRow.Font.Bold = True
Range("A3").EntireRow.HorizontalAlignment = xlRight
```

```
        Range("A3").HorizontalAlignment = xlLeft

        Range("A2").Select
        MsgBox "CEO Report has been Created"
End Sub
```

The Top 5 Markets report actually contains two snapshots of a pivot table. After using the AutoShow feature to grab the top five markets with their totals, the macro went back to the pivot table, removed the AutoShow option, and grabbed the total of all markets to produce the Total Company row.

ShowDetail **to Filter a Recordset**

Take any pivot table in the Excel user interface. Double-click any number in the table. Excel inserts a new sheet in the workbook and copies all the source records that represent that number. In the Excel user interface, this is a great way to ad-hoc query a dataset.

The equivalent VBA property is ShowDetail. By setting this property to True for any cell in the pivot table, you will generate a new worksheet with all the records that make up that cell:

```
PT.TableRange2.Offset(2, 1).Resize(1, 1).ShowDetail = True
```

Listing 12.7 produces a pivot table with the total revenue for the top three stores and ShowDetail for each of those stores. This is an alternative method to using the Advanced Filter report. The results of this macro are three new sheets. Figure 12.19 shows the first sheet created.

Figure 12.19

Pivot table applications are incredibly diverse. This macro created a pivot table of the top three stores and then used the ShowDetail property to retrieve the records for each of those stores.

	A	B	C	D	E	F	G	H	I
1	Detail for 35034014 (Store Rank: 1)								
2									
3	REGION	MARKET	STORE	IN BALANCE DATE	FISCAL PERIOD	MODEL	LINE OF BUSINESS	REVENUE	UNITS SOLD
4	South	Illinois	35034014	6/30/2007	200310	2500P	Printer Sale	54889	10
5	South	Illinois	35034014	12/30/2007	200404	3002P	Parts	21439	0
6	South	Illinois	35034014	12/29/2007	200404	3002P	Service Plan	252636	0
7	South	Illinois	35034014	12/26/2007	200404	3002C	Parts	77	0
8	South	Illinois	35034014	12/21/2007	200404	3002C	Parts	861	0
9	South	Illinois	35034014	12/19/2007	200404	4055T	Parts	2446	0
10	South	Illinois	35034014	12/18/2007	200404	4500C	Service Plan	165648	0
11	South	Illinois	35034014	12/17/2007	200404	2500C	Copier Sale	31136	7
12	South	Illinois	35034014	12/15/2007	200404	3002C	Service Plan	65311	0
13	South	Illinois	35034014	12/14/2007	200404	5001C	Parts	21987	0
14	South	Illinois	35034014	12/12/2007	200404	3002P	Parts	2897	0
15	South	Illinois	35034014	12/11/2007	200404	3002C	Parts	99	0

Listing 12.7   Code That Uses the ShowDetail **Method to Provide Detail for the Top Three Customers**

```
Sub RetrieveTop3StoreDetail()
    ' Retrieve Details from Top 3 Stores
    Dim WSD As Worksheet
    Dim WSR As Worksheet
    Dim WBN As Workbook
    Dim PTCache As PivotCache
    Dim PT As PivotTable
    Dim PRange As Range
```

```
Dim FinalRow As Long
Set WSD = Worksheets("PivotTable")

' Delete any prior pivot tables
For Each PT In WSD.PivotTables
    PT.TableRange2.Clear
Next PT

' Define input area and set up a Pivot Cache
FinalRow = WSD.Cells(Application.Rows.Count, 1).End(xlUp).Row
FinalCol = WSD.Cells(1, Application.Columns.Count). _
    End(xlToLeft).Column
Set PRange = WSD.Cells(1, 1).Resize(FinalRow, FinalCol)
Set PTCache = ActiveWorkbook.PivotCaches.Add(SourceType:= _
    xlDatabase, SourceData:=PRange.Address)

' Create the Pivot Table from the Pivot Cache
Set PT = PTCache.CreatePivotTable(TableDestination:=WSD. _
    Cells(2, FinalCol + 2), TableName:="PivotTable1")

' Turn off updating while building the table
PT.ManualUpdate = True

' Set up the row fields
PT.AddFields RowFields:="Store", ColumnFields:="Data"

' Set up the data fields
With PT.PivotFields("Revenue")
    .Orientation = xlDataField
    .Function = xlSum
    .Position = 1
    .NumberFormat = "#,##0"
    .Name = "Total Revenue"
End With

' Sort Stores descending by sum of revenue
PT.PivotFields("Store").AutoSort Order:=xlDescending, _
    Field:="Total Revenue"

' Show only the top 3 stores
PT.PivotFields("Store").AutoShow Type:=xlAutomatic, Range:=xlTop, _
    Count:=3, Field:="Total Revenue"

' Ensure that you get zeroes instead of blanks in the data area
PT.NullString = "0"

' Calc the pivot table to allow the date label to be drawn
PT.ManualUpdate = False
PT.ManualUpdate = True

' Produce summary reports for each customer
For i = 1 To 3
    PT.TableRange2.Offset(i + 1, 1).Resize(1, 1).ShowDetail = True
    ' The active sheet has changed to the new detail report
    ' Add a title
    Range("A1:A2").EntireRow.Insert
    Range("A1").Value = "Detail for " & _
```

```
                 PT.TableRange2.Offset(i + 1, 0).Resize(1, 1).Value & _
                 " (Store Rank: " & i & ")"
        Next i

        MsgBox "Detail reports for top 3 stores have been created."

    End Sub
```

Create Reports for Each Region or Model

A pivot table can have one or more page fields. A page field goes in a separate set of rows above the pivot report. It can serve to filter the report to a certain region, a certain model, or a certain combination of region and model.

To set up a page field in VBA, add the `PageFields` parameter to the `AddFields` method. The following line of code creates a pivot table with Region in the page field:

```
PT.AddFields RowFields:="Model", ColumnFields:="Data", PageFields:="Region"
```

The preceding line of code sets up the Region page field set to the value (All), which returns all regions. To limit the report to just the North region, use the `CurrentPage` property:

```
PT.PivotFields("Region").CurrentPage = "North"
```

One use of a page field is to build a user form where someone can select a particular region or a particular product. You then use this information to set the `CurrentPage` property and display the results of the user form.

Another interesting use is to loop through all `PivotItems` and display them one at a time in the page field. You can quickly produce top 10 reports for each region using this method.

To determine how many regions are available in the data, use `PT.PivotFields("Region").PivotItems.Count`. Either of these loops would work:

```
For i = 1 To PT.PivotFields("Region").PivotItems.Count
    PT.PivotFields("Region").CurrentPage = _
            PT.PivotFields("Region").PivotItems(i).Name
    PT.ManualUpdate = False
    PT.ManualUpdate = True
Next i

For Each PivItem In PT.PivotFields("Region").PivotItems
    PT.PivotFields("Region").CurrentPage = PivItem.Name
    PT.ManualUpdate = False
    PT.ManualUpdate = True
Next PivItem
```

Of course, in both of these loops, the three region reports fly by too quickly to see. In practice, you would want to save each report while it is displayed.

So far in this chapter, you have been using `PT.TableRange2` when copying the data from the pivot table. The `TableRange2` property includes all rows of the pivot table, including the

12

page fields. There is also a `.TableRange1` property, which excludes the page fields. You can use either statement to get the detail rows:

```
PT.TableRange2.Offset(3, 0)
PT.TableRange1.Offset(1, 0)
```

Which you use is your preference, but if you use `TableRange2`, you won't have problems when you try to delete the pivot table with `PT.TableRange2.Clear`. If you were to accidentally attempt to clear `TableRange1` when there are page fields, you would end up with the dreaded "Cannot move or change part of a pivot table" error.

Listing 12.8 produces a new workbook for each region, as shown in Figure 12.20.

Figure 12.20
By looping through all items found in the Region page field, the macro produced one workbook for each regional manager.

	A	B	C	D	E
1	Top 5 Stores in the South Region				
2					
3	STORE	Revenue			
4	35034014	18,635K			
5	35034054	15,606K			
6	63163013	11,825K			
7	74076026	10,832K			
8	16115015	9,729K			
9	Top 5 Total	66,627K			

Listing 12.8   Code That Creates a New Workbook per Region

```
Sub Top5ByRegionReport()
    ' Produce a report of top 5 stores for each region
    Dim WSD As Worksheet
    Dim WSR As Worksheet
    Dim WBN As Workbook
    Dim PTCache As PivotCache
    Dim PT As PivotTable
    Dim PRange As Range
    Dim FinalRow As Long

    Set WSD = Worksheets("PivotTable")

    ' Delete any prior pivot tables
    For Each PT In WSD.PivotTables
        PT.TableRange2.Clear
    Next PT

    ' Define input area and set up a Pivot Cache
    FinalRow = WSD.Cells(Application.Rows.Count, 1).End(xlUp).Row
    FinalCol = WSD.Cells(1, Application.Columns.Count). _
        End(xlToLeft).Column
    Set PRange = WSD.Cells(1, 1).Resize(FinalRow, FinalCol)
    Set PTCache = ActiveWorkbook.PivotCaches.Add(SourceType:= _
        xlDatabase, SourceData:=PRange.Address)

    ' Create the Pivot Table from the Pivot Cache
    Set PT = PTCache.CreatePivotTable(TableDestination:=WSD. _
        Cells(2, FinalCol + 2), TableName:="PivotTable1")

    ' Turn off updating while building the table
```

```
PT.ManualUpdate = True

' Set up the row fields
PT.AddFields RowFields:="Store", ColumnFields:="Data", _
    PageFields:="Region"

' Set up the data fields
With PT.PivotFields("Revenue")
    .Orientation = xlDataField
    .Function = xlSum
    .Position = 1
    .NumberFormat = "#,##0,K"
    .Name = "Total Revenue"
End With

' Sort stores descending by sum of revenue
PT.PivotFields("Store").AutoSort Order:=xlDescending, _
    Field:="Total Revenue"

' Show only the top 5 stores
PT.PivotFields("Store").AutoShow Type:=xlAutomatic, Range:=xlTop, _
    Count:=5, Field:="Total Revenue"

' Ensure that you get zeroes instead of blanks in the data area
PT.NullString = "0"

' Calc the pivot table
PT.ManualUpdate = False
PT.ManualUpdate = True
Ctr = 0

' Loop through each region
For Each PivItem In PT.PivotFields("Region").PivotItems
    Ctr = Ctr + 1
    PT.PivotFields("Region").CurrentPage = PivItem.Name
    PT.ManualUpdate = False
    PT.ManualUpdate = True

    ' Create a new blank workbook with one worksheet
    Set WBN = Workbooks.Add(xlWBATWorksheet)
    Set WSR = WBN.Worksheets(1)
    WSR.Name = PivItem.Name
    ' Set up Title for Report
    With WSR.[A1]
        .Value = "Top 5 Stores in the " & PivItem.Name & " Region"
        .Font.Size = 14
    End With

    ' Copy the pivot table data to row 3 of the report sheet
    ' Use offset to eliminate the page & title rows of the pivot table
    PT.TableRange2.Offset(3, 0).Copy
    WSR.[A3].PasteSpecial Paste:=xlPasteValuesAndNumberFormats
    LastRow = WSR.Cells(65536, 1).End(xlUp).Row
    WSR.Cells(LastRow, 1).Value = "Top 5 Total"

    ' Do some basic formatting
```

```
        ' Autofit columns, bold the headings, right-align
        WSR.Range(WSR.Range("A2"), WSR.Cells(LastRow, 3)).Columns.AutoFit
        Range("A3").EntireRow.Font.Bold = True
        Range("A3").EntireRow.HorizontalAlignment = xlRight
        Range("A3").HorizontalAlignment = xlLeft
        Range("B3").Value = "Revenue"

        Range("A2").Select

    Next PivItem

    ' Clear the pivot table
    PT.TableRange2.Clear
    Set PTCache = Nothing

    MsgBox Ctr & " Region reports have been created"

End Sub
```

Manually Filter Two or More Items in a PivotField

In addition to setting up a calculated pivot item to display the total of a couple of products that make up a dimension, it is possible to manually filter a particular PivotField.

For example, you have one client who sells shoes. In the report showing sales of sandals, he wants to see just the stores that are in warm-weather states. The code to hide a particular store is

```
PT.PivotFields("Store").PivotItems("Minneapolis").Visible = False
```

You need to be very careful to never set all items to False; otherwise, the macro will end with an error. This tends to happen more than you would expect. An application may first show products A and B, then on the next loop show products C and D. If you attempt to make A and B not visible before making C and D visible, you will be in the situation of having no products visible along the PivotField, which causes an error. To correct this, always loop through all PivotItems, making sure to turn them back to Visible before the second pass through the loop.

This process is easy in VBA. After building the table with Line of Business in the page field, loop through to change the Visible property to show only the total of certain products. Use the following code:

```
    ' Make sure all PivotItems along line are visible
    For Each PivItem In _
        PT.PivotFields("Line of Business").PivotItems
        PivItem.Visible = True
    Next PivItem

    ' Now - loop through and keep only certain items visible
    For Each PivItem In _
        PT.PivotFields("Line of Business").PivotItems
```

```
         Select Case PivItem.Name
             Case "Copier Sale", "Printer Sale"
                 PivItem.Visible = True
             Case Else
                 PivItem.Visible = False
         End Select
     Next PivItem
```

Control the Sort Order Manually

If your company has been reporting regions in the sequence of South, North, West forever, it is an uphill battle getting managers to accept seeing the report ordered North, South, West just because this is the default alphabetical order offered by pivot tables.

Strangely enough, Microsoft offers a bizarre method for handling a custom sort order in a pivot table. It's called a *manual sort order*. To change the sort order in the user interface, you simply go to a cell in the pivot table that contains "North," type the word "South," and press Enter. As if by magic, North and South switch places. Of course, all the numbers for North move to the appropriate column.

The VBA code to do a manual sort involves setting the Position property for a specific PivotItem. This is somewhat dangerous because you don't know whether the underlying data will have data for "South" on any given day. Be sure to set Error Checking to resume in case South doesn't exist today:

```
On Error Resume Next
PT.PivotFields("Region").PivotItems("South").Position = 1
On Error GoTo 0
```

Sum, Average, Count, Min, Max, and More

So far, every example in this chapter has involved summing data. It is also possible to get an average, minimum, or maximum of data. In VBA, change the Function property of the data field and give the data field a unique name. For example, the following code fragment produces five different summaries of the quantity field, each with a unique name:

```
   ' Set up the data fields
   With PT.PivotFields("Revenue")
       .Orientation = xlDataField
       .Function = xlSum
       .Position = 1
       .NumberFormat = "#,##0,K"
       .Name = "Total Revenue"
   End With

   With PT.PivotFields("Revenue")
       .Orientation = xlDataField
       .Function = xlCount
       .Position = 2
       .NumberFormat = "#,##0"
```

12

```
            .Name = "Number Orders"
        End With

        With PT.PivotFields("Revenue")
            .Orientation = xlDataField
            .Function = xlAverage
            .Position = 3
            .NumberFormat = "#,##0"
            .Name = "Average Revenue"
        End With

        With PT.PivotFields("Revenue")
            .Orientation = xlDataField
            .Function = xlMin
            .Position = 4
            .NumberFormat = "#,##0"
            .Name = "Smallest Order"
        End With

        With PT.PivotFields("Revenue")
            .Orientation = xlDataField
            .Function = xlMax
            .Position = 5
            .NumberFormat = "#,##0"
            .Name = "Largest Order"
        End With
```

The resultant pivot table provides a number of statistics about the average revenue, largest order, smallest order, and so on.

Report Percentages

In addition to the available choices, such as Sum, Min, Max, and Average, there is another set of pivot table options called the *calculation options*. These allow you to show a particular field as a percentage of the total, a percentage of the row, a percentage of the column, or as the percent difference from the previous or next item. All these settings are controlled through the .Calculation property of the page field.

The valid properties for .Calculation are xlPercentOf, xlPercentOfColumn, xlPercentOfRow, xlPercentOfTotal, xlRunningTotal, xlPercentDifferenceFrom, xlDifferenceFrom, xlIndex, and xlNoAdditionalCalculation. Each has its own unique set of rules. Some require that you specify a BaseField, and others require that you specify both a BaseField and a BaseItem. The following sections have some specific examples.

Percentage of Total

To get the percentage of the total, specify xlPercentOfTotal as the Calculation property for the page field:

```
' Set up a percentage of total
With PT.PivotFields("Revenue")
    .Orientation = xlDataField
    .Caption = "PctOfTotal"
```

```
    .Function = xlSum
    .Position = 2
    .NumberFormat = "#0.0%"
    .Calculation = xlPercentOfTotal
End With
```

Percentage Growth from Previous Month

With ship months going down the columns, you might want to see the percentage of revenue growth from month to month. You can set this up with the `xlPercentDifferenceFrom` setting. In this case, you must specify that the `BaseField` is `"In Balance Date"` and that the `BaseItem` is something called (`previous`):

```
' Set up % change from prior month
With PT.PivotFields("Revenue")
    .Orientation = xlDataField
    .Function = xlSum
    .Caption = "%Change"
    .Calculation = xlPercentDifferenceFrom
    .BaseField = "In Balance Date"
    .BaseItem = "(previous)"
    .Position = 3
    .NumberFormat = "#0.0%"
End With
```

Note that with positional calculations, you cannot use the `AutoShow` or `AutoSort` method. This is too bad; it would be interesting to sort the customers high to low and to see their sizes in relation to each other.

Percentage of a Specific Item

Many companies have a goal to have service revenue exceed a certain multiplier of copier sales. You can use the `xlPercentDifferenceFrom` setting to express revenues as a percentage of the copier product line:

```
' Show revenue as a percentage of hardware
With PT.PivotFields("Revenue")
    .Orientation = xlDataField
    .Function = xlSum
    .Caption = "% of Copier"
    .Calculation = xlPercentDifferenceFrom
    .BaseField = "ProductLine"
    .BaseItem = "Copier Sale"
    .Position = 3
    .NumberFormat = "#0.0%"
End With
```

Running Total

It is not intuitive, but to set up a running total, you must define a `BaseField`. In this example, you have In Balance Date running down the column. To define a running total column for revenue, you must specify that `BaseField` is `"In Balance Date"`:

12

```
' Set up Running Total
With PT.PivotFields("Revenue")
    .Orientation = xlDataField
    .Function = xlSum
    .Caption = "YTD Total"
    .Calculation = xlRunningTotal
    .Position = 4
    .NumberFormat = "#,##0,K"
    .BaseField = "In Balance Date"
End With
```

Figure 12.21 shows the results of a pivot table with three custom calculation settings, as discussed earlier.

Figure 12.21

This pivot table presents four views of Sum of Revenue. Column O is the normal calculation. Column P is % of Total. Column Q is % change from previous month. Column R is the running total.

	M	N	O	P	Q	R
2			Data			
3	Years	IN BALANCE DATE	Sum of REVENUE	PctOfTotal	%Change	YTD Total
4	2006	Jan	32,684K	4.0%		32,684K
5		Feb	34,091K	4.2%	4.3%	66,775K
6		Mar	34,649K	4.3%	1.6%	101,424K
7		Apr	33,959K	4.2%	-2.0%	135,383K
8		May	35,113K	4.3%	3.4%	170,496K
9		Jun	33,704K	4.1%	-4.0%	204,200K
10		Jul	33,134K	4.1%	-1.7%	237,334K
11		Aug	32,991K	4.1%	-0.4%	270,325K
12		Sep	32,305K	4.0%	-2.1%	302,631K
13		Oct	34,445K	4.2%	6.6%	337,076K
14		Nov	33,745K	4.1%	-2.0%	370,821K
15		Dec	33,051K	4.1%	-2.1%	403,872K
16	2007	Jan	33,743K	4.1%		33,743K
17		Feb	33,483K	4.1%	-0.8%	67,226K
18		Mar	35,841K	4.4%	7.0%	103,067K
19		Apr	33,710K	4.1%	-5.9%	136,777K
20		May	34,459K	4.2%	2.2%	171,236K
21		Jun	33,492K	4.1%	-2.8%	204,728K
22		Jul	33,751K	4.1%	0.8%	238,479K
23		Aug	34,229K	4.2%	1.4%	272,708K
24		Sep	32,836K	4.0%	-4.1%	305,543K
25		Oct	35,219K	4.3%	7.3%	340,762K
26		Nov	35,704K	4.4%	1.4%	376,467K
27		Dec	33,056K	4.1%	-7.4%	409,523K
28	Grand Total		813,395K	100.0%		

12

CASE STUDY

Special Considerations for Excel 97

Pivot tables and VBA took a radical turn in Excel 2000. In Excel 2000, Microsoft introduced the PivotCache object. This object allows you to define one pivot cache and then build many pivot reports from the pivot cache.

Officially, Microsoft quit supporting Excel 97 a few years ago. But, in practical terms, there are still many companies using Excel 97. If you need your code to work on a legacy platform, you should be aware of how pivot tables were created in Excel 97.

In Excel 97, you would use the PivotTableWizard method. Take a look at the code for building a simple pivot table showing revenue by region and line of business. Where current code uses two steps (add a PivotCache and then use CreatePivotTable), Excel 97 would use just one step, using the PivotTableWizard method to create the table:

```
Sub PivotExcel97Compatible()
    ' Pivot Table Code for Excel 97 Users
```

```
        Dim WSD As Worksheet
        Dim PT As PivotTable
        Dim PRange As Range
        Dim FinalRow As Long

        Set WSD = Worksheets("PivotTable")

        ' Delete any prior pivot tables
        For Each PT In WSD.PivotTables
            PT.TableRange2.Clear
        Next PT

        ' Define input area
        FinalRow = WSD.Cells(Application.Rows.Count, 1).End(xlUp).Row
        FinalCol = WSD.Cells(1, Application.Columns.Count). _
            End(xlToLeft).Column
        Set PRange = WSD.Cells(1, 1).Resize(FinalRow, FinalCol)

        ' Create pivot table using PivotTableWizard
        Set PT = WSD.PivotTableWizard(SourceType:=xlDatabase, _
            SourceData:=PRange.Address, _
            TableDestination:="R2C13", TableName:="PivotTable1")

        PT.ManualUpdate = True
        ' Set up the row fields
        PT.AddFields RowFields:="Region", ColumnFields:="Line of Business"

        ' Set up the data fields
        With PT.PivotFields("Revenue")
            .Orientation = xlDataField
            .Function = xlSum
            .Position = 1
            .NumberFormat = "#,##0,K"
            .Name = "Total Revenue"
        End With

        PT.ManualUpdate = False
        PT.ManualUpdate = True
End Sub
```

Next Steps

In Appendix A, "Solutions to Common Questions and Issues with Pivot Tables," you will learn a myriad of techniques for handling common questions and issues with pivot tables.

Solutions to Common Questions and Issues with Pivot Tables

A

This appendix covers solutions to the following questions and issues:

- What does "The PivotTable field name is not valid" mean?
- When I refresh my pivot table, my data disappears.
- When I try to group a field, I get an error message.
- Why can't I group my month fields into quarters?
- My pivot table is showing the same data item twice.
- Why are deleted data items still showing up in the page field?
- When I type a formula referencing a pivot table, I cannot copy the formula down.
- How can I sort data items in a unique order that is not ascending or descending?
- How do I turn my pivot table into hard data?
- Is there an easy way to fill the empty cells left by row fields?
- Is there an easy way to fill the empty cells left by row fields in multiple columns?
- How do I add a rank number field to my pivot table?
- Why does my pivot chart exclude months for certain data items?
- Can I create a pivot chart on the same sheet as my pivot table?
- How can I turn my pivot table report into an interactive web page?

What does "The PivotTable field name is not valid" mean?

Problem

When you try to create a pivot table, you get the following error message:

"The PivotTable field name is not valid. To create a PivotTable report, you must use data that is organized as a list with labeled columns. If you are changing the name of a PivotTable field, you must type a new name for the field."

Solution

This message means that one or more of the columns in your data source does not have a header name. To correct this problem, go to the dataset you are using to create the pivot table and make sure that all columns have a header name.

When I refresh my pivot table, my data disappears.

Problem

After you refresh your pivot table, the field you placed into the data area disappears, effectively removing the data in your pivot table.

Solution

You will run into this behavior when you change the name of the field you placed into the data area. For example, if you created a pivot table and placed a field called Revenue into the data area, your pivot table will show revenue numbers in the data area. If you were to go to your source data and change the Revenue column heading name to "Dollars" and then refresh your pivot table, the numbers in the data area would disappear. This is because when you refreshed your pivot table, it took a new snapshot of your data source and determined that there is no longer a field called "Revenue"—and it cannot calculate a field that is not there.

To resolve this issue, open your pivot table field list and simply drag your new field into the data area.

When I try to group a field, I get an error message.

Problem

When you try to group a field in your pivot table, you get the following error message: "Cannot group that selection."

A

Solution

One of the following scenarios can trigger this error message:

- The field you are trying to group is a text field.
- The field you are trying to group is a date field but contains text or blank cells.
- The field you are trying to group is a date field but is being recognized by Excel as text.
- The field you are trying to group is in the page area of your pivot table.

To resolve this issue, take the following steps:

1. Go to your data source and make sure the field you are trying to group is formatted as Date and does not contain blanks cells or cells with text in them. Remove all text, format the cells in the field as Date, and fill in all blank cells with a dummy date.

2. Highlight the column that contains the field you are trying to group. Go up to the application menu and select Data, Text to Columns. This will activate the Text to Columns Wizard. All you have to do in this wizard is click Next, click Next again, and then click Finish.

3. Go back to your pivot table, right-click, and select Refresh Data.

4. If the field you are trying to group is in the page area of your pivot table, move the field to the row or column area.

5. At this point, you will be able to group the data items in your field. After the field is grouped, you can move it back to the page field if needed.

Why can't I group my month fields into quarters?

Problem

Instead of having one field that contains months, you have several fields that represent each month. Your pivot table looks similar to the one shown in Figure A.1.

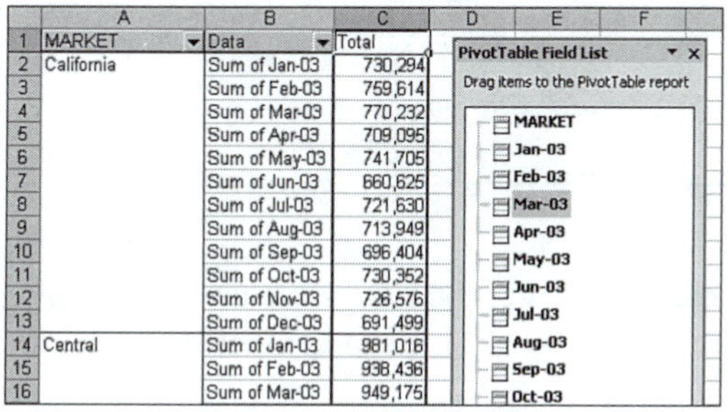

Figure A.1
Instead of one field that contains months, each month is its own field.

The issue is that there is no way for you to group these months into quarters because pivot tables can only group the data items within a field; they cannot group fields together. Because each month is separated into its own field, you will not be able to group them in their current state.

Solution

The source of this problem is the table structure of the data source. The table shown in Figure A.2 has a flawed structure. A general rule when working with pivot tables is that none of the column names in your data source should double as data items that will be used as filters or query criterion (for example, names of months, dates, years, names of locations, names of employees).

Figure A.2

The table structure of the data source is flawed. Most of the column names in this table double as criterion used to identify the month.

	A	B	C	D	E	F
1	MARKET	Jan-03	Feb-03	Mar-03	Apr-03	May
2	California	$730,294	$759,614	$770,232	$709,095	$741
3	Central	$981,016	$938,436	$949,175	$934,094	$928
4	Colorado	$540,837	$553,479	$592,669	$574,104	$560
5	Florida	$455,060	$408,010	$449,666	$451,639	$384
6	Great Lakes	$420,761	$422,123	$415,914	$410,464	$438
7	Gulf Coast	$280,487	$288,974	$364,922	$314,447	$321
8	Illinois	$321,835	$291,195	$320,365	$300,862	$302
9	Indiana	$226,568	$285,434	$302,631	$286,715	$254
10	Kentucky	$379,327	$378,018	$384,176	$452,715	$463
11	New England	$415,067	$423,408	$448,268	$465,639	$476
12	New York North	$292,538	$308,697	$357,592	$384,183	$367
13	New York South	$734,261	$764,568	$731,455	$766,360	$759
14	North Carolina	$584,545	$519,211	$528,393	$538,249	$604
15	North West	$220,118	$232,836	$253,672	$225,071	$158
16	Ohio	$451,660	$532,884	$550,965	$509,350	$519
17	Shenandoah Valley	$541,947	$516,790	$517,964	$519,944	$537
18	South Carolina	$411,743	$437,459	$470,820	$429,479	$463
19	Southwest	$617,615	$576,157	$600,807	$618,345	$617
20	Tennessee	$797,573	$821,957	$843,722	$806,500	$891
21	Texas	$519,277	$462,635	$463,517	$440,761	$489
22	Topeka	$664,475	$724,166	$689,518	$616,225	$666

As you can see in Figure A.3, the solution to this problem is to change the structure of your data source to contain three columns: Market, Month, and Revenue.

Figure A.3

Creating separate columns for market and revenue will allow you to use month names as data items in your pivot table, instead of fields.

	A	B	C
1	**Market**	**Month**	**Revenue**
2	California	January-03	$730,294
3	California	February-03	$759,614
4	California	March-03	$770,232
5	California	April-03	$709,095
6	California	May-03	$741,705
7	California	June-03	$660,625
8	California	July-03	$721,630
9	California	August-03	$713,949
10	California	September-03	$696,404
11	California	October-03	$730,352
12	California	November-03	$726,576

Luckily, there is an easy method to alter the table structure from Figure A.2 to the one shown in Figure A.3. Strangely though, this method involves the creation of a pivot table.

1. Place your cursor anywhere inside your table and then go up to the application menu and select Data, PivotTable and PivotChart Report.

2. When the PivotTable Wizard activates, select Multiple Consolidation Ranges and then click Next.

3. Select I Will Create the Page Fields and then click Next.

4. The dialog box that pops up will ask you for the range of your data source. Enter the range in the Range input box and click Finish.

5. At this point, you will have created a pivot table that doesn't make much sense. In the pivot table you just created, double-click on the intersection of the grand totals, as shown in Figure A.4.

Figure A.4
Double-click the intersection of grand totals to
get your final table.

	L	M	N
16	794369	723894	8959737
17	544568	521774	6585373
18	172210	150836	2224062
19	531587	481886	6241795
20	553248	497228	6397371
21	492683	445715	5431354
22	665826	588650	7200391
23	931193	939933	10466016
24	521500	451708	5756746
25	675886	709575	8033558
26	11305371	10725252	129907370

The final result, shown in here in Figure A.5, is a brand-new table that is structured exactly the way you need it in order to group months. Keep in mind that you will have to do some slight formatting of this table before using it in a pivot table (that is, you will need to change the date format and rename column headers).

Figure A.5
After you format and
rename the columns in
your final table, you can
create a new pivot table
from it. This table structure will allow you to
group your months by
quarter.

	A	B	C
1	Row	Column	Value
2	California	January-03	730294
3	California	February-03	759614
4	California	March-03	770232
5	California	April-03	709095
6	California	May-03	741705
7	California	June-03	660625
8	California	July-03	721630
9	California	August-03	713949
10	California	September-03	696404
11	California	October-03	730352
12	California	November-03	726576
13	California	December-03	691499

My pivot table is showing the same data item twice.

Problem

Your pivot table is showing the same data item two times, effectively treating each instance of the data item as a separate entity. Figure A.6 demonstrates an example of this error.

Solution

You are getting this behavior because, although the two data items look the same to you, there is something different between them. Excel is picking up this difference and deciding that they are two different data items. In order to fix this issue, you will have to ensure that the problem data items are exactly the same. Follow these steps to correct this problem:

1. Go to your data source and sort your table on the problem field. In the example shown in Figure A.6, the problem field is the Date field.

2. Find all instances of the problem data item (1/3/2003, in this case) and make sure they are all the same. You can do this by copying the first instance of the data item and pasting over the other instances.

3. Highlight the column that contains the problem data item. Go up to the application menu and select Data, Text to Columns. This will activate the Text to Columns Wizard. All you have to do in this wizard is click Next, click Next again, and then click Finish.

4. Go back to your pivot table, right-click, and select Refresh Data.

Figure A.6
Notice that 1/3/2003 is shown in the pivot table twice. There is something wrong here. If these dates are the same, they should be grouped together to give you one calculation, not two.

	A	B	C	D	E	F	G	H
1	STORE	(All)						
2								
3	Sum of REVENUE		DATE ▾					
4	REGION ▾	LINE OF BUSINESS ▾	1/3/2003	1/3/2003	1/4/2003	1/5/2003	1/6/2003	1/7/2003
5	West	Copier Sale					25348	26822
6		Parts			56212	6413	28074	10934
7		Service Plan	23343	3382		45712	298997	10960

Why are deleted data items still showing up in the page field?

Problem

You deleted a data item from your data source and refreshed your pivot table. However, the data item still appears in your pivot table. In the example shown in Figure A.7, you see four regions, including Midwest, in the page field.

Figure A.7
The issue here is that the Midwest region does not exist any longer, and your data source does not have records tagged as Midwest. Your pivot table is holding on to this data item in its pivot cache.

	A	B	C
1	REGION	(All)	
2			
3	Sum of REVENUE	(All)	
4	LINE OF BUSINE ▾	West	
5	Copier Sale	North	
6	Parts	South	
7	Service Plan	Midwest	
8			
9			
10			
11			
12			
13		OK	Cancel
14			

Solution

To clear these phantom data items from your pivot table, completely remove the field that contains the old items (in this example, the Region field) from the pivot table. Refresh the pivot table and then drag the field back to its original position. The phantom data items will be gone.

When I type a formula referencing a pivot table, I cannot copy the formula down.

Problem

If you are working with Excel 2002 or a later version, you will find that Excel has an annoying default setting that revolves around the GetPivotData function.

Excel automatically inserts the GetPivotData function into any cell where you are trying to enter a formula referencing your pivot data. The issue is that the GetPivotData function automatically references the cells in your pivot table as absolute references, making it impossible to simply copy your formulas down and get the right answer.

Solution

To resolve this issue, take the following steps:

1. Go to the application menu bar and select Tools, Customize.
2. In the Commands tab, select Data.
3. Find Generate GetPivotData and drag it to any one of your toolbars.
4. Click Close.
5. Click the Generate GetPivotData button to turn off this feature.
6. Re-enter your formula with this feature turned off.

How can I sort data items in a unique order that is not ascending or descending?

Problem

Figure A.8 shows the default sequence of regions in a pivot table report. Alphabetically, the regions are shown in sequence of North, South, West. If your company is based in California, company traditions might dictate that the West region should be shown first, followed by North and South.

Figure A.8
Company traditions might dictate that the Region field should be in West, North, South sequence. Unfortunately, neither an Ascending sort order nor a Descending sort order can help you.

	A	B	C	D	E
1					
2					
3					
4	Revenue	REGION ▼			
5	LINE OF BUSINESS ▼	North	South	West	Grand Total
6	Copier Sale	25,893,618	36,711,470	23,976,601	86,581,689
7	Parts	29,063,171	31,205,269	23,670,053	83,938,493
8	Printer Sale	20,621,317	28,153,264	19,594,197	68,368,778
9	Service Plan	201,414,511	223,750,307	149,341,261	574,506,079
10	Grand Total	276,992,617	319,820,310	216,582,112	813,395,039

Solution

You can rearrange data items in your pivot table manually by simply typing the exact name of the data item where you would like to see its data. You can also drag the data item where you want it.

To solve the problem in this example, you would simply type the word "West" in cell B5 and then press Enter. The pivot table will respond by resequencing the regions. The $216 million in sales for the West will automatically move from column D to column B. The remaining regions will move over to the next two columns.

How do I turn my pivot table into hard data?

Problem

You only created your pivot table in order to summarize and shape your data. You do not want to keep the source data, nor do you want to keep the pivot table with all its overhead.

Solution

Turning your pivot table into hard data allows you to utilize the results of the pivot table without having to deal with the source data, or a pivot cache. How you turn your pivot table into hard data depends on how much of your pivot table you are going to copy.

If you are copying just a portion of your pivot table, follow these steps:

1. Select the data you want to copy from the pivot table. Then go up to the application menu and select Edit, Copy.

2. Right-click anywhere on a spreadsheet and select Edit, Paste.

Here's what to do if you are copying your entire pivot table:

1. Select the data you want to copy from the pivot table. Then go up to the application menu and select Edit, Copy.

2. Right-click anywhere on a spreadsheet and select Paste Special.

3. Select Values and then click OK.

Is there an easy way to fill the empty cells left by row fields?

Problem

When you turn a pivot table into hard data, you are not only left with the values created by the pivot table, but you are also left with the pivot table's data structure. For example, the data shown in Figure A.9 came from a pivot table.

Notice that the Market field kept the same row structure it had when this data was in the row area of the pivot table. It would be unwise to use this table anywhere else without filling in the empty cells left by the row field, but how do you easily fill these empty cells?

Figure A.9

Notice that the Market field keeps the same row field structure it had when this data was in a pivot table. It would be impractical to use this data anywhere else without filling in the empty cells left by the row field.

	A	B	C
1	MARKET	LINE OF BUSINESS	Total
2	California	Copier Sale	$4,020,385
3		Parts	$8,720,027
4		Printer Sale	$3,570,593
5		Service Plan	$45,325,727
6	Central	Copier Sale	$3,506,717
7		Parts	$2,487,047
8		Printer Sale	$3,414,010
9		Service Plan	$21,096,068
10	Colorado	Copier Sale	$3,113,591
11		Parts	$1,862,325
12		Printer Sale	$3,124,724
13		Service Plan	$18,116,561

Solution

Although the first thought that comes to your head is to copy each market and paste it into the appropriate empty cells, keep in mind that there are 20 markets. You do not want to waste your time pasting market names into empty cells.

The best solution here is to use a simple formula. This formula, shown in Figure A.10, is entered next to the first data item in the row field. The idea is to create a column next to the empty cells and fill it with a value. That value, in this case, is a market name.

Figure A.10

The formula, =IF(B2="",A1,B2), states that if the cell next to the formula is empty, use the cell above the formula. Otherwise, use the cell next to the formula.

	A	B	C	D
1		MARKET	LINE OF BUSINESS	Total
2	=IF(B2="",A1,B2)	California	Copier Sale	$4,020,385
3			Parts	$8,720,027
4			Printer Sale	$3,570,593
5			Service Plan	$45,325,727
6		Central	Copier Sale	$3,506,717
7			Parts	$2,487,047
8			Printer Sale	$3,414,010

After you enter the correct formula, copy it down to the end of your dataset. As you can see in Figure A.11, this method is a lot more efficient than copying and pasting market names for 20 markets.

Figure A.11

After your formula is entered, you can copy it all the way down to the end of your dataset to fill in the gaps.

	A	B	C	D
1		MARKET	LINE OF BUSINESS	Total
2	California	California	Copier Sale	$4,020,385
3	California		Parts	$8,720,027
4	California		Printer Sale	$3,570,593
5	California		Service Plan	$45,325,727
6	Central	Central	Copier Sale	$3,506,717
7	Central		Parts	$2,487,047
8	Central		Printer Sale	$3,414,010
9	Central		Service Plan	$21,096,068
10	Colorado	Colorado	Copier Sale	$3,113,591

A

You're not done yet. After you filled in the gaps with your formula, highlight the entire column by clicking on the column letter, as shown here in Figure A.12, and then go up to the application menu and select Edit, Copy. Right-click on the column letter and select Paste Special, Values. Then click OK.

Figure A.12
Turn your formulas into hard data using Paste Special functionality.

	A	B	C	D
1		KET	LINE OF BUSINESS	Total
2	California	California	Copier Sale	$4,020,385
3	California		Parts	$8,720,027
4	California		Printer Sale	$3,570,593
5	California		Service Plan	$45,325,727
6	Central	Central	Copier Sale	$3,506,717
7	Central		Parts	$2,487,047
8	Central		Printer Sale	$3,414,010
9	Central		Service Plan	$21,096,068
10	Colorado	Colorado	Copier Sale	$3,113,591

The last step, shown in Figure A.13, is to delete the column with the empty cells and add a header to the column you just created.

Figure A.13
After a little formatting, you have the result you are looking for.

	A	B	C
1	MARKET	LINE OF BUSINESS	Total
2	California	Copier Sale	$4,020,385
3	California	Parts	$8,720,027
4	California	Printer Sale	$3,570,593
5	California	Service Plan	$45,325,727
6	Central	Copier Sale	$3,506,717
7	Central	Parts	$2,487,047
8	Central	Printer Sale	$3,414,010
9	Central	Service Plan	$21,096,068
10	Colorado	Copier Sale	$3,113,591

Is there an easy way to fill the empty cells left by row fields in multiple columns?

Problem

When you turn a pivot table into hard data, you are left with several blank columns. The previous method works fine for one column, but it could get tedious if you have to fill in several columns, such as with the pivot table shown in Figure A.14.

Figure A.14
You will want to fill in all blanks in columns A through C.

	A	B	C	D
1	MARKET	LINE OF BUSINESS	IN BALANCE DATE	Total
2	California	Copier Sale	Jan	295819
3			Feb	302261
4			Mar	327455
5			Apr	331489
6			May	339592
7			Jun	351133
8			Jul	335742
9			Aug	312499
10			Sep	382426
11			Oct	362035
12			Nov	320288
13			Dec	359646
14		Parts	Jan	670949
15			Feb	717046

Solution

This solution is not as intuitive as the previous method, but it works nicely when you have several columns of blanks to fill.

You will select a range in columns A, B, and C that extends from the first row with blanks to the row just above the grand total. In the present example, this is A3:C1009.

Select Go To from the Edit menu. In the lower-left corner of the Go To dialog box, click the Special button.

The Go To Special dialog box is a powerful feature that allows you to modify your selection based on various conditions. In this example, choose the option for Blanks, as shown in Figure A.15.

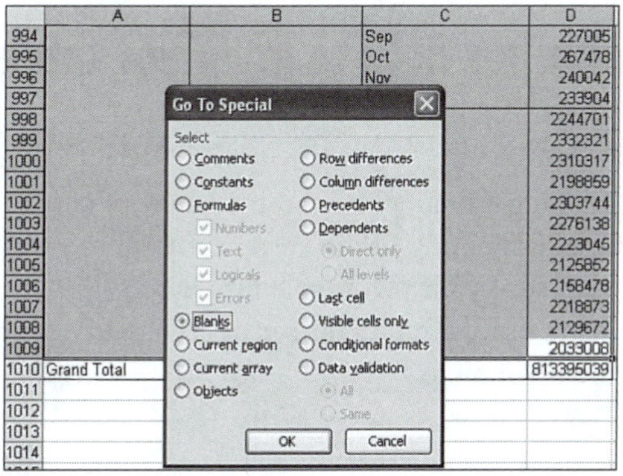

Figure A.15
Using the Go To Special dialog box allows you to select all the blank cells to be filled.

The result will be that only the blank cells within your selection will be selected.

Enter a formula that will copy the pivot item values from the cell above to the blank cells. You can do this with four keystrokes, but it helps if you don't look at the screen while you perform them. Type an equals sign, press the up-arrow key, and then hold down the Ctrl key while pressing Enter.

The equals sign tells Excel that you are entering a formula in the active cell. Pressing the up-arrow key points to the cell above the active cell. Using Ctrl+Enter tells Excel to enter a similar formula in all the selected cells instead of just the active cell. As you can see in Figure A.16, you will have entered a formula to fill in all the blank cells at once.

You still will want to convert those formulas to values. However, if you attempt to copy the current selection, Excel will present an error—you cannot copy a selection that contains multiple selections. By using Go To Special Blanks, you actually selected many areas of the spreadsheet.

You will have to reselect the original range of A3:C1009. You can then use Ctrl+C to copy and use Edit, Paste Special, Values to convert the formulas to values.

Figure A.16
With just a few keystrokes, you have the result you are looking for.

	A	B	C	D
1	MARKET	LINE OF BUSINESS	IN BALANCE DATE	Total
2	California	Copier Sale	Jan	295819
3	California	Copier Sale	Feb	302261
4	California	Copier Sale	Mar	327455
5	California	Copier Sale	Apr	331489
6	California	Copier Sale	May	339592
7	California	Copier Sale	Jun	351133
8	California	Copier Sale	Jul	335742
9	California	Copier Sale	Aug	312499
10	California	Copier Sale	Sep	382426
11	California	Copier Sale	Oct	362035
12	California	Copier Sale	Nov	320288
13	California	Copier Sale	Dec	359646
14	California	Parts	Jan	670949
15	California	Parts	Feb	717046
16	California	Parts	Mar	684975

This method provides a quick way to easily fill in the outline view provided by the pivot table.

How do I add a rank number field to my pivot table?

Problem

When you are sorting and ranking a field with a large amount of data items, it can be difficult to determine the number ranking of the current data item you are analyzing. Furthermore, you may want to turn your pivot table into hard values for further analysis. An integer field that contains the actual rank number of each data item could prove to be helpful in analysis outside the pivot table.

Solution

Select a cell in your pivot table. From the PivotTable toolbar, use the Pivot Table dropdown and select Formulas, Calculated Field.

Figure A.17 shows the Insert Calculated Field dialog box. Give the field a name such as MarketRank. The formula should be =1. Click the Add button to create the field.

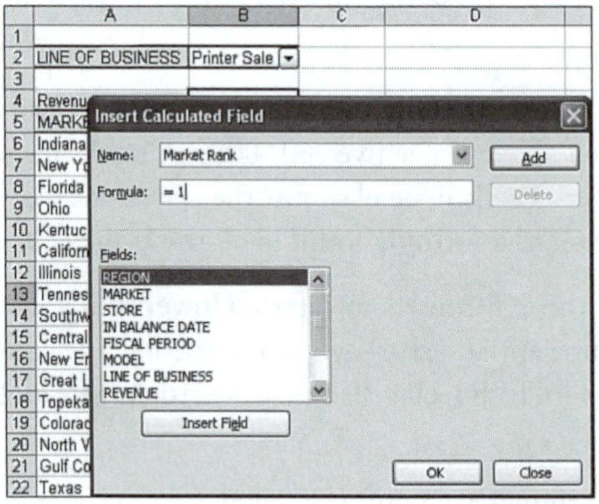

Figure A.17
Adding a rank field requires a simple calculated field that will assign a value of 1 to each market.

Initially, the MarketRank field looks fairly useless, reporting that all markets have a rank of 1. Right-click the Sum of MarketRank heading and choose Field Options.

In the PivotTable Field dialog box, give the field a name such as Rank_. Click the Options button to expand the dialog box.

In the expanded dialog box, change the setting for Show Data As to be Running Total In. Because this field is used to rank the markets, change the base field to be Market. Figure A.18 shows the completed dialog box.

Figure A.18
Change the rank field to be a running total within Market.

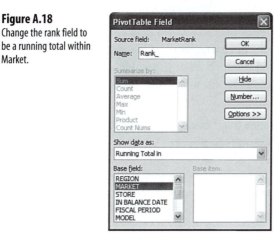

The result will be a new data field that reports the relative rank of each market, as shown in Figure A.19.

Figure A.19
After you change the setting to Running Total In, the calculated field properly shows the rank of each market.

	A	B	C
1			
2	LINE OF BUSINESS	Copier Sale ▼	
3			
4		Data ▼	
5	MARKET ▼	Rank	Revenue
6	Tennessee	1	6,323,837
7	New England	2	6,011,684
8	Kentucky	3	5,872,430
9	Gulf Coast	4	5,830,888
10	South Carolina	5	5,751,497
11	Topeka	6	5,624,620
12	Southwest	7	4,532,147
13	Texas	8	4,531,085
14	Shenandoah Valley	9	4,244,770
15	California	10	4,020,385
16	New York North	11	3,932,881
17	Florida	12	3,783,617
18	North Carolina	13	3,763,158
19	Indiana	14	3,616,687
20	Central US	15	3,506,717
21	North West	16	3,179,141
22	Colorado	17	3,113,591
23	Illinois	18	2,989,768
24	Ohio	19	2,381,299
25	Great Lakes	20	1,929,517
26	New York South	21	1,641,970
27	Grand Total		86,581,689

A

```
┌─ CAUTION ─────────────────────────────────────────────────────────────┐
│  The rank field will only work for the Market field. If you reshape the report to have Region replace │
│  Market, you will have to change the field options to change the base field to Region.                 │
│                                                                        │
└────────────────────────────────────────────────────────────────────────┘
```

Why does my pivot chart exclude months for certain data items?

Problem

If you are plotting trends over time with a pivot chart, and there is no occurrence of a particular month, the pivot chart excludes that month all together. However, in most cases, you will want to show your audience a placeholder for that month, illustrating that there is no data there.

For example, the chart in Figure A.20 shows a trend from January through December, but you will notice that May through June is not shown.

Figure A.20
There is no data for May through June, so this pivot chart excludes these months. However, it would be nice if this pivot chart would show all 12 months regardless.

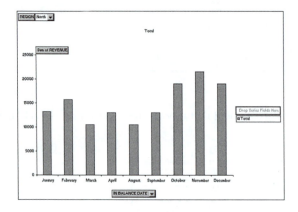

Solution

The solution to this problem is to set the pivot field to show all items with no data.

In this example, you would double-click on In Balance Date and then place a check in the Show Items with No Data check box, as shown in Figure A.21.

After your pivot field is set to show all items, your pivot table will show all 12 months, regardless of whether there is data in those months. The net effect is that you see May, June, and July, even though there is no data in those months, as shown in Figure A.22.

Figure A.21
Clicking on Show Items with No Data will ensure that all months are shown, whether data exists for that month or not.

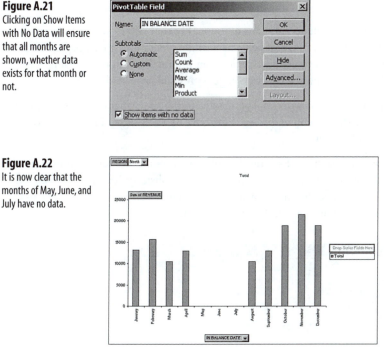

Figure A.22
It is now clear that the months of May, June, and July have no data.

Can I create a pivot chart on the same sheet as my pivot table?

Problem

By default, Excel creates all pivot charts on their own worksheet. However, you can get around this default and create a pivot chart on the same worksheet as your pivot table.

Solution

Place your cursor in a cell outside your pivot table and launch Excel's Chart Wizard. In step 1 of the wizard, select the type of chart you want to use. In step 2 of the wizard, click on your pivot table and then click Finish. A new pivot chart will be created on your worksheet, just as a normal chart would. All you have to do at this point is format the chart.

How can I turn my pivot table report into an interactive web page?

Problem

You have a pivot table report that you would like to share with clients on your department website. You need to create a web page that allows your clients to retain all the interactive functionality of your pivot table.

Solution

The good news is that Excel contains inherent functionality that allows you to turn an entire workbook, a single spreadsheet, a range of cells, or a single object into a web page. You can use the Save as Web Page option to create a static or an interactive web page. Using this option, you can easily create an interactive web page with your pivot table on it.

To start this process, open up your workbook and activate the sheet that contains the pivot table. Go up to the application menu and select File, Save as Web Page. The dialog box shown in Figure A.23 will activate.

As you can see, you have the option of saving the entire workbook or a selection in your workbook. In this case, because you are only interested in publishing your pivot table, you will select Selection: Sheet. In addition, because you need your web page to be interactive, you will need to place a check in the Add Interactivity box.

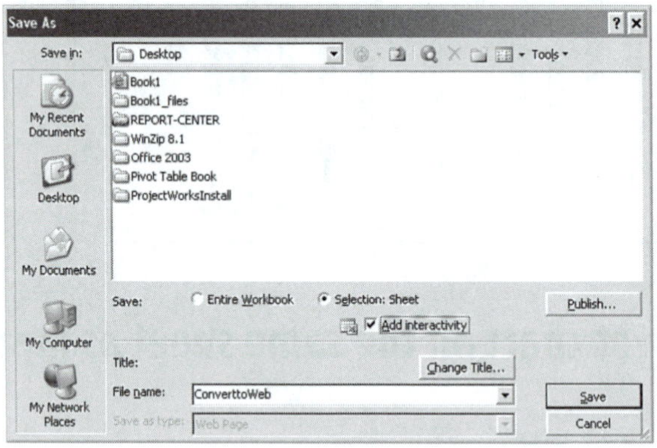

Figure A.23
Start the process of creating a web page by activating the Save as Web Page dialog box.

You will also see the Change Title button in Figure A.23. Clicking this button will allow you to enter a title for your web page. This title helps your clients identify the nature of the report they are reviewing.

Finally, the File Name input box allows you to change the name of your resultant web page files. In most instances, this name defaults to the name of your spreadsheet. When you are comfortable with your initial settings, click on the Publish button to continue the process.

After you click Publish, the Publish as Web Page dialog box, shown in Figure A.24, will be activated. You will notice that this dialog box has three main sections: Item to Publish, Viewing Options, and Publish As.

The first thing you will have to do is to identify which items you would like to publish. That is, you will have to choose what object or objects you want to bring into your web page. In the example in Figure A.24, you only want to show the pivot table that is contained in the Summary tab of your workbook. Therefore, you will select Items in Summary from the Choose drop-down list and then select PivotTable.

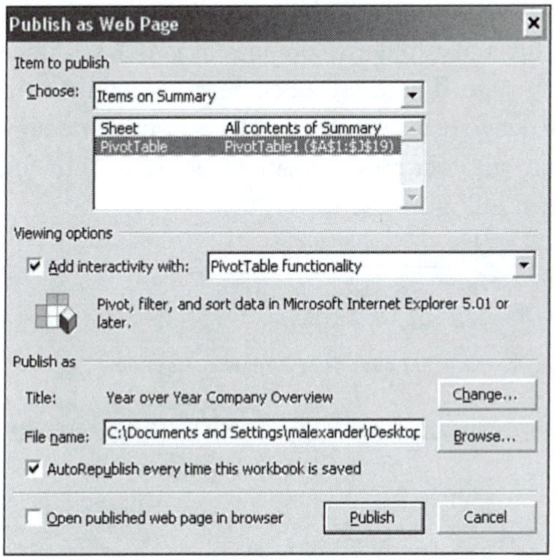

Figure A.24
Activate the Publish as
Web Page dialog box.

You will notice that selecting PivotTable in the Item to Publish section will force Viewing Options to default to PivotTable Functionality. This is perfect, because that is exactly the functionality you need.

CAUTION

Be careful not to remove the check from the Add Interactivity With check box. If you do, pivot table functionality will be disabled, effectively giving you a static web page.

In the Publish As section, you will select a location to output your web page and its supporting documents. In addition, you can place a check in the AutoRepublish check box. This will ensure that your web pages are automatically republished each time this workbook is saved.

NOTE

After you enable the AutoRepublish feature, you will receive the following message the next time you save the workbook after publishing:

"This workbook contains items that are automatically republished to Web pages each time the workbook is saved."

You will have two options to select from: Disable AutoRepublish and Enable AutoRepublish. To ensure that you AutoRepublish your web page after changes, you will have to select the Enable AutoRepublish option.

A

To finish, click on the Publish button. Go to the location you specified for the output, andyou will see an HTML file and a folder that contains two XML documents. The HTML file is your final web page. The XML documents contain the pivot cache and the components necessary to make your web page go. Place all these documents on your web server to allow your clients to hit your newly created web page. Your final web page will look similar to the one shown in Figure A.25.

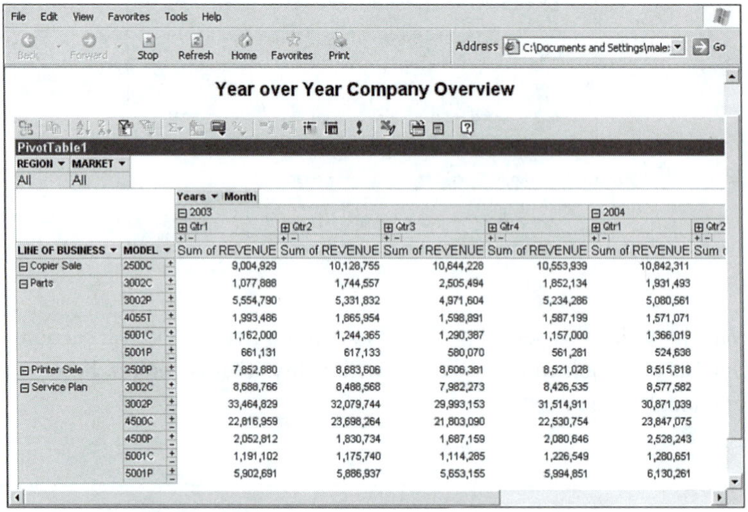

Figure A.25

You have successfully created your first interactive web-based pivot table!

A Word About Microsoft Office Web Components

In order for clients to be able to properly use your web page, they will have to have Microsoft Office Web Components installed. Microsoft Office Web Components is a collection of Component Object Model (COM) controls that are installed with Microsoft Office. This means that clients who do not have Microsoft Office installed on their system will not be able use the interactive functionality of your web page.

In order to get the complete functionality of Office Web Components, your clients must use Internet Explorer 5 or later. Also, if you create your web page using Office 2003, your clients who are using previous versions of Office should update their Web Components by installing the owc11.exe package available for free at Microsoft's website.